ORGANISATION STRUCTURES AND PROCESSES

05

ORGANISATION STRUCTURES AND PROCESSES

Jon Sutherland and Diane Canwell

PITMAN PUBLISHING

London · Hong Kong · Johannesburg · Melbourne · Singapore · Washington DC

To Vera and John Sutherland

PITMAN PUBLISHING
128 Long Acre, London WC2E 9AN
Tel: +44 (0)171 447 2000
Fax: +44 (0)171 240 5771

A Division of Pearson Professional Limited

First published in Great Britain 1997

ISBN 0 273 62509 8

British Library Cataloguing in Publication Data
A CIP catalogue record for this book can be obtained from the British Library.

10 9 8 7 6 5 4 3 2 1

Typeset by 🖋 Tek-Art, Croydon, Surrey
Printed and bound in Great Britain by Clays Ltd, St Ives plc

The Publishers' policy is to use paper manufactured from sustainable forests.

# Contents

Contents

Contents

# Preface

This book takes both a theoretical and a practical approach to the study of organisational structure and associated processes. Above all, it aims to analyse the effectiveness of organisations and how their structures often reflect their ability to cope with a wide range of different influences and environments. With the principal focus on the internal nature of organisations, we hope that we have identified the various alternative structures and their common patterns of behaviour.

Organisations are dynamic and varied, often making it difficult to state absolutes about the ways in which they might deal with structural difficulties, change and innovation, the challenges of communication and the ability to influence and adapt their own organisational culture.

Although this book is written primarily for the BTEC HNDC Core Module: Organisation Structures and Processes, there is a solid framework for any broader study of the nature of organisations and their operations.

The book has been written with the aim of avoiding the use of overly technical terms and jargon. Obviously some knowledge or understanding of the nature of organisations would be an advantage at this level of study, but we have not assumed prior knowledge at any point. Although this book should be seen as taking a broad sweep across the topic area, no doubt the reader will want to refer to some of the theorists mentioned for a more in-depth analysis of the subject.

It is hoped that the book will be able to provide the reader with:

◆ the ability to identify and describe different organisational structures.

◆ sufficient knowledge to be able to evaluate their appropriateness.

◆ the ability to appreciate how organisations are established and designed.

◆ the understanding to be able to analyse the relationship between different structures and the organisational performance and development.

◆ an understanding of the nature and management of change.

◆ an ability to evaluate different communications systems, the implications of technology and channels of communication.

◆ an ability to identify organisational cultures, rules and norms, the factors which influence the development of organisational culture and its relationship with the structure and performance of an organisation.

We hope that the systematic way in which we have approached the four main sections of the syllabus will enable the reader to access the information that they need. The format of the book follows a tried and tested structure which has proved popular with readers in the past.

Finally, it is our hope that you find this book to be a useful and accessible tool in your studies or personal reading.

Jon Sutherland & Diane Canwell
March 1997

All figures appearing in this title are the original work of the authors.

Section 1

IDENTIFYING STRUCTURES

After reading this section you should be able to:

◆ identify and describe different organisational structures.

◆ evaluate the appropriateness of different organisational structures.

◆ participate in the design of different structures to meet identified needs.

Types of organisation and associated structures

An organisation is a pattern or network of interrelationships of behaviour and activities. The organisation represents a constant interchange of many variables that incorporate the individuals involved, the technology used, the tasks undertaken and the methods employed. In short, it is the means by which a group of individuals organise themselves in order to carry out a series of functions; it is how they are managed and how the group deals with the external environment.

The structure of an organisation reflects the pattern of relationships between the various members of that organisation. In some way, the structure needs also to reflect the nature and division of the work carried out by the individuals. This needs to be established to ensure that they can achieve the goals and objectives of the organisation, with careful co-ordination and direction by the management.

Without a clear structure, it would be extremely difficult to have any form of effective management. It is therefore essential that the organisation develops a series of layers or levels through which the orders and commands can pass to direct and control the activities of the individuals. Careful consideration needs to be given as to the nature of the structure. It must incorporate clear allocation of tasks, it must state who has responsibility and authority, and it needs to establish the relationships between the individuals in that organisation. There are some straightforward objectives that can be identified, regardless of the size of the organisation and the exact activities and operations involved.

It would be true to say that all organisations have particular functions to perform. While doing this, they have a series of objectives which they are required to meet. In addition, they need to attempt to satisfy the needs of the individuals working for the organisation. If these individuals were working on their own, they would have little chance of being able to achieve the objectives; co-operation and the division of the work allow the individuals to perform to the best of their abilities and assist the organisation in reaching its objectives. Obviously, the nature of the activities in which the organisation is involved will determine the type of structure and its management component. The success or failure of the organisation will depend upon the manipulation and use of the resources at the organisation's disposal.

Broadly, we can identify two resources, which at this stage we can call *human* and *non-human*. The human aspect covers the abilities, the experience and skills of those employed, or involved in some way, with the organisation. The second grouping includes all of the assets, materials, machinery and facilities owned or used by the organisation.

We will gradually begin to realise that there are as many different ways of employing these resources as there are organisations. Each and every organisation will have its own distinctive way of managing the various assets at its disposal: some will be well managed and effective; a great many more will not make full use of the assets it has and as a consequence may face problems of its own making.

Classification of organisations

As we have already mentioned, the organisation is a means by which groups of individuals work together to reach a series of common goals. At this point, we need to identify some of the key characteristics of organisations that help us understand their creation and proposed function. All organisations will have the following in common:

◆ a structure which is designed to facilitate the most effective use of the resources available to the organisation.

◆ activities which will be grouped in some way, with a manager who has authority to supervise and make decisions.

◆ relationships which have been established with regard to functions, roles, jobs and tasks.

◆ tasks which will have been sub-divided and delegated to individuals within the organisation.

As we can see from Fig. 1.1, there are three main areas that need to be considered in the structuring of an organisation. We will develop each of these three strands

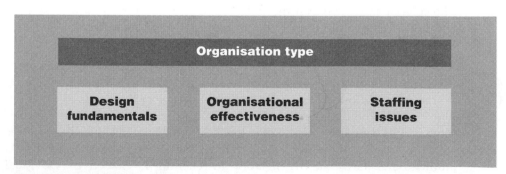

Fig. 1.1 Classifying organisations

in some detail in this part of the book, although many of the concepts will need to be revisited later.

Design fundamentals

There are a number of key concepts that affect the design of the organisation, and we will look at some of the more important ones, as detailed in Fig. 1.2.

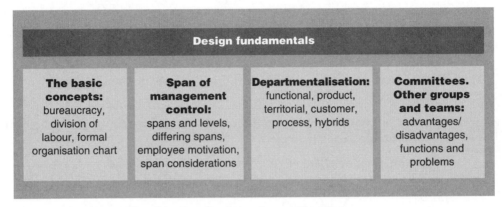

Fig. 1.2 Factors affecting the design of organisations

The basic concepts

Bureaucracy

It was Max Weber who brought forward the concept of bureaucracy some years ago. It is true to say that this is still a very important consideration. We can identify some of the main bureaucratic characteristics, as follows:

◆ tasks in the organisation are divided into specialisms.

◆ a strict set of regulations controls all activities in order to ensure a level of predictability and performance.

◆ the authority and responsibility within the organisation are clearly defined.

◆ most managers adopt an impersonal approach to the supervision of their subordinates.

◆ there is a strict adherence to merit as being the principal means of promotion.

◆ the organisation expects a lifelong devotion from its employees.

Some bureaucratic organisations can be very effective; they are well-controlled and somewhat predictable. It is this very fact that causes many of the problems that are associated with these types of organisation. Rules tend to be too restrictive, employees get bored and restless, and the organisation finds great difficulty in recognising the qualities of the employees and making good use of them.

There is a tendency for organisations to become more and more bureaucratic as they get 'older'.

Division of labour

Given the fact that (in most cases) two people work better as a pair than two individuals working alone, we create something called *synergy*. This relies on having some form of division of labour, or specialisation, so that the qualities and abilities of the individuals working in the group complement each other.

Formal organisation chart

An organisation chart will show a number of elements which we will be looking at later in the chapter, but essentially these are:

◆ the chain of command (the authority and responsibility that link the individuals).

◆ unity of command (the fact that each individual should only be ultimately accountable to one manager).

◆ communication channels.

◆ departmentalisation.

◆ the span of control of the management.

◆ the division of labour (by denoting the job title etc.).

Departmentalisation

Departmentalisation offers the organisation the opportunity to design itself around the various activities and operations that are common to the nature of its business. We can readily identify the following types of classification:

Functional departmentalisation – that groups together similar areas of activity such as marketing, finance and production (*see* Fig.1.3). The main advantages of this approach include the ability to concentrate the specialisms and facilitate easier managerial control. Although this minimises the duplication of functions throughout the organisation, it does mean that there are often difficulties in co-ordinating the functions as the organisation grows. Equally, there is a danger of the specialist areas becoming too short-sighted and concerned with the performance of their own area rather than the organisation as a whole.

Product departmentalisation – this is often seen as a main alternative to the functional approach (*see* Fig. 1.4). Many organisations favour this approach which enables them to identify individuals who can be given the responsibility of handling all the activities related to a particular product line. This means that a number of smaller 'sub-organisations' are brought into existence with their functions revolving around a particular product or range of products. Operating to strict guidelines, these sub-groups are part of a complex network within the organisation. Attention can then be given to particular products and services,

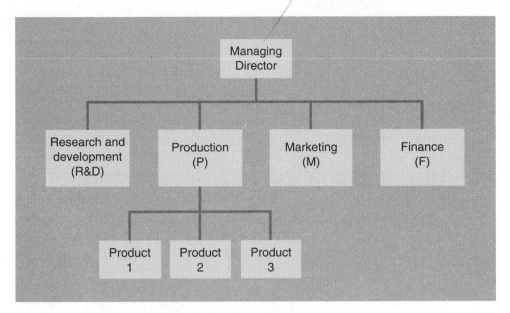

Fig. 1.3 Functional departmentalisation

allowing better co-ordination of the functions and placing a profit responsibility on the department. The more general management functions are carried out by centrally placed individuals who have a more 'macro' view of the operations. This approach does mean that there is a tendency to have a series of duplicated roles within the organisation, and coupled with this is the danger that the different departments are following diverse approaches in terms of policy and action. This can be eliminated by close supervision and adherence to the controls.

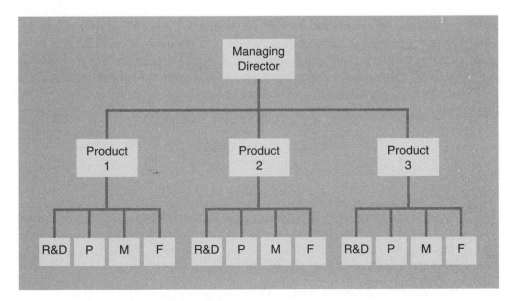

Fig. 1.4 Product departmentalisation

Territorial departmentalisation – this form of departmentalisation is also known as regional, area or geographical departmentalisation. Large organisations favour this approach as it enables them to concentrate a full range of functions within a specified area (*see* Fig. 1.5). There will be a degree of duplication, but in most cases the duplication occurs at sales and marketing level. Organisations have found this approach to be particularly useful as it allows them to focus on the unique nature of an area and develop specific skills and approaches to suit the needs of the region.

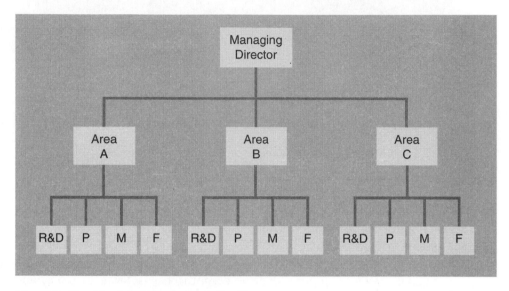

Fig. 1.5 Territorial departmentalisation

Customer departmentalisation – in many respects this approach can be seen as being rather similar to product departmentalisation. In essence, it goes one stage further. Rather than focusing on the product or service itself, it identifies customer types and product and service ranges aimed at these groups. In this way, the organisation may have a business-to-business orientated department, a direct sales department and another that is concerned with retailing in the conventional sense. While this approach enables the organisation to adapt to the needs of specific customers, there is still a duplication of effort leading to co-ordination problems, under-utilisation of resources and the danger of competition between managers.

Process departmentalisation – this approach focuses on the production process and is often found in organisations that have a strong manufacturing base. There are obvious advantages related to the utilisation of skills and equipment which facilitate economic use of them; indeed it is often economic considerations that lead to the formation of this type of organisation.

Hybrids – as we will see later, some organisations favour the use of project teams to facilitate the successful completion of various activities and projects. The key to project teams is the successful blending of skills and specialisms and the full integration of the individuals within the group. The matrix structure, which we will investigate in greater depth later, involves superimposing conventional functional departments over the specialist project teams. This is seen as a 'quick response' organisation type that is common in the technically orientated businesses that involve large numbers of scientists and engineers.

Finally, in this section, we will look at the nature of committees and other groups that are involved in the co-ordination of the activities of the organisation.

Committees

Committees have three main functions:

1 Co-ordination – aiming to integrate the various areas of the organisation and assist the interrelationships.

2 Advisory – offering advice and recommendations to the management of the organisation.

3 Decision-making – making decisions and ensuring that they are carried out.

Committees are common in all areas of business: over 80 per cent of all senior executives serve on committees, as do over 70 per cent of middle managers and 50 per cent of supervisors and junior managers. Essentially, there are two types of committee:

1 Structural or standing committees – that are a permanent part of the organisational structure (these will be pay review bodies, development committees and project committees, for example).

2 Ad hoc committees – that are created to perform a specific function and are then disbanded, unlike the more permanent standing committees.

Committees are seen as an opportunity to pool the experience of various individuals so that alternatives and solutions can be created. This is another example of synergy. The main advantages are that:

◆ participation increases the possibility of acceptance of new ideas.

◆ dispersion of power can counteract abuses of power.

◆ unpopular decisions are not the responsibility of one individual.

◆ they provide an excellent opportunity for aspiring managers.

Given the fact that any meeting can be dominated by forceful individuals, committees can suffer the same fate. Compromises are common and recommendations are often diluted to ensure that there is agreement. Committees are also seen as being rather expensive in terms of time taken and the diversion from the normal business of the managers. The strongest criticisms revolve around lost opportunities and poorly organised committees that are seen as a complete waste of time and resources.

Organisational effectiveness

The second classification focus considers the ways in which organisational effectiveness can be facilitated through the appropriate distribution of responsiblity at the various levels of the organisation (*see* Fig. 1.6).

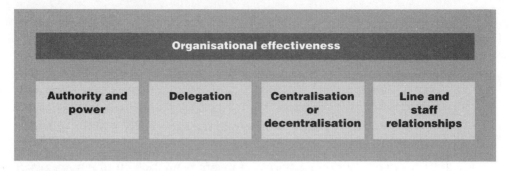

Fig. 1.6 Organisational effectiveness

Authority and power

Authority is perhaps one of the most important considerations, and the delegation and use of authority is of particular concern. Authority is the right to command others to act or not to act in a particular way in order to achieve objectives. There are two differing opinions regarding the legitimacy of authority:

The *formal view* takes the approach that all authority is given by the ultimate source of the power. In most organisations this source will be the owners, whether they are shareholders or members of the board of directors. There is an inherent notion that all authority has been granted to a particular individual or group and this is to be accepted by the other members of the organisation.

The *acceptance view* is in direct contradiction to the formal view of authority. Taking this stance, the authority is only seen as viable once those over whom the authority will be exercised accept its legitimacy. If an individual chooses to disobey the orders directed toward them, then the legitimacy of the authority is challenged.

The most important issue concerning authority is that it is used effectively, as the possession of authority is not in itself sufficient to ensure that others accept it. The manager needs to have the power to exercise authority. There are several different sources of this power:

◆ *reward power* – this comes from the positive reinforcement of being rewarded for good service to the manager; subordinates perceive that they can receive positive rewards that are controlled by the manager.

◆ *coercive power* – typified by the possibility that the subordinate could be punished if they do not follow the strict instructions of the manager.

◆ *legitimate power* – developed through the subordinate's acceptance of the manager's right to make decisions.

◆ *information power* – with access to privileged information the manager has a better view of the situation.

◆ *symbolic power* – managers have certain desirable traits that make them charismatic.

◆ *expertise power* – the manager's position is derived from knowledge gained by study or from previous experience.

We will return to the subject of power and authority a number of times throughout this book, particularly with reference to the fact that the breadth of power and authority diminishes the lower we go down the chain of command.

Delegation

The delegation of authority – which means that managers allocate authority downwards to individuals who will report to them – is common in most organisations. There is usually some form of objective setting involved along with the need to allocate the necessary authority to a subordinate who is then responsible for carrying through these objectives once they have accepted the delegation. The obvious reasons for delegation lie in the fact that even the most efficient manager could not possibly accomplish everything that has to be done. If, by delegation, the manager can focus upon the more important tasks or obtain a wider view of the tasks in hand, then these will be carried out with greater efficiency. Equally, the manager needs to consider the fact that delegation provides subordinates with opportunities to develop.

Despite the obvious advantages of delegation and how critical it is to effective management, many managers fail to delegate or cannot delegate very well. There are a number of reasons for this:

◆ many managers feel more powerful by retaining their decision-making privileges.

◆ some managers do not wish to face the possibility that their subordinates will use the authority poorly.

◆ managers often believe that subordinates lack the ability to exercise good judgement and feel that they can always do better themselves. They have a sense of being indispensable.

◆ managers also feel that their subordinates don't wish to have broader decision-making possibilities.

◆ some managers feel that subordinates will perform their tasks so effectively that their own position may well be threatened in the future.

At the same time, managers may find themselves with subordinates who actively resist delegation. There are a number of reasons for this. Primarily, however, is the fact that they do not wish to have additional responsibilities and to be more accountable. If in the past the subordinates have been able to seek the advice of their manager to solve a problem then they may find it difficult to make the necessary adaptation. Coupled with this more common set of circumstances is the fact that many subordinates feel that once they have been given the authority they will exercise it poorly and be criticised as a result. This lack of self-confidence and additional pressure makes them shy away from decision-making situations.

Centralisation and decentralisation

The effectiveness of an organisation is often measured by the degree of centralisation or decentralisation of authority. These two considerations are a way in which you can measure the concentration or dispersion of authority. As we have seen, delegation refers to the level of delegated authority and responsibility. Decentralisation is a rather broader concept. It refers to the extent to which the upper levels of management delegate authority to the lower level organisational units, divisions, branches or managers. Centralisation, on the other hand, concerns the concentration of power and authority towards the top of the organisation. There are rare cases of organisations which are either completely centralised or decentralised. The vast majority of businesses will be somewhere between a high level of centralisation and a high level of decentralisation.

Organisations with senior managers who are very *autocratic* will tend to wish to have a strong central control. With help from closely monitored support staff they will make most of the major decisions particularly at the higher levels. On the other hand, some managers may believe that decentralised organisations are far more effective. This is particularly true of managers who have a functional role. They have access to information which allows them to make good decisions and take immediate action. If authority is delegated then it needs to be coupled with the responsibility and the accountability required so that full co-operation and integration can be facilitated at all levels.

For organisations that have enjoyed considerable internal growth over a number of years there is a tendency for centralisation to be the main way of exercising authority. Conversely, organisations which have grown externally through take-overs and mergers will tend to be rather more decentralised. This is largely due to the fact that the acquired businesses are somewhat more loosely managed by the parent company and will remain this way providing results continue to be acceptable. It is only when these organisations need to be brought more closely under the umbrella of the parent company that centralisation will become the primary driving force behind authority.

In cases when organisations are widely dispersed geographically there is a greater tendency for decentralisation. This decentralisation will allow lower level managers to have a higher degree of involvement in decision making so that they can adapt to local conditions which affect their particular part of the business.

If an organisation recognises the fact that it does not have effective control of the lower tiers of management, then it will tend to become more centralised as this will make it easier to monitor performance at the lower levels. Certainly in the 1980s there was a tendency for large organisations which had previously engaged in decentralisation schemes to institute a recentralisation system to reverse the problems which had become all too apparent. This meant that many middle managers in these large organisations found that their jobs were becoming much more structured and far more routine. At the same time, these middle management jobs lost some of their status and pay differentials were being eroded. Many commentators put this trend down to the introduction of information technology. However, these circumstances were not common in all organisational structures. A sizeable minority of organisations actually increased the number of middle managers, improved their status and pay and, in many cases, their responsibilities too. Certainly information technology has had an effect on the decentralisation of many organisations. It has enabled the top levels of management to acquire a broader and more systematic means of monitoring decision making at all levels of the organisation.

Organisations which engage in decentralisation find themselves in great need of quality managers. These managers need to have a broad range of decision-making skills even at low levels. The need for the manager to be innovative and creative is paramount and many organisations have found it difficult to recruit highly qualified managers and specialists in order to feed their decentralisation schemes. If an organisation has a wide range of products and services then there will also be a tendency for the structure to be decentralised. Specific specialist knowledge of a particular product or service may be seen to come first before managerial skills. It is important, therefore, that the organisation recruits specialists who also have good managerial skills as opposed to specialists who are not managers, or managers who do not have these specialist skills. If either of the latter two conditions exist then decentralisation could be a problem. If the organisation does not have a wide range of products and services then there is little need for it to be decentralised: the majority of functions and activities can be controlled centrally as they lack any major degree of differentiation.

Line and staff relationships

The concept of line and staff relationships within an organisation can be somewhat confusing. The line organisation for a particular section or department of an organisation indicates those who are directly responsible for accomplishing the major activities of the organisation. In other words, the line organisation would run from the chief executive officer through the various tiers of management to the production employees working on the shop floor. This would form an unbroken chain of command and authority with each layer or level of management assuming direct responsibility for all those subordinate to that position. The majority of smaller organisations operate a line organisation system. Each particular individual would carry out a major activity within the business, such as sales or production. There would only be one supervisor: one ultimate manager.

This would ensure unity of command. Once an organisation grows beyond this it may feel that it needs to take on the skills and expertise of specialists to perform specific functions or services within the organisation. These new employees will not have line activity responsibility and are therefore referred to as staff. The organisational structure then becomes somewhat more complex. It will consist of the traditional line relationships which run from the top to the bottom of the organisation but overlaying this will be a series of staff posts. The general bench-mark for identifying staff posts is that these individuals working in particular departments or areas of the business are not directly involved in the organisa-tion's mainstream activities. Maintenance staff, for example, while involved in ensuring that plant and machinery are running efficiently, are not directly involved in selling the products and services which the organisation deems to be its main area of activity. These distinctions are not always clear and there is often a blurring between the line and staff employees.

In the vast proportion of cases, the line activities take precedence in terms of attention and finance. It is of course essential that the integrity and the influence of these particular parts of the organisation remain paramount, and it would be foolish to restrict the performance of the line departments by giving too much authority over to the staff areas. It is interesting to note that, in times of difficulty, the line areas are the ones which are affected the most since they are more directly linked with productivity and performance. However, in situations where pro-ductivity and performance are still quite strong but the overall profitability of the organisation remains low, it is the staff areas which are affected by cuts.

Staff employees generally fall into two categories. We have already mentioned the fact that certain specialist staff would naturally fall in this area. Generally their function is fairly narrow. They may be involved in personnel perhaps, or health and safety or legal aspects. The main point of the exercise is that these individuals' experience and skills are available throughout the whole of the organisation. They are there to advise, assist or counsel the line managers as and when necessary. The second area where staff employees are common is that of personal assistance. Many managers require the assistance of an individual in order to help them fulfil the various tasks which are required of them. This indi-vidual will not have line responsibilities. They are there to help, advise and service a particular manager. Note that the role of a personal assistant should not necessarily be confused with the role of a secretary, since a PA tends to have a broader administrative and deputising function with clear areas of responsibility and associated decision-making authority.

As we mentioned earlier, authority implies a clear understanding of the right to make decisions and impose an individual's will upon another. When we con-sider that there are line and staff relationships within an organisation, we must also realise there will be line and staff authority. The type of authority which we have already discussed would generally fall under the category of line authority. This corresponds almost exactly to the chain of command usually directed down-ward through the organisation's levels. The manager is able to exercise authority over the immediate subordinates and all managers in this mode would exercise line authority over all of their subordinates. Staff authority is based on the right for particular individuals to offer specialist advice, counselling or recommendations. They do not necessarily have the right to dictate or command line individuals to take particular courses of action. The relationship between staff employees and line departments will be based upon traditional acceptance of each other's authority. This will determine the level of influence which the staff employees have over the line functions. In certain cases, senior management may consider that staff employees need a degree of functional authority. They will have the right in certain circumstances to command line management to take account of their instructions. This would be particularly true of health and safety individuals who will have an overriding responsibility within the organisation. Other examples include the requirements of an accounts department to demand certain financial information from line departments, and an individual who is responsible for quality control throughout the organisation requiring satisfactory completion and submission of sample products and additional data. If senior management decides to give functional authority to staff employees then this may be at variance with the principal of unity of command, thus causing a wide variety of organisational conflicts. If staff employees are tempted to over-use their functional authority then this may seriously undermine the integrity of the line departments. It is the line departments, after all, which have a degree of accountability in areas other than those which are the concern of the staff employees.

Line and staff conflicts are probably inevitable. Since staff employees will tend to be more specialist they may also be younger and more highly educated than traditional line managers. This will, of course, be a potential source of continuing conflict. There is also the temptation for staff employees to exceed their authority and attempt to give orders directly to line personnel. Given the fact that line personnel may feel that the staff specialists are unable to understand the complexities and problems of the line functions, they may consider that the advice given is unusable. There is also a certain degree of inevitability in positive changes made in the functions of the organisation being hijacked by staff employees who may claim credit for being able to resolve certain long-term problems.

There may be a sense of separation between the line and staff individuals if the latter have greater access to information and consequently are unable to use language and technical terms which are not understood by line management.

Perhaps the biggest problem is when senior management does not explain fully the extent to which staff employees have authority over line management. The exact relationship may have never been clearly defined. This is compounded by the fact that many of the more senior staff positions will appear to occupy relatively senior positions within the organisation, which only serves to reinforce the confusion. Senior management must clearly convey the extent of the delegation of responsibility to these staff employees. At the same time the staff employees and departments need to be made aware of the fact that they must justify their existence by making a positive contribution to the smooth running of the line functions. Their role is to assist the line functions and not, as happens in many cases, the reverse. It is worth bearing in mind, of course, that staff specialists have no function at all without the line departments. True performance and productivity can only be assessed in terms of the success or failure of the line departments, since it is only at this level that there will be targets set against which performance can be measured.

Staffing issues

Staffing and broader personnel issues can also be seen as the third valuable means by which organisations are classified. The policies and procedure adopted by an organisation will reflect many of their core values.

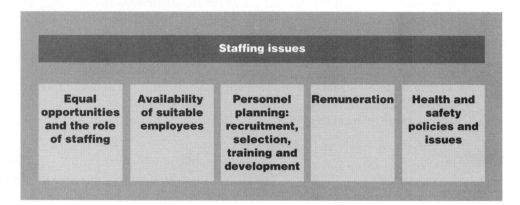

Fig. 1.7 Factors affecting the staffing of organisations

Equal opportunities and the role of staffing

The significance of personnel and staffing has increased considerably over the past few years. There have certainly been enormous changes arising from government legislation, the impact of technology and more general demands from employees who wish to receive considered managerial leadership. Of course the staffing function is carried out by all managers from large corporation executives to the owners of small businesses. The main problem with this is that the majority of managers are inadequately trained in order to fulfil many of the staffing requirements. The gradual emergence of equal opportunities as a key issue has perhaps highlighted this most. Traditionally women, elderly people, people with disabilities and people from various ethnic minority groups occupied lower status, lower paid jobs. Legally, particularly in relation to equal opportunity policies, this is no longer acceptable. Staffing is certainly affected enormously by equal opportunities. Controls regarding equal opportunities span from the recruitment period all the way through employment to termination. There can be no decisions, particularly prejudicial ones, based on race, colour, religion, gender or national origin. The legislation allows individuals or their representatives to take legal action should any of these abuses arise.

Availability of suitable employees

You should have already appreciated the fact that organisations do not operate in isolation. They need to consider themselves as an integral part of the overall environment. An organisation must therefore look to the availability of suitable employees within the broad geographical area in which the business is located. There is, of course, a national demand for and supply of employees. However, there are regional and local fluctuations which an organisation needs to be aware of. One of the greatest influences certainly on the availability of employees has been the increasing number of women who have been entering the workforce. It is said that around two out of every three new employees in the last couple of decades have been women. In fact, women account for more than 50 per cent of the workforce.

Obviously the availability of individuals within the employment pool is one thing but these employees need to be suitable; they not only need to match the skill or experience requirements of the available posts but also need to be within a certain profile as identified by the organisation itself.

Personnel planning

Organisations need to find competent individuals as soon as possible. This is particularly true of specialist areas where a degree of future planning needs to be carried out in order to ensure that there are sufficient individuals to fill probable vacancies. This *personnel planning* essentially means that the organisation is geared up to providing the right types of individuals and employees to reach the organisation's objectives. Obviously, personnel planning is a complex issue but effectively it covers three main areas. These are:

◆ to determine the jobs which need to be performed, the abilities needed by employees to do the jobs and how many employees will be needed;

◆ knowing where to look for potential employees; and

◆ consideration regarding the demand for and supply of potential employees.

Let us have a look at these in a little more detail beginning with the determining of job needs.

Larger organisations have more complex staffing issues because of the large number of different job posts and titles. They will of course determine particular job specifications which will identify the types of jobs that need to be performed and the skills required to match these. They will then attempt to estimate the total number of employees that they need for a given time period. This will take into account labour turnover. They will also make an inventory of individuals who are already available to perform these particular jobs. This will enable the organisation to make an assessment of how many individuals need to be taken on and when their contracts will need to start.

It is important that this early stage of the personnel planning function incorporates many of the more general aspects including the objectives and plans of the organisation. Obviously, many of the objectives will determine or at least influence the number and types of individuals that will need to be hired. This will allow the organisation to determine the overall personnel needs of the organisation. There can then be an analysis of particular occupational specialities, job skills, personal characteristics and of course the number of employees needed. Perhaps one of the easiest ways of doing this is to study the current employee pool. The organisation can make an inventory of the present personnel and assess and identify the particular abilities and skills which these currently employed individuals have. The difference between the overall needs of the organisation in terms of employees and the present employee inventory is the net new personnel requirement that needs to be filled by immediate recruitment. Many organisations will set up a recruitment action plan based on the findings from their studies.

Recruitment and selection

Obviously, in order to acquire additional employees as and when the organisation needs them, it is imperative that the personnel department develops its sources of supply of personnel. Naturally, a number of individuals can be recruited internally through upgrading or at least repositioning. External sources can be somewhat more complex. In addition to the individuals who will make the first contact with the organisation on a purely speculative basis, there are employment agencies, both public and private, generally available to help fill vital job vacancies. An organisation which is keen to maintain its competitive edge will obviously look towards its competitors and similar organisations in the market-place in order to poach staff or at least give them some inducements to transfer. Many organisations have also established long-term relations with educational institutions such as colleges and universities. Although the relationships may have become close over a number of years, the organisations do not necessarily undertake to accept individuals who have passed through the particular educational institution's process. However, in many cases these individuals are given priority in their recruitment drives. One of the more common trends in allowing organisations to cater for changing employment needs has been the increase in the number of part-time employees. This process has continued at a pace throughout the 1990s and is one of the more dominant features of women's employment patterns, particularly in the service and manufacturing sectors.

Although this is not the place to consider the complexities of recruitment and selection, the nature of the organisation's approach to this may give some indication as to the intended organisational structure and how the organisation can be classified. Some organisations by virtue of their business activity have little or no choice about their recruitment techniques. They may require a continuous stream of low-skilled employees with little experience of working in this area of operations. It may be the nature of the business that determines the longevity of the employee's stay with the organisation. In cases where the skill level requirements are low and the period of retention of individual employees is also short, the organisation will need to have a rolling recruitment programme in order to continually fill vacant positions. Organisations which have a more stable employee base can perhaps be rather more sophisticated in the way in which they recruit. To this end they may have established a series of filtering systems which ensure that the correct employee for the particular post is selected. Returning to the organisation which has less opportunity to be selective, the personnel function may be geared to mass rather than quality and in this respect the recruitment process is rather like a batch or flow production system rather than a bespoke selection system.

Once the individual has been selected, the nature of the organisation itself needs to be impressed upon the new recruit. Many organisations will have integral induction programmes which aim to orientate the new employee and reduce the difficulties and frustrations which may become apparent. While the new employee will be qualified to do the job, the situation in which they now find themselves will be radically different from anything else that they have already experienced. If the individual has not been correctly orientated then any enthusiasm or effort which is put in at the beginning of their employment will be wasted. Research has certainly shown that effective orientation programmes such as induction schemes can certainly reduce labour turnover as well as reducing employee anxiety or uncertainty. In addition to this, induction schemes save current employees from having to spend large amounts of their time involving themselves in orientating the new employee. Finally, the positive work values of the organisation can be directed towards the new employee and this will improve their motivation and job satisfaction even in the short term.

Training and development

The way in which the organisation trains and develops its employees is of course a crucial concern. Many organisations will have formalised systems which allow access to training and development at regular periods for all employees regardless of their status. Training and development is absolutely essential since it allows the employees to have access to information and skills which will, of course, lead to greater personal satisfaction, making them more dynamic and considerably more satisfied with their jobs. Some large organisations obviously favour on-the-job training methods where coaching or planned progression is encouraged by involving employees in some form of guidance and counselling system. In addition to this, other organisations will favour job orientation where individuals will be rotated through a number of diversified or differentiated job posts. Off-the-job training is largely restricted to the upper echelons of organisations where senior managers and executives will be given the opportunity to develop their managerial skills at university or other educational institutions. For small organisations, off-the-job training may be the only option and as such many of these smaller businesses will allow their employees to attend subsidised day release or evening classes. At the end of the day training and development is extremely important. Not only will it develop the individual employee but it will also have a marked effect on the overall effectiveness of the organisation itself. True personnel planning will identify the importance of training and development and this should not be seen in any way as a diversion from the day-to-day activities of the organisation.

Remuneration

Remuneration is an extremely important consideration for most employees as it is a measure of how they value themselves. In this respect organisations need to be acutely aware of the comparative remuneration between different individuals in a variety of job roles. Ultimately the level of income which an individual enjoys will determine their standard of living, their status, their prestige, and influence their sense of worth. Since organisations will obviously have to pay employees in the form of salaries, wages and benefits, this is often the highest cost item. An average organisation will clearly state that salaries and wages and other allied costs account for some 50 per cent of all sales income.

Relating remuneration directly to the organisation and its structure, individuals need to be able to accept that their level of income is fair and that they are valued relative to others. Employees will of course accept pay differentials which are based on concepts such as responsibility, knowledge, productivity, ability or managerial activities. However, there are a vast number of differentials which cannot be justified on any basis whatsoever. Often the production of an organisation chart will only serve to reinforce the unjustified nature of many of the pay differentials. On paper, the relative position in the organisation of particular individuals will belie their true worth and their true contribution to the organisation itself. What will be clear is that some will have a comparative worth. This is usually arrived at by allocating points or grades based on skills, education and responsibility. This does not necessarily mean that an individual will receive equal pay for equal work. In fact women can receive considerably less than equal pay for equal jobs. On average a woman will only receive around two-thirds of a salary of a male holding a similar post.

Health and safety

The final issue in this section refers to health and safety. Although this is not an appropriate point to discuss the intricacies of health and safety policies and issues, it is important to establish that management has specific responsibilities in these areas. Legislation is certainly forcing employers and employees towards ever safer and healthier working conditions. Obviously the nature of the organisation's areas of activity will determine the level and complexity of health and safety policy and practice within the organisation itself. There are considerably more health and safety issues to be considered in manufacturing than perhaps in the service sector. This will influence the degree to which health and safety impinges upon the day-to-day operations of the organisation.

As you will have appreciated, the complexity and diversity of different organisations mean that it is difficult to determine any general characteristics of all organisations. Many of the structural choices which have been made by individuals in establishing the nature of their organisations are purely individual to that organisation itself. The internal and external influences which have conspired to create an organisation are peculiar to that organisation alone. We can make a number of generalisations regarding the nature and classification of particular organisations. However we will discover that even within the same broad area of operations or market-place there are a wide variety of different organisations operating significantly different systems equally as effectively.

Organisation charts

The organisation chart, as you will have already realised, represents the organisation's best attempts to configure itself in order to meet its declared objectives. At the very least, the organisation chart will show the following:

◆ the *chain of command* illustrating the authority–responsibility relationships that link the supervisors/managers to their subordinates. This chain of command flows naturally down the organisation chart, as shown in Fig. 1.8.

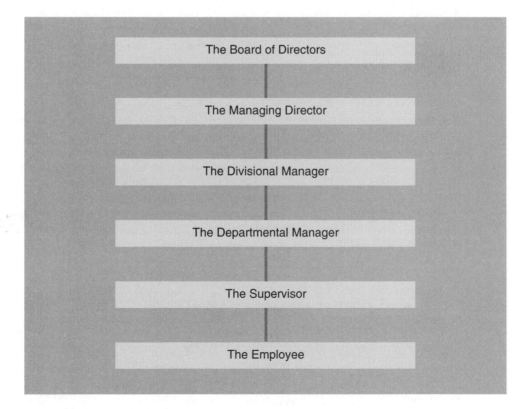

Fig. 1.8 The chain of command

◆ the *unity of command* which, as Henri Fayol stated, is essential as it clearly shows to whom an individual is responsible and ensures that there is a reduction in the chance of an individual receiving mixed messages. In other words, it simplifies the lines of communication.

◆ the formal *channels of communication* which become evident if we trace the lines of responsibility and authority. It should not be assumed that the channels of communication necessarily follow the chain of command. In more complex organisational charts, these channels of communication are shown as dotted lines.

The larger the organisation, the more chance there will be of a degree of *departmentalisation*. This is undertaken to ensure that the larger and unwieldy nature of some of the areas of activity are split to facilitate easier management and operations.

The *hierarchical levels* within the organisation should be clear by the ability to identify individuals who are at the same level of the organisation. These will be evident by noting those who are at the same level of the chain of command. Their position should denote their relative authority and power within the structure.

The *span of control* (which we will consider later in more detail), enables the individual to appreciate the number of subordinates for whom they have a direct line management responsibility. Technically, all those who are shown as subordinate at the next level down on the chart are within the span of control. Those who appear as subordinates of those within the span are the responsibility of that next level of management (although the senior manager will have ultimate responsibility for them). It is the span of control that will determine whether the organisation structure is a flat or tall one.

The *division of work* or specialisation is translated as part of the organisation chart by the number of specific functions or job roles that are identified. The higher the degree of specialisation, the more complex the chart is likely to be.

In the second section of this book, we will be returning to the subject of organisation charts in relation to the differing types of organisation that are commonly used. We will see that the nature of the internal workings of the organisation and management's attempts to configure these will have a crucial impact on how the organisation structure will look.

 ## Spans of control

The number of individuals reporting to one person is known as the *span of control*. A single person can only directly supervise the activities of a limited number of individuals. To this end, a business will divide up the work that needs to be supervised among a number of managers. These managers, in turn, are supervised by another manager whose span of control is also limited by the practical number of individuals that can be supervised effectively. Particularly in

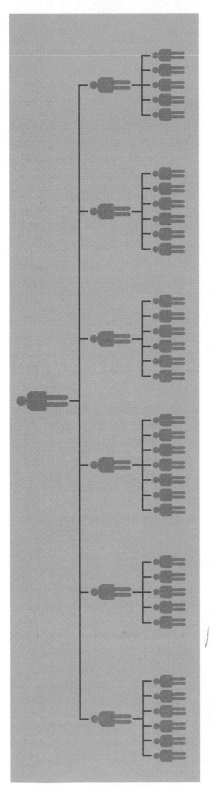

Fig. 1.9(a) Flat organisational structure resulting from broad span of control

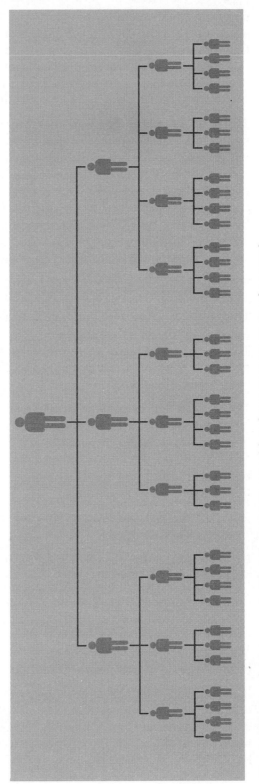

Fig. 1.9(b) Pyramidal organisational structure resulting from narrow span of control

larger and more complex organisations, the span of control will determine the shape of the hierarchy. If an organisation opts for fairly broad spans of control, then the organisation will have a flat appearance. If the organisation considers that the spans of control should be narrow, then the inevitable consequence is an organisation that appears to be much more peaked (*see* Fig. 1.9(a) and (b)). Narrow spans of control mean lots of managers and many levels of management.

The spans of control throughout an organisation are rarely uniform, as typified by the fact that the span of control narrows towards the top of the organisation, with senior managers only having a span of control over two or three individuals. At the bottom of the organisation, where the numbers of individuals are greatest, the spans of control are broader. It is also true to say that the spans of control at the same level of the organisation will not be the same. It is unlikely that the managers will have the same number of subordinates; this will depend upon the nature of the activities carried out by that manager and the traditional spans of control that have existed for a while.

Essentially, there are two schools of thought regarding the width or breadth of span of control. First, there are those who favour the narrow spans of control. This is based on the assumption that an average individual can only cope with a certain number of subordinates. Psychologists would probably agree with this. The manager that has a large number of subordinates to handle is likely to try to deal with them on a one-by-one basis. There will be a resulting lack of overall control and direction.

The number of relationships, or interrelationships, increases arithmetically. If the manager has just three subordinates, there are 42 possible relationships. With five subordinates, this increases to 100. At ten, the number is a staggering 5210. Most theorists who favour the narrower span of control cite four as being the optimum number, but state that five or six is the absolute maximum. They base this opinion on two key factors:

1 All of the possible relationships between the manager and the subordinates are real and are used.

2 The manager *does* actually supervise all of the subordinates.

In reality, the fact that there is a *possibility* of interaction between individuals does not mean that there *is* an interaction. Many of the interactions and interrelationships that could occur on paper do not occur in practice. Some subordinates may not need supervision at all and the manager may not be concerned with their activities on a daily basis. However, in theory, the addition of any extra subordinates could mean a geometric addition to the number of relationships.

It is the theoretical nature of the number of interrelationships that make many other theorists sceptical about the narrow span of control approach. Merely calculating the number of interrelationships on a geometric basis is considered too tenuous. Above all, the narrow span of control approach misses the fact that individuals are controlled as effectively by their peers as they are by their manager. In this way, the manager does not have to have a direct input into the control function; the group itself would do much of this monitoring and control. Equally, many subordinates operate effectively if they are not closely supervised, taking the responsibility given to them very seriously without having to be monitored. If this approach is accepted then the natural conclusion is that, by broadening the span of control, close supervision is impossible leaving the subordinates with a greater degree of independence.

As we have said earlier, the spans of control will vary within an organisation, usually typified by a narrower span at the top of the organisation and a broader span at the bottom. Larger organisations have the option to do something about the span of control: they can vary the number of subordinates to suit the circumstances. In smaller organisations, there is a tendency to have a broader span of control than is really effective. For the larger organisations, the broader span leads to greater efficiency and increased morale, coupled with a flatter management structure. This is more commonly known as decentralisation where the level of responsibility is greater and the opportunities to have autonomous decision making are enhanced. The flatter the structure, the more opportunities the lower level members of the organisation will have relative to the senior management. In these flatter organisations, there is a development of the differentiation between the work of the manager and the subordinates, with each of the subunits operating with greater effectiveness.

With these two widely differing stances, we have on the one hand a broader span of control meaning that the subordinates have more freedom to make their own decisions, but on the other hand the manager needs to be aware of what is going on. Certainly, the broadening of the span of control has led to decentralisation, but also to job enrichment for the subordinates. The net result offers a useful compromise between the two approaches. Organisations that have increased the breadth of the span of control have noted that their managers and subordinates share many common objectives, and roles have changed from that of supervisor and supervised to helper and helped.

Obviously, new technology has made this move far more effective, and the production process is often seen as a key determining factor. The higher the level of technology used (for example, mass production as opposed to process or unit production), the broader the span of control. This is coupled with the number of levels of management common to those organisations using particular production techniques. The more complex the operation (with the broader spans of control), the higher the number of management levels.

Technology, size of organisation and the nature of the hierarchy of an organisation are key determinants of the span of control. On a theoretical basis this is understandable, but there are a number of more closely related factors that will influence the span of control:

◆ the functions of the manager and the subordinates need to be broadly similar for the manager to be able to understand how the tasks will be performed.

Equally, the fact that the subordinates work is broadly similar will greater simplify the manager's role. There will be less chance of confusion if the manager can understand the functions and roles of each subordinate.

◆ the geographical dispersion of the subordinates can either lead to a broader span of control or greatly reduce it. Interdependence is the key to this: in organisations that are production orientated, the span of control is narrower, whereas sales orientated organisations have a broader span of control that is not so reliant on the operations of others. Distance does mean difficulties for the manager, as they may be unable to exercise clear control over their subordinates. Moderate dispersion of the operations of the organisation means that the span of control is generally decreased, while substantial dispersion means that the span of control is greatly increased.

◆ managers who have a personal assistant find that dealing with a broad span of control is greatly improved. The personal assistant is able to collect data and information on the manager's behalf. This leads to more of the manager's time being available for the supervision of subordinates.

◆ a vital feature of many organisations is the fact that a number of subordinates are also supervised in some way by managers who have a cross-organisational role (particularly in the matrix style organisation – *see* pp. 30–2). It is not uncommon for individuals to receive as much as half of their supervision from managers who are not their direct line manager. Although this complicates matters as far as the span of control is concerned, there is a greater enhancement of the overall management of the organisation. The only problems that may arise as a result are conflicts in the nature of the supervision, but this can be eradicated by a notion of 'unity of command' throughout the organisation.

The level of discretion that a subordinate is given to make decisions (for example, the range of areas covered and the time allowed before bringing a matter to the attention of the manager) can add a further dimension to the span of control. The discretion rests upon two key issues:

1 The capabilities of the subordinate, in other words their ability to cope with the demands of the job.

2 The motivational status of the subordinate and their desire to be fully involved in the job.

Both of these concerns rest upon the perceptions of the manager and several key assumptions. Among these are the manager's views on the initiative, maturity and ability of the subordinate. If the manager is not prepared to accept the subordinate's abilities in these areas then the level of control and supervision needs to be higher.

The relative stability of the organisational environment will also have an affect on the span of control. Any objectives and goals that have been relayed and agreed by the manager and the subordinates can be assumed as being covered. If the environment changes, the sub-objectives and sub-goals may be considered as inappropriate and may need to be redefined. When a crisis looms, there is a tendency for the decision making to be taken back by the management and further up the hierarchy.

The accepted pyramidal nature of the majority of organisations is somewhat challenged by the concept of spans of control. For organisations that have both staff and line relationships, there is a tendency for a reverse pyramidal form to exist. In others, there is an indefinable pattern that does not conform with the hypothetical structures. The concept of linked command groups allows us to appreciate the fact that a manager will simultaneously have a number of conventional relationships with subordinates and a series of horizontal (or peer) relationships with others at the same level of the hierarchy. The demands of these roles are often conflicting or at least contradictory. A manager needs to be capable of handling a diverse range of roles to reduce or eliminate the resulting stress and confusion.

Formal and informal groups and relationships within an organisation

Groups and teams are very common within organisations. Groups, technically speaking, are two or more individuals who come into personal and meaningful contact on a continued basis. A team on the other hand is a group of individuals who are empowered to participate in decision making and exercise some degree of influence over how their objectives are met. Within an organisation there are essentially two different types of group: the *formal group* whose purpose is directly related to the attainment of stated organisational objectives; and the *informal group* which develops around shared day-to-day activities or interactions and enables the members to meet their own needs.

Formal groups

Formal groups tend to be used to pass on and share information. They are also used to gain commitment, help make decisions and train individuals. They are often seen as an official part of the organisation structure. In this respect they will of course include quality circles, project groups, boards of directors and various committees. Some of the formal groups will exist for a long period of time, whereas others will be given a short life span in order to carry out specific tasks.

The majority of managers and supervisors will be members of teams or groups. We can identify three main types of formal group which will be most common. These are:

1 Problem-solving teams – consist of a variable number of employees from different areas of the organisation who are given the responsibility and authority to implement ideas in order to address a particular concern.

2 Special purpose teams – will possibly be rather more broadly based in terms of their membership and will attempt to assist the introduction of changes in

working practices and new technologies into the organisation. They will facilitate the linkage of the specialist functions within the organisation such as marketing, human resources and manufacturing, and be able to give valuable inputs as to the probable impact of changes in technology or working practices on specific areas of the organisation.

3   The self-managing teams – usually consist of a number of individuals who meet on a daily basis in order to carry out a series of managerial tasks including work scheduling. It is common for organisations which have a fluctuating work load to have self-managing teams meet each morning in order to allocate and prioritise the work for the rest of the employees for the day or the remaining part of the week.

One of the overriding considerations in many of these formal teams is that there is still a notion of hierarchy. While many organisations will take steps to level out or eradicate the more inhibiting problems which are associated with working with individuals of considerably higher rank, in a team this is not always possible. There may be a sense of reluctance from more junior members to involve themselves fully.

Informal groups

As we mentioned earlier, the second major category of group is the informal group which may develop to support particular activities both within or outside the organisation. This is seen as a vital network of individuals who will co-operate and collaborate with one another in order to implement particular tasks and fulfil certain roles.

Line and staff relationships within an organisation

In most organisations there is certainly a blurring of the distinction between line and staff responsibilities and relationships. Strictly speaking, line relationships imply that these individuals have a direct supervisory role which is based on formal authority. The staff relationships imply something rather more informal and suggest a right to advise. Line functions as we have seen are more closely linked to the organisational objectives and perhaps the means or methods of production. The particular functions obviously differ from one organisation to another. Staff departments as we have also seen provide more specialist tasks and skills which are designed to be in co-operation with the line management. Whatever the relationships between the line and staff employees, it is certainly the case that the staff employees should restrict their activities to the support of the line functions.

Obviously the location of staff departments within an organisation will reflect the degree to which these departments are required as a necessary day-to-day function of operations. Indeed the managers responsible for the smooth running of the staff functions of an organisation may find themselves to be relatively high in the hierarchy. This will enable them to co-ordinate the staff support mechanisms rather more effectively. This is particularly true of finance and administration functions. In recent years the inclusion of an individual manager responsible for the implementation and monitoring of information technology systems has also proved to be invaluable at board level. Staff departments do provide necessary services for specific line functions and they are generally located physically close to the line employees involved as well as being available for direct and permanent access.

There will always be a degree of conflict between the line and staff roles because the majority of the managers involved do not necessarily see their functions as being perfectly complementary. Staff managers, for example, may be rather more imaginative, co-operative and adaptable since they do not have a direct linkage to the overall performance of the organisation which can be measured in a specific manner. Line managers, on the other hand, may be rather more independent and forceful. This difference between the two management approaches inevitably causes a degree of conflict. Being relatively higher in the hierarchical structure of the organisation, the staff managers have access to information which the line managers would not normally see. In this way they are able to analyse more global data and report on the effectiveness of particular line managers. This informal authority can cause a degree of uncertainty and paranoia on the part of the line managers. They see the staff function as being a way in which their own decision making and operations are controlled by the hierarchy of the organisation. There are a number of references throughout this book to the nature of line and staff relationships within an organisation and you will find some useful specific information in respect of the matrix structure as well as the combinations of individuals used in teams.

Project teams

As we will see, the matrix structure offers great flexibility, but has a degree of permanence about it. Project teams, on the other hand, are temporary structures designed to complete a specific task often in an unstable environment. Individuals are selected from a variety of different departments, the choice being based on their expertise and technical ability related to the project in hand rather than their rank or status within the organisation. Many project teams are based on the need to work very closely with clients or customers and will have the relevant expertise in their chosen areas as well as experience in close client liaison. Some project teams are an amalgam of in-house experts and external specialists brought in on a fixed short-term contract basis.

Often, the project team will duplicate the normal functions of other individuals within the organisation. This is deliberate, as the in-house departments may not be able to handle the project at short notice or they may have differing priorities that preclude their involvement. Above all, the project team needs to be operating with clear objectives and goals within a specified time-frame. In larger organisations a number of different project teams will be in existence, operating at various levels and complexity.

Matrix relationships

As we will see in the second section of this book when we consider the different structures prevalent in the different organisations, matrix relationships are based on multiple levels of authority and multiple support systems. The matrix structure was evolved in the aerospace industry in order to facilitate easier control of particular projects.

In essence there are two different lines of authority within a matrix structure: one is the functional departmental authority which in effect runs vertically and the other is the project or product authority which runs horizontally, as illustrated in Fig. 1.10. In this way the matrix structure has three very different sets of relationships. The first is between the project manager and the functional and product managers. The second is the relationship between the functional and product managers who share a number of subordinates. The third is between the subordinates themselves and their various managers.

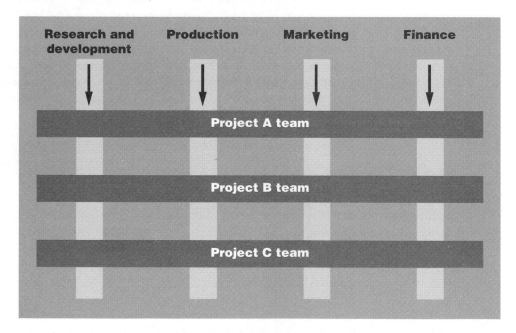

Fig. 1.10 Matrix organisational structure

Advantages and disadvantages of matrix structures

The matrix structure attempts to incorporate many of the advantages which can be seen in functional and product forms while minimising the disadvantages associated with them. It also helps to break down barriers by allowing employees from different functional departments to pool their skills and resources in solving common problems. In other words, the matrix structure tries to maximise use of human and financial resources making it more adaptable to changing sets of circumstances.

It is comparatively difficult, of course, to transfer from a functional or product orientated organisational structure to a matrix structure. It requires a great degree of flexibility and co-operation throughout the organisation. In addition to this, the managers need to acquire a new range of skills not least involving the resolution of interdepartmental conflicts. If the organisation is operating in an environment which requires an innovative approach then the management needs to give strong consideration to the matrix structure. This will enable the organisation to co-ordinate the marketing, production and personnel functions. Managers will also have access to a wider range of information which they will need in order to respond to rapidly changing markets and technologies.

Providing the organisation can use its resources in an efficient manner then it may find that the matrix structure makes it far easier for them to transfer skills, personnel and effort from one product range to another. The prime advantage of the matrix structure is that it allows the organisation to use the specialist skills from a number of different areas within the organisation for the benefit of wider areas of the organisation itself. It does lessen the co-ordination problems which would be associated in a structure which is geared to functions or products. Project managers will be able to gain considerable experience particularly in interpersonal, information-related and decision-making roles through their involvement with other areas of the organisation. This should in turn improve the quality of decision making, innovation and problem solving.

One of the principal problems associated with matrix structures is that individuals can find it extremely difficult to decide where their loyalties actually lie. Should precedence be given to the department in which the individual is normally employed or to their project team, bearing in mind that the project team may be of short duration? Certain departmental or functional heads may consider that their requirements are paramount and that matrix responsibilities which have been given to their subordinates should take a lower level of priority. This 'office politics' will inevitably lead to stress and put strains on relationships. It is common for conflicts in loyalty to actually erode the effectiveness of particular project teams. Once a project team has been established then it needs to be given the opportunity to develop as an effective decision-making and problem-solving unit. Inevitably team moral will be effected if there are changes in personnel. Projects will begin and end causing the break-up of project teams. In addition to this, as a project changes over a period of months, it may be difficult to ensure that the personnel involved in that particular project remain constant throughout the duration. There will also be a degree of inertia arising from the move of project team members back into more functional roles. Individuals who are in constant demand as members of project teams will find that their stay within a functional departmental structure is a short one, not really allowing them enough time to re-establish themselves in their previous hierarchy.

The influence of technology on the organisational structure

Technology has had and will continue to have a dramatic effect on the organisational structure of a business. The first major influence that we can identify is associated with productivity increases. This is coupled with the relevant changes in motivation of individuals. Certainly we can readily see that changes in the production systems used by an organisation will have a marked effect if machines become a substitute for humans.

Many jobs are determined by the technology used within an organisation. With the introduction of technology and machines, jobs are changed. This process of mechanisation may eliminate or replace the lower skilled jobs and create fewer but newer higher skilled jobs. In some cases, however, the exact reverse is true. The introduction of machinery has reduced the number of higher skilled individuals replacing them with a smaller number of lower skilled employees whose main purpose is to monitor and replenish the stocks fed into the machine. It is certainly the case that, as technology has developed and organisations which have embraced this new technology have become more conversant with its possibilities there is less opportunity for competitors to enter the market-place. Organisations which use sophisticated technologies have made considerable investments over a number of years that many other organisations will find difficult to replicate.

With the continued development of technology there will be a time lapse before even the most committed organisation can readily and easily incorporate new developments into its systems. Then by the time they are in a position to implement the necessary changes, technology will have moved on again. This gradual adjustment from the technology used at present to the type of technology available for the future will be a continuing problem. Given the nature of many of the different technologies it is very difficult to institute a system by which the technology can gradually evolve. In many sets of circumstances the technology has to be completely replaced.

Defining technology

We need to identify exactly what we mean by the term technology. Broadly speaking technology represents a body of knowledge. There is also a notion that it has a scientific basis. To this end technology is not only the knowledge but it is the way in which tools, machinery, devices and other gadgets can be used within the organisational environment. Technology is often related to problem solving or at least producing a particular desired outcome whether it is a product or piece of data. There also needs to be some linkage between the use of machines and the individuals who will operate these machines.

Technology then can be more clearly defined as equipment or machines which operate in a particular way to produce a series of activities, methods or processes. This is perhaps an abstract way of looking at technology. However, it is impossible to be specific about the use or at least the level of use of technology within a particular organisation. It is true to say that there are some commonalities between the use of technology from one organisation to another. This would be particularly true of information technology and the use of desktop computers. Once our investigation goes beyond the use of basic information technologies we are considering specialist uses of specialist technologies.

Technical and social systems

If we consider technology to be of paramount importance within an organisation, we could say that the organisational structure is something more of a socio-technical system than a social system. Bearing in mind that the social system is a web of behaviour of individuals, if we incorporate the use of technology into that equation then we have an overlying system based on technology.

Systems theory would support this notion. In fact it would go further and state that technical and social systems within an organisation are interdependent. They both influence one another; they both determine one another's form and function. In addition to this the social system may well set limits on the technology that can be used. However, in other sets of circumstances it is the technology that will determine the nature of the social system. There is no natural match between particular technical systems and social systems. They will vary from organisation to organisation but one thing for certain is that the organisational structure will either determine the use of technology within the business or the technology will have had a marked influence on the organisational structure itself.

Whether the social system has determined the technical system or vice versa they must be compatible with one another. Obviously when new technologies are overlaid onto an existing social system within an organisation there will be periods of uncertainty and friction. Over a period of time however the technology will become part of the social system forming, as we said earlier, a socio-technical system. The technology will then have been accepted and will be as much a part of the organisational structure and its overall functions as any individual employee.

Introducing and applying technology

The use of technology within an organisation will obviously be dependant on its worth to that business. The technology needs to work but beyond that it also needs to accomplish particular and specified outcomes. Primarily these outcomes will be economic in nature related to the efficient use of resources or perhaps the greatest possible return on investment. Technologies will not necessarily be chosen by an organisation purely on the basis of whether they work within the organisational structure and are suitable for a particular purpose; they need to be somewhat more sophisticated than that. They need to minimise costs or maximise gains, otherwise there may be little point in introducing them. By purely spending large amounts of money on technology, the organisation is not guaranteed a greater level of efficiency.

On an evaluation level then we can look at the technology and say clearly whether it fits a particular purpose, but beyond this we need to look at the costs. We need to determine whether the technology allows the organisation to be more profitable or more efficient. Ultimately this will determine whether the organisation is more or less profitable in general terms than similar organisations. As you will appreciate, it is very difficult to determine performance in a purely abstract manner. This requires a great deal of experience, judgement and knowledge of the situations and the available technologies before any meaningful statement can be made.

Technical systems tend to be closed systems or at least more closed than the organisation itself. The organisation will have to be structured in such a way that it can accommodate a wide variety of different inputs. The technology or the technical system itself will only constitute a very small part of the overall operations of the organisation. In this respect the function of the technology is very clear. If we extend the closed nature of technical systems to the actual functions of the individuals involved we will also note that in the majority of cases when technology is used exclusively, the nature of the jobs involved are somewhat more limited. A department which, for example, is responsible for ensuring quality control, may use a series of technologies in order to establish benchmarks. This is their sole and only purpose. Technology is perfectly suitable in these cases, however; it is only when the application of the individual has been overlaid onto the technical system that we get any sense of openness and relevance to the organisation as a whole.

If an organisation is in a position to break down the work process into clearly defined subsections then it is possible that technology could be used to replace or improve certain parts of that production process. This is known as systematising. During this process the most efficient and effective way of carrying out a particular task is identified with the sole purpose of increasing productivity. This means that any implementation of technology related in this sense is made in a purely rational and productive manner. Mechanisation within certain areas of industry has continued apace. Not only this, the service sector has seen considerable amounts of mechanisation leading to enormous job losses. Naturally, both of these processes in the manufacturing sector and the tertiary sector have led to enormous changes in organisational structures. Machinery or technology is used to carry out many of the core activities of the organisation leading, as we have said, to substantial reductions in the number of individuals required to work within the organisation. There are a number of key elements which determine the degree to which the mechanisation process has been incorporated within the organisation.

From the basic introduction of technology, the organisation may choose to spread technology throughout the whole of the organisation at every level. With the introduction of desktop computers as a departmental resource we can now see that they are commonplace on nearly all desks within the majority of organisations. This progressive increase in the amount of technology employed is inevitable since not only do organisations readily appreciate the advantages, they also realise that they must incorporate the use of technology in order to remain efficient.

Organisations need to be explicit about the importance of technology and the long-term effects it will have on the structure of the organisation itself. It may be necessary to determine the scope or the spread of technology throughout the organisation and to address the question of how much penetration into support activities technology will have. As a result of this the organisation needs to consider how sophisticated the technology will need to be in order to support the needs which they have identified.

In organisations where the central function of the business is to produce products and services then mechanisation or the introduction of technology is somewhat more inevitable. By substituting machines for direct human labour, the organisation can attempt to establish a more regular level of production and achievement. This means that there will be considerable changes in the organisational structure, not least in terms of what happens to all the individuals whose job roles have been subsumed by technology. Skilled craftsmen may become machine minders leading to a reduction in their prestige, security, remuneration and status within the organisation. However, more complex machinery does need higher skilled workers. This means that these individuals need to be able to perform at a higher skill level than perhaps they had done in the past. Many of the negative effects of de-skilling which we have already mentioned are reversed in this scenario. Automation is of course inevitable in a number of process-orientated organisations. The first level of replacement of humans begins at the lowest level of unskilled or semi-skilled manual posts. There has been a considerable rise in the amount of technology which has been introduced in this manner. It has been an expensive and long-term process, requiring commitment by the organisation; however, they appreciate the long-term benefits.

So how is the organisational structure influenced by the use of technology? It is certainly true that there is a thinning out of employees at the bottom end of the organisational structure. There is also a reduced need for hands-on supervisors and managers at the lowest levels since the number of employees involved has been drastically reduced. Naturally this has a knock-on effect as we look further up the hierarchical levels of the organisation. Managers who had considerable line management responsibilities in the past will have a reduced role to play. This may mean that some form of downsizing or rationalisation of the middle to senior management can also occur. In some respects this means that the organisation will certainly become far leaner in terms of employees from senior level to shop floor. It also probably implies that the majority of individuals are either extremely highly skilled or unskilled in relation to production. The net result and effect on management is that, although they will have fewer individuals to manage as such, they will have to carry out a wider variety of functions and roles particularly in relation to the monitoring of performance and productivity. For more general functions carried out by managers in the past, staff appointments can now be made to take account of the lower levels of employment within the organisation. It is therefore more convenient to establish a centralised personnel department, for example, which can take responsibility across the board for all employees. This means that duplication within each department or division is no longer necessary since the number of individual employees has been reduced.

It was originally assumed that the introduction of information technology to organisations would mean that large numbers of lower middle-level managerial jobs would have been eliminated. There was also the anticipation that there would be a re-centralisation of decision making within the organisation. The original forecasts of the effects of information technology have proved to be inaccurate. Computers, for the most part, are still under-utilised. The social system within the organisational structure has not yet developed enough, generally speaking, to take full advantage of the uses of information technology. Those at the bottom end of the hierarchy find it difficult to defend their jobs or roles against information technology; those who are higher in the hierarchy may have the power and authority to resist its introduction and effects.

What information technology has been able to do is to expose the true performance of many managers and departments. In the past it would have been relatively easy for an individual to mask the true performance of his or her department, or at the very least prepare some sort of defence to explain a particular level of performance. Computers do enable the organisation to make more global decisions which would affect all areas of the business. Although these decisions are somewhat generalised, they can enable the decision makers to be far more consistent.

In terms of technology's net effect upon the organisational structure itself we can see that the manager's power and authority over subordinates have both been increased in certain areas and decreased in others. Direction of effort can be determined by the information technology: technology, being systematic and procedural in nature, leads to greater personal control over an individual's workload. For automated systems, the fact that the machinery will continue the pace throughout the day may have considerable effects on the way in which the organisation needs to be structured. The business may need to consider providing the machinery with a constant level of human manning in order to ensure that productivity remains constant. With the introduction of technology the level of decision making left under the control of individuals is sharply reduced. This again is very much related to the level of productivity which is expected as a result of the level of automation. Although there is a constant set of changes which are inevitable in all organisations as a result of the introduction of technology, machinery has certainly increased this pace. There are smaller numbers of employees moving into higher skilled jobs while the majority are moving into less skilled positions. This again will have a drastic effect on the overall organisational structure.

Depending upon the nature of the technology involved we can identify a number of different ways in which it can affect the structure and the business itself. For manufacturing organisations, the technology is often referred to as 'long-linked'. This means that the technology introduced involves many hundreds if not thousands of different individual acts which are carried out in order to produce a final product. The degree of repetition in producing the product is the foundation upon which the technology was initially introduced. The large numbers of products which are produced can all be manufactured within fairly narrow limits of variation. Banking and insurance are examples of areas of business activity which involve the bringing together or standardisation of various complex procedures. In this example, we can refer to the technology as being 'mediating' which means that the various procedures have been standardised in order to allow the technology to handle the large number of transactions and procedures. Each individual transaction, although it will be unique, contains many similar elements to that of the standard transaction.

Intensive technology

Intensive technology refers to situations where the specialist nature of the work carried out determines the highly sophisticated level of technology which would be employed. Specialist functions or specialist tasks carried out by the technology will differ from situation to situation. There will be no degree of standardisation or indeed pre-planning of requirements. Typically, intensive technologies would include the various hospital treatments which are reliant upon the use of technology, and the use of design-based technologies in the arts. In the former example we can see that it is impossible for doctors or technology-based employees working in a hospital to predict the level of treatment or repeat use of the technology for a particular patient. They will not be able to plan the sequence of uses of technology related to a particular individual, neither will they be able to determine the length of time the individual requires to use that technology.

Further structural considerations

We can certainly see that in the majority of manufacturing organisations the introduction of technology has radically affected all levels of the organisational structure. There are different patterns of spans of control, there are radically different ratios between management and staff and there are variations in the levels of management within the organisation. In some cases we can make a direct link between the type of production predominantly used within an organisation and some of these factors. For organisations which use batch production we can see that the number of levels of management tend to be no more than three. For mass production organisations this average number of levels increases to four. It is in the organisations which have a more continuous process of production that we see a higher number of levels of management averaging out at around six. The natural assumption is that as we move from unit or batch production which is less reliant upon technology, to mass or continuous production which is more reliant on technology, the organisation needs a considerably more complex management structure. It appears at the very least that the number of levels of authority have been considerably increased.

Referring to the span of control within these similar types of manufacturing organisation, line managers in unit or batch production organisations have tended to have a span of control of no more than 20 to 30. Mass production organisations have required their managers to have a span of control of up to 50. However, the interesting point is that continuous production organisations have dropped the span of control to less than 20. There are a number of things that we can read into this set of data. Certainly there is a correlation between the size or nature of the production process and the span of control. We could say to some extent that mass production requires less personal supervision since the technology accounts for much of the control. As more and more activities of individual employees are dictated or controlled by the machinery or the technological system, the direct span of control of the manager is less crucial. In the continuous process systems, where nearly all of the activities have been taken over by technology, the nature of the jobs in which the employees are involved are not as predictable. Their main role will be to maintain the machinery and carry out a series of routine checks. In this respect, the activities are far more varied. This implies that the managerial span of control needs to be somewhat narrower. The diversity of the activities undertaken by the employees will make it difficult for managers to keep a close eye on them, hence the narrower span of control.

In mass production situations where an employee's job has become basic and highly repetitive, the individual can acquire a high level of skill at that particular job very quickly. This means that close supervision is unnecessary. As we have already mentioned, in process systems where the variety of different jobs required of the individual are somewhat more varied, it is difficult for managers to predict exactly what kind of skills and experience their employees will need. It is therefore essential that a close level of management is placed upon these individuals.

Without doubt the application of technology within an organisation will certainly determine the way in which the structure develops. In addition to this we can see that the level of technology operating within an organisation will also determine the number of employees necessary to carry out the various functions. This is particularly true of manufacturing organisations or organisations which have experienced considerable developments in the technology used. We can see that in the tertiary sector, activities such as banking, insurance and tourism have been radically affected by the introduction of technology. Computerised banking, record keeping and monitoring have drastically reduced the number of employees. In the tourist industry the introduction of technology and the streamlining of bookings have also similarly affected the number of employees. We can also see that, up to a certain point, the introduction of mass production technologies will reduce and drastically affect the organisational structure. However, once a certain point has been reached and the organisation shifts from mass production to a continuous process production there is a slight return to a narrower span of control together with a reduction in the overall number of levels of management.

Review questions

1 Outline the key features of a bureaucratic organisation.

2 What is departmentalisation? Describe its various forms or classifications.

3 Explain the process of delegation and comment on how it could increase organisational effectiveness.

4 Outline the key advantages and disadvantages of centralisation and decentralisation.

5 What are the key differences between line and staff relationships in an organisation?

6 What is the principal aim of personnel planning?

7 Outline the key stages of the recruitment, selection and training process aimed at ensuring that the individual fits into the existing organisational structure.

8 What is the chain of command and how does this influence the organisational structure?

9 Explain the nature of spans of control. How is this illustrated in a typical organisation chart?

10 Describe the nature of formal groups within an organisation and identify three different types of formal group.

11 Explain the terms 'systemising' and 'mechanisation'.

12 Outline the probable effects of the introduction of new technology on a typical organisation.

1.2

Structural factors which influence the success or failure of an organisation

A number of theorists have attempted to study the relationship between structure and performance. Typically, this would involve the comparison of organisations that have a low or high profit level.

Joan Woodward (1965) identified a close relationship between organisations that had introduced technology (enabling them to use batch production) and better management control. This relationship between technology, a more adaptable structure and success is a recurrent one.

The next year saw Burns and Stalker (1966) noting that different organisations in particular areas of the economy had distinctive forms of structure. The more technical ones had an organic structure, while the organisations in more traditional areas of activity tended to have rigid structures that were quite bureaucratic.

Perhaps it was Khandwalla, in his 1970s study consisting of several articles, who identified the fact that a number of different approaches can be made. He did not find a discernible relationship between structure and performance but there were, however, a number of similarities between those successful organisations or the highest performers. The principal similarities were that:

◆ the functional elements of the organisation had their own separate departmental structure (some 75 per cent).

◆ the organisation had favoured splitting the various parts of their operations into clearly definable divisions (30 per cent).

◆ the organisation had opted for some form of vertical integration to rationalise the structure and the operations (30 per cent).

◆ the board and senior managers encouraged and supported delegation of the decision-making (40 per cent).

◆ the organisation positively encouraged participation in decision making at all levels of the company (60 per cent).

◆ the management still used formal controls over the organisation (50 per cent).

The truly successful organisations design themselves to match the situation in which they find themselves, or the way in which they intend to operate. This is known as *congruence theory*, indicating that there is a relationship between the contingency factors and the design possibilities of the organisation. *Configuration theory*, as we will see later, demands that there has to be a very close relationship between the different aspects of the design and that this design is consistent throughout the whole of the organisation. Before we turn our attention to configuration theory, it is worth investing a little time in considering congruence theory.

Many organisations will have to trade off consistency in structure with situational needs and sometimes situational factors. It very much depends on contingency factors such as the technical systems used or perhaps the size of the organisation. As we will see later, the effectively structured organisation has a high degree of consistency in design and in its contingency factors, when worked through to their logical conclusion. The closer the relationship between the contingency factors and the design parameters, the greater the degree of congruence there will be in the organisation.

◆ Configuration

Following the theories of Mintzberg, we can readily identify five major configurations that need to be described. He called these:

◆ the simple structure.

◆ the machine bureaucracy.

◆ the professional bureaucracy.

◆ the divisional form.

◆ the adhocracy.

Before we begin to investigate each of these proposed forms, it would be useful to identify the key differences between each of the different configurations and see whether there are any broad categorisations that would be useful. Mintzberg suggests that there are three aspects that will help to summarise the differences between the configurations. The first is the 'prime co-ordinating mechanism', which refers to the main reasoning behind the choice of organisation type; in other words, the actual nature of the work carried out within the organisation itself. The second he refers to as the 'key part of the organisation'. By this, he means that a specific part of the organisation has a major role in the operations of the organisation. The final criterion is referred to as the 'type of decentralisation'. This pinpoints the exact nature of the delegation of responsibility and operations within the organisation. We can now see how these criteria overlay and interact with one another in our description of the five organisational types.

The simple structure is primarily co-ordinated by direct supervision, the most important part of the organisation being the top or apex of the structure where the majority of decisions are made (*see* Fig. 1.11). There is vertical and horizontal centralisation which tends to inhibit the ability of subordinates to make decisions themselves. The existence of a strategic apex means that the major determining factor is one of centralisation: the key players in the organisation need to maintain control over the decision-making process.

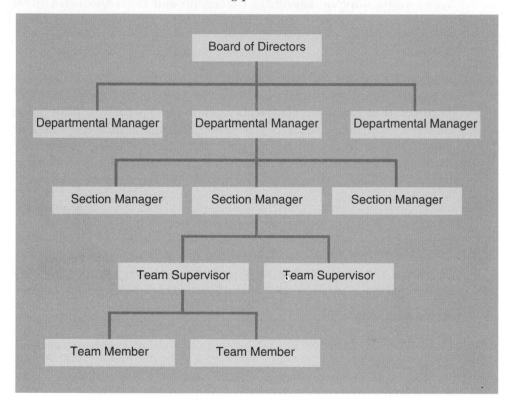

Fig. 1.11 Simple organisation chart

The machine bureaucracy by virtue of its reliance on technology as a primary means of production will tend to standardise the work processes. This means that the organisational structure can be called a 'techno-structure', as it is very much machine-orientated. There needs to be some degree of horizontal decentralisation but this is often limited as individual work processes have their own sub-structure.

In a professional bureaucracy there is still a standardisation of skills with much of the administration being undertaken centrally. This is known as 'the operating core'. Most of the professionals working in this type of organisation will be comparatively autonomous, relying on the core administrative support of a number of individuals. To this end, there is a degree of vertical and horizontal decentralisation, which allows this level of autonomy.

Organisations which exhibit a divisionalised form of structure, as shown in Fig. 1.12, will have a tendency to have standardised outputs, with clearly identified sub-divisions that have sole responsibility for meeting targets and adhering to budgets. This process is known as *balkanisation*. In this respect organisations such as these will have a number of similar sub-structures within the main structure which replicate operations. Middle management hold the key positions in these organisations as they have responsibility for discrete divisions. There will also be a limited amount of vertical decentralisation in order to facilitate day-to-day decision making.

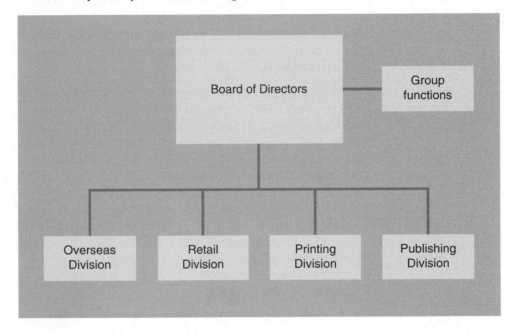

Fig. 1.12 Divisional structure

In an adhocracy there needs to be a high level of collaboration and mutual assistance between different parts of the organisation. Each discrete area of the organisation will need to be flexible enough to make adjustments to their work schedules in order to accommodate the needs of other parts of the organisation. There tends to be a reliance on support staff in such organisations, as their efforts will underpin the activities of the specialists. They, too, will need to be flexible and responsive so that they can adjust their work schedules accordingly. These organisations exhibit selective decentralisation, allowing co-ordination between the various parts of the organisation without the involvement of senior management.

We can now, therefore, identify five key 'pulls' on an organisation. These are:

1   The pull to centralise.

2 The pull to standardise.

3 The pull to professionalise.

4 The pull to balkanise.

5 The pull to collaborate.

Having considered the key aspects of each of these five configurations, we should now look in some greater detail at each of them.

Simple structures

The simple structure, as we have seen, has little or no techno-structure. It tends to be very light on support staff, with no clear definition of divisions of labour. Above all, simple structures do not have a complex management team. Many of the activities revolve around dealing with situations on a needs basis. For the most part the simple structure is an organic one.

With the majority of key decisions being made by a single individual at the strategic apex of the organisation, this means that the rest of the organisation is involved in operations rather than decision making. The job structure of each employee is flexible, and tends to be unspecialised and interchangeable with others. For the most part decision making is also flexible, albeit centralised at the strategic apex. This allows for tighter co-ordination of decision-making, but also for intuitive decisions to be made, facilitating a true entrepreneurial approach. The individual at the strategic apex has to be a true leader in all aspects. They will have to directly supervise, monitor, operate as a figure-head, allocate resources and undertake all other managerial roles. As Khandwalla stated, the simple structure exhibits the following tendencies:

◆ a lack of product and marketing research.

◆ a lack of training and staff development.

◆ a very loose grip on finances.

◆ an entrepreneurial approach.

◆ a power-orientated structure.

◆ a somewhat conservative approach to decision making and development.

◆ a 'seat of the pants' managerial style.

The simple structure often operates in what could be described as a dynamic environment. In other words, the environment is so fluid that there is no opportunity or desire to standardise operations. This would be a pointless exercise since the nature of the environment in which the structure operates is constantly changing, requiring the organisation to make rapid changes to its operations. There is a tendency for many organisations to be simple structures in the first few years of their existence. For the most part, organisations which remain small will retain the vestiges of a simple structure. It is only when the size of the operation increases that repetition of work can lead to standardisation.

Perhaps one of the more interesting variations on the simple structure is the organisation that constantly operates in a state of crisis. In these organisations there is a need to be able to respond rapidly to changing situations, meaning that power is always held by those at the strategic apex and the organisation cannot allow bureaucratic functions to get in the way of operations. The synthetic organisation as described by James Thompson is, in effect, a crisis organisation. However, these operate in very extraordinary circumstances. Typically, we would see a synthetic organisation brought into existence to cope with a natural disaster or some other similar problem in need of attention.

The autocratic organisation can also be a simple structure. There is a high degree of formalised behaviour and all decision-making power is held by a single individual. A very similar set of circumstances can be found in a charismatic organisation where all decisions are made by an individual, but by mutual consent rather than terror.

Analysts have identified the fact that the simple structure predominates in less developed countries, where there is a distinct lack of educated individuals capable of carrying out the bureaucratic functions. This means that the majority of work has to be undertaken under direct supervision, thus reducing the ability of the organisation to proceed beyond that of a simple structure.

Given the fact that many simple structures are entrepreneurial and dynamic, they often lack the necessary ability to survive in the long term. There is an incredibly high attrition rate for these simple structures. Many are unable to make the transition into another structure. This does not mean, however, that organisations that cannot adopt a bureaucratic form are doomed to failure; they may just lack the skills to put some of the bureaucratic features into operation.

With most of the power held at the strategic apex, the organisation can be flexible and adaptive as only one individual needs to act to have an impact on the situation. However, we can see that this centralisation of power can cause confusion between strictly strategic decisions and operating issues. As we have said, over-reliance on a single individual can cause problems for the organisation. If that individual, who is aware of all activities within the organisation, is unable to make a decision for one reason or another, the structure is left in limbo.

Finally, there are two conflicting viewpoints regarding the simple structure. On the one hand many individuals enjoy working in an intimate organisation and for a leader who may be charismatic and approachable. To some extent this is a perfect social system, rather like a family. On the other hand, simple structures can be seen as being rather restrictive, with all decisions being made by a single individual, allowing no scope for personal development. However, the simple structure is still one of the most common forms of organisation. While some organisations will inevitably move from this configuration to a more complex configuration, there are always new organisations starting out as simple structure.

Machine bureaucracies

The machine bureaucracy exhibits a number of common features, which include:

◆ involvement in highly specialised markets.

◆ a high degree of routine operations.

◆ a series of formalised procedures.

◆ an overabundance of rules and regulations.

◆ formalised communication systems within the organisation.

◆ functional organisation of employees.

◆ centralised decision-making.

◆ fussy and elaborate administrative structures.

◆ noticeable differences between line and staff employees.

The machine bureaucracy relies very heavily on the standardisation of its operating procedures (*see* Fig. 1.13). Based on a techno-structure, there is considerable scope for standardisation. Without individuals whose sole responsibility it is to analyse the work processes, there would be no opportunity to standardise. In this respect, researchers, engineers, planners and designers can all be found within the machine bureaucracy. They will institutionalise the working practices. In order to support this, the rules and regulations will be somewhat inflexible to ensure that standardisation proceeds without interruption. Equally, there is a tendency for the formal chain of authority to be at the centre of all decision making and communications.

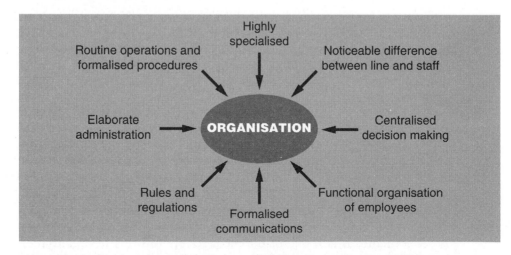

Fig. 1.13 Features of a machine bureaucracy

The managers who have formal authority over the workforce will operate in a distinctly different environment to that of the staff employees. The latter will have no direct input into the supervision of operatives. Above all, a sense of control permeates throughout the organisation. Each manager will be charged with the task of ensuring that their subordinates are performing according to the operational rules and regulations at each level.

The machine bureaucracy needs to be efficient. As the name implies, there needs to be a smooth and uninterrupted flow of work throughout the organisation. Unfortunately this tends to mean that there is a distinct difference between the control systems and the reality of production which will inevitably throw up a series of conflicts at both horizontal and vertical points throughout the organisation.

At the strategic apex of the organisation the key role of these individuals is that of fine tuning. They know precisely what is required of the organisation and have an understanding of the necessary outputs. As Hunt suggested, they have a problem between balancing performance against necessary problem solving. This conflict between performance and problem solving takes up most of the time of the key decision makers. It is readily apparent that there is considerable power at this strategic apex. Only the analysts and other staff members have any real input in to or impact on the standardisation process. Most decisions are top-down, with very little scope for suggestions to be brought on board from lower tiers of the organisation.

Ideally, a machine bureaucracy would operate in an environment that is stable and simple to understand. Most machine bureaucracies have existed long enough to have incorporated a high level of standardisation, arising out of repetitive work. Above all, the required quality standards will have been established. It is in mass production that we find the majority of machine bureaucracies, where a high level of standardisation is possible and all other operations have been segmented in such a way as to facilitate economies of scale and a clear hierarchy. Once a machine bureaucracy has established its key standardisation criteria, it can then reduce the level of administration within the structure. It no longer requires elaborate administrative structures to control and produce the information to build the standardisation system.

Many government departments and local authority structures exhibit features of a machine bureaucracy. The standardisation of processes such as tax collection can mean that routine operations are easily established. They are bureaucracies, but involved in work flow rather than production.

It is said that the most efficient structure to control simple repetitive tasks is the machine bureaucracy. This structure allows consistent output with a machine-like efficiency. Unfortunately, it does not favour the general welfare of the employees who are, to all intents and purposes, part of the machinery itself. For societies that demand cheap mass-produced products, there may be no alternative to the machine bureaucracy. On the one hand this configuration allows efficient production, but on the other hand it ignores individual employee satisfaction.

Providing the administrative core of the machine bureaucracy operates in an efficient manner which incorporates co-ordination and supervision, the routine activities are adequately addressed. It is only when non-routine or unexpected situations arise that the machine bureaucracy finds difficulty in coping. There is a need, therefore, for the inflexible administrative core to become rather more adaptive. This also means that those at the strategic apex need to be able to predict the unexpected. Without these two pre-conditions the machine bureaucracy appears to be much more cumbersome and unable to respond than, perhaps, is true. Many of these problems can be solved by the incorporation of a flexible management information system which is available at all decision points within the organisation.

The chain of authority, as the primary means by which decisions are made, can become over-burdened in times of change. Many decisions will appear to address problems in a superficial manner. This also needs to be resolved by making the chain of command rather more flexible. The implementation of strategy and decisions has to have the ability to be reformulated as it moves up or down the hierarchical structure. Without this, the machine bureaucracy appears to be ill-suited to change and non-adaptive in many respects. The solution may be to revert back to that of a more simple structure.

Professional bureaucracies

The structural configuration known as the professional bureaucracy is bureaucratic without being centralised. It has been able to standardise its behaviour, but the operations are controlled by the individuals who actually carry out the tasks. There is a need for standardised skills to be an integral part of all individuals' work methods. While individuals operate autonomously, they must adopt a consistent or corporate approach. The main point of contact between the customer and the organisation will be at individual level. The standardised operating procedures ensure that a similar approach is made in all cases. As with other organisations which are bureaucratic in their nature, the standards predetermine what needs to be done in identified circumstances. Rather than relying on a set of internally generated standards, the professional bureaucracy is often bound by a set of regulations or rules which are common to a profession or area of expertise.

The standardisation process in relation to a professional bureaucracy is somewhat more complex than that of a machine bureaucracy. There needs to be a broader range of standard responses to a number of different contingencies or situations. The professional, of course, operates according to the needs of the customer or client and needs to diagnose a particular response or solution to the customer's requirements. Having identified the particular course of action relevant to the situation, the professional also needs to know how to implement or apply the solution. Typical examples of professional bureaucracies would, of course, include doctors, solicitors, accountants and chartered surveyors.

Professionals will need to provide a functional as well as a market-based service. This means that the structure has to account for the basic requirements in order to provide a functional service, as well as catering for the intricacies of the market. Professional bureaucracies are, of course, supported by other employees, but these take very much a subservient role and purely act as a backup to the professionals. As we mentioned earlier, professional bureaucracies tend to be highly decentralised, providing, of course, the standardisation of procedures has already been agreed. Rather than the administrative support having any direct bearing on the decision-making ability of the professional, it is the latter that seek to have control over the former. However, we must make a proviso that the administrative staff may know more about the regulations and procedures than the professionals.

In larger professional bureaucracies, where there is a need for a complex administrative hierarchy, there can be a conflict between the staff function and the provider function. In this respect there will be a bottom-up decision-making hierarchy for the professionals, and a top-down hierarchy for the administrative support. Many of these larger organisations will have professional administrators. This hybrid role seeks to encompass the requirements of the administrative support and the professional function. There is a tendency for professionals to become reliant on efficient and effective administrators and this can lead to conflicts of interest. However, the majority of administrators may have been professional specialists before they embraced the administration function. Individuals which have this balance and experience will be able to wield considerable power within the organisation since they have a working knowledge of the needs of the professional, coupled with an ability to manage the administrative necessities. In most respects, administrators need to be rather more democratic than would be expected in other forms of configuration. They need to be able to address the requirements of the professional, while ensuring that the administrative tasks are undertaken correctly.

Being dominated by skilled workers whose functions are well-defined, yet difficult to learn, this is an environment which is both stable and complex. There may be an ability to standardise the application of skills through training programmes, providing that there is a stable enough environment. Knowledge is the key factor, and it is difficult to establish a technical system able to apply knowledge of this sort. As the professional bureaucracy is reliant upon numerous skilled workers, it tends to be rather more democratic than other configurations. With autonomy, professionals need not co-ordinate their activities with others. This allows them to concentrate on the job at hand and on improving their skill levels. Professionals are, to a large extent, self-regulating. They need to address their own deficiencies rather than having an external agency impose regulations and conditions upon them. At the same time, it is difficult to deal with professionals who cannot cope with the autonomous nature of the job or the intricacies involved in acquiring the skills. By giving individual professionals discretion to make their own decisions, they may ignore the needs of their customers. This, in turn, means that the needs of the organisation are likewise ignored.

For all of the democratic advantages of a professional bureaucracy, there is a tendency for them to be rather inflexible. A general practice in medicine would standardise responses to various ailments. However, they would find it difficult to embrace alternative treatments unless they were required to consider these by an external agency.

While there may be some pressure to control the activities of professionals by the government, non-professional administrators, or society itself, they can only attempt to standardise the outputs. However, complex work of this nature can only really be performed by the professional. In other words, the control needs to be in the hands of the individual who does the work. Inevitably, professionals will seek to offset any external influences. It would be impossible to impose wholesale changes on the way in which these professional bureaucracies operate. Change happens gradually rather than suddenly or in a radical way.

Divisional forms

In a divisionalised form, an organisation seeks to hold together a number of disparate activities and operations with a central core of administration. Typically, we will see that this configuration has a number of divisions and a central administration or headquarters. This is the most common configuration in the private sector, particularly when we look at larger organisations.

In divisionalised forms, groups of activities are concentrated under an individual at the top end of middle management. There will be a number of duplications of functions in each of the divisions. Having said this, some functions will be carried out within the central core of administration. The main point of the exercise is to create a series of quasi-autonomous operations which are free of central control, particularly in day-to-day matters. The span of control, particularly at the strategic apex of the organisation, will be wide. Decentralisation, therefore, is at its optimum level. This tendency is certainly true at the top end of each of the divisions, particularly in relation to that of the strategic apex. However, each division may have centralised its decision making. The headquarters will have delegated the majority of its power to the divisions, but it will have maintained a degree of control in order to justify its existence. Typically, the headquarters would allow each division to make their own decisions within certain broad objectives, but would be active in the monitoring of the results of these decisions.

The reason for the creation of the separate divisions will normally be related to the standardisation of outputs within that division. In this way each division can impose a performance control system.

Each division needs to be considered as a single integrated system. Above all, any goals for that division need to be related to operations, particularly if the goals can be quantitatively measured. In other words, the divisions have the ability to run their own 'businesses'. They are responsible for the operations and strategies that fall within their particular area.

At the strategic level the headquarters will determine whether to establish, expand, sell or close down each of the divisions. There is a clear delineation between the headquarters and the operations of each division. Ultimately, it is the headquarters that holds the purse strings and allocates the financial resources of the overall organisation. They will also be involved in the design of any performance control system. In order to maintain complete control of each division, the headquarters will also take the responsibility of hiring and firing divisional managers. When there is a need for support common to each division, the headquarters will provide this service. This ensures that there is no unnecessary duplication of effort and activity in each division.

Divisionalisation is a natural occurrence arising out of diversification. Where an organisation is involved in a number of markets which are difficult to fully integrate into one division, there will be a tendency to increase the number of sub-divisions. In this way partial replicas of existing divisions can be set up in alternative markets. Divisionalisation is only as effective as the organisation's ability to create a technical system to control the divisions. Since each division may be operating in a radically different business environment, there can be no standardisation of response to change and challenge. Some environments will be dynamic and complex, whereas others may be stable and simple. While some divisions may take the guise of a machine bureaucracy, others may have to adapt to a more simple form. Organisations will also institute divisionalisation when they grow. This is equally true of organisations which have been in existence for a number of years. As the organisation moves into less traditional markets, the management may consider that divisions are the way in which to adapt to the changes required.

The question of power within the structure is a complex one. At the strategic apex of the organisation there can be a considerable weight of power resting in the hands of a few individuals. They will have responsibility for controlling a number of divisions of variable sizes. At the divisional level the managers will have considerable power, albeit restricted to the division itself. The larger, functional administrative systems that form the core of the headquarters can become extremely powerful. They will be able to control finance and supply, for example, to each of the divisions.

Organisations which have diversified vertically will be able to embrace divisionalisation in order to streamline their functions. An organisation which processes raw materials and then retails them can experience significant savings if, as a natural part of the diversification process, it is able to create or acquire separate divisions for each stage of the production and sales process. Equally, if a particular division is not performing or does not conform with the requirements of the organisation, it can be disposed of without adversely affecting the overall running of the organisation and its operations. This allows considerable scope for central planning at headquarters.

Many larger organisations have a number of unrelated divisions, known as conglomerates. There are no significant interdependencies between the separate divisions. However, there are considerable advantages to be had by pooling resources.

If the headquarters attempts to centralise decisions related to the product or the market in which the division operates, then the whole purpose of divisionalisation is undermined. Managers within the headquarters function will have considerably less autonomy than their colleagues in the divisions. In this instance, divisionalisation may have occurred as a result of the managers at the strategic apex of the organisation not understanding the intricacies of a particular market. If they seek to usurp the power of the managers in the divisions then they will have defeated the main purpose of divisionalisation. Although control systems need to be incorporated in order to monitor each division, these systems need to be flexible enough to cater for the intricacies of each of the different products or markets involved. In other words, the overall policy needs to be broad enough or bland enough to suit each division's purposes.

Clearly, one of the reasons why organisations configure in a divisionalised form is to combat the danger of being too big. There is a tendency for large organisations to become overly bureaucratic. It is said that divisionalised forms do not work well in the public sector. Nonetheless, governments are inclined to split larger public sector services into 'divisions'.

In conclusion, we can see that the divisionalised form does suit diversified organisations, but it leans very heavily on other configurations in terms of the structure of each of the divisions. The exercise of control over each of the divisions needs to be deftly handled in order to ensure that the organisation as a whole maintains its integrity.

Adhocracies

The adhocracy is, perhaps, the most organic of the configurations. Typically, there is no formalised behaviour, no rigid job specification or specialisation and very little centralisation. The adhocracy tends to consist of functional units of individuals. These will be related to special projects needing the attention of a variety of different specialists and experts. Unlike many other configurations, there will be little consideration of the unity of command. The organisation relies on experts who are able to use their knowledge and skills. There can be no reliance on standardisation: innovation is the key. It is for this reason that many adhocracies adopt a matrix structure. The design of the organisation encourages close liaison between different individuals in order to facilitate the successful conclusion of the various projects. Having said this, there are a great number of managers within the structure. These will be functional managers, integrating managers or project managers. Each will have a narrow span of control. Decisions are made at each and every level of the organisation so decentralisation is common, both in its horizontal and vertical form. Above all, an adhocracy needs to be able to adapt and respond to the problems and requirements of its customers. In this respect adhocracies are similar to professional bureaucracies. However, the scope is broader since adhocracies encourage an innovative approach to problem solving.

There is a blurring of distinction between the administration and the operations functions. Within each project area there will be administrative support as an integral part of the team effort. This ensures that in some way the project team is accountable to the administrative core of the organisation. For some adhocracies which operate in a dynamic environment, the operating core can be established as a distinctly separate organisation. In other adhocracies the operating (or production) core is contracted out to an independent third party.

As we said, the support staff play a key role in the adhocracy. They have to be able to operate in a constantly changing set of circumstances with different project teams, so in this respect they need to be as responsive as the team members themselves.

The individuals at the strategic apex of the adhocracy need to give clear instructions as to the priority of the various strategic options. Given the fact that their organisation is a fluid one, they may find it difficult to establish any sense of continuity in decision making. Their central role will be that of monitoring and co-ordination; equally they will need to operate as the main liaison between the organisation and the external environment. As the majority of adhocracies operate in dynamic and complex environments, there is a need to produce innovative work in unpredictable sets of circumstances. It would be impossible for top management to exert rigorous control in such circumstances.

There is a tendency for adhocracies to take on the guise of bureaucracies. In fact, adhocracies tend to become bureaucracies as they age. Once an organisation has established a reputation for innovation and adaptability, top management may seek to replicate this success by instituting a series of bureaucratic measures. Inevitably most attempts to do this will fail since they will stifle the autonomous nature of the organisation and the freedom enjoyed by the individuals responsible for the innovation. Trying to find a formula for innovation is difficult, if not impossible, particularly given the fact that the organisation is still operating in a complex and dynamic environment. On the other hand, there may be a pull towards adhocracy in markets which are highly competitive, requiring the organisation to adopt a temporary adhocracy in order to cope with special conditions.

It is said that adhocracies are tomorrow's configuration, while the other configurations are outdated and outmoded. Given the fact that the majority of people in economically developed countries are educated, they can cope with the sophisticated demands of an adhocracy. Not only will they be able to cope with complex technical systems, but they will also be able to handle the varied demands of different project groups. For individuals who cannot operate well in bureaucratic situations or when there is a high level of structural rigidity, adhocracies offer a far more democratic environment. However, this is not to say that members of adhocracies can necessarily understand or easily accept the ambiguous nature of relationships within an adhocracy.

Adhocracies do have a number of disadvantages, and these primarily include the following:

◆ the majority of members of an adhocracy are not capable or comfortable with routine operations.

◆ adhocracies tend to have inefficient and high cost communications systems.

◆ adhocracies are inefficient due to the fact that they will have unbalanced workloads. There will be periods of intense activity followed by periods of relative quiet.

From theory to practice

Obviously, each of the main configurations that we have examined are extremes. In reality, the majority of organisations have a number of characteristics from a variety of these different configurations. While we can make some broad generalisations regarding the evolution of organisations, in terms of their most appropriate configuration, there is an inevitable difference between the theory and the practice. Most organisations exhibit a number of different characteristics effectively making them hybrids.

Mintzberg suggests that the configurations are merely representative of the five main forces that pull organisations in different structural directions. These are:

1   The pull from the strategic apex to centralise and co-ordinate by supervision.

2   The pull by the techno-structure to standardise.

3   The pull by employees to professionalise.

4   The pull by middle managers to balkanise.

5   The pull by support staff to collaborate and co-ordinate.

Most organisations will gradually gravitate towards a configuration that suits their structure in terms of smooth operation and consistency in approach. Each configuration offers considerable benefits to particular preferred management and organisational styles. Ideally, organisations will seek to identify the key elements of each different configuration that will enable them to operate in the most efficient and effective manner. They may appear to have adopted contradictory features, although this may only be on a superficial basis.

Above all, the key structural configurations are useful to the analyst in any attempts to understand why organisations choose to move from one structural type to another. Given the fact that most organisations are in a constant state of transition, dependent upon internal needs and the external environment, we can see that all organisations will pass through key stages at some point in their history. It is inevitable that any changes in the configuration of an organisation will lag behind the impetus that gave cause to that change. In effect, organisations are continually transforming and remodelling themselves on the basis of out-dated information and needs. It is only when all members of an organisation have fully accepted and internalised the norms of that organisation that we can begin to identify a structure which is capable of responding to innumerable variables without having to resort to drastic transitions in their configuration.

Symptoms of an efficient or deficient organisation

Analysing management systems

It may be readily apparent that any discussion of efficient or deficient organisations must begin with some analysis of the managerial system used within that organisation. Strictly speaking, efficiency is directly concerned with making sure that decisions, processes and operations are carried out correctly, but, in addition, efficiency relates more broadly to inputs and exactly what the managers do. There is a need to address the effectiveness of actions as these will relate directly to outputs. This is a way of measuring the performance of the management. It is also apparent that the majority of organisations will have both formal and informal goals. While striving for these goals, both internal and external variables need to be taken into account.

Defining the efficiency or effectiveness of management is no easy task. Ideally, the manager not only needs to be measured against specific performance targets, but also needs to be judged in terms of their behaviour, adaptability and willingness to adopt alternative techniques and systems. Depending upon the organisation itself, efficiency and effectiveness can be measured formally, informally, or by some form of self-assessment.

Some of the suggestions that we have made with regard to the measurement of efficiency may seem somewhat subjective and difficult to quantify. It is for this reason that many organisations will resort to using a series of ratios in order to make precise judgements regarding efficiency. Although it is not appropriate to investigate these in any great detail in this module, it would be wise to identify some possibilities. These will include:

◆ average collection period.

◆ average credit period.

◆ rate of stock turnover.

◆ liquidity.

◆ profitability.

◆ earnings per share.

Relating efficiencies and deficiencies to functions

Given the fact that organisations are a series of interconnected elements which will depend on the nature of the organisation in question, the identification of efficiencies and deficiencies must be related to functions. Simply stating that the organisation is a set of interconnected elements is to miss the point. All of the elements must contribute towards the performance of a function. If we define the system from the point of view of the functions rather than the elements, it will help us understand what those elements mean and their importance within the organisation itself.

We can begin by considering the various types of system:

◆ deterministic and probabilistic systems.

◆ progressive specialisation.

In the first instance we are considering an organisation where the operations appear to be completely predictable or *deterministic*. In other cases, some organisations are fairly predictable, but not always so, which means we can call them *probabilistic*. Alternatively, we can look at systems which have been developed as a result of the realisation that something was not being accomplished correctly or completely. Generally speaking, this means that a specific individual has not been identified to carry out, or at least monitor, the whole operation from start to finish. Perhaps all of the individuals within the organisation had very blurred job roles. This is addressed by *progressive specialisation*, where certain individuals are given the responsibility of overseeing a specific aspect of the organisation's operations. This can be amply illustrated by the fact that most large organisations have a proliferation of specialist departments to carry out a series of expert functions.

Most organisations will have a probabilistic basis, rather than a deterministic one, but will inevitably move towards progressive specialisation as they grow, or as they become aware of the need to accommodate and react to the external environment and change.

In order to ensure that an organisation is created in such a way as to fulfil the majority of the functions required of it, a number of factors need to be in place. These, of course, include the employees, or more broadly the individuals involved in the organisation, having a willingness to contribute fully to the organisation itself and its declared objectives. Equally, their commitment needs to be consistent so that they can contribute more fully in the long term. There also needs to be a clear understanding of what the organisation intends to accomplish. This will be an integral part of the employee's willingness to contribute. Just as an organisation needs to have a purpose, so, too, do the individuals involved. At the very least the organisation should be able to fulfil employees' basic needs, but on a more long-term basis it needs to be able to offer them a sense of achievement and fulfilment. Obviously, those involved in the organisation must communicate in order to share their common objectives. Given the fact that most communication is verbal in nature, there needs to be a constant interchange of views and opinions. Once this has been established, the organisation has to develop the ability to pass on information in a number of other different ways.

Relating efficiencies and deficiencies to organisational systems

When considering probable efficiencies and deficiencies, we also need to give some thought to the properties of the organisational system itself. The vast majority of organisations will have a clear hierarchical structure. This will enable individuals within that organisation to clearly understand where they are within the system. In addition to this, the hierarchical system allows external analysis to be undertaken in order to identify key posts which hold positions of authority.

If we accept that an efficient system is greater than the sum of all of the parts of the organisation, and that greater levels of output can be enjoyed as a result of co-operation, then we must also realise that it is the organisation as a whole which will create efficiencies or establish deficiencies. This is known as a *synergistic effect*. By adding the skills of various specialists together, it is possible to enjoy greater levels of productivity and efficiency than would normally be anticipated if those individuals operated on their own. Organisations do strive to create synergistic effects in their attempts to become efficient.

When analysing a system, it is often useful to focus upon the nature of the system itself. To this end, we can identify the fact that some systems are closed and others are open. A closed system operates in an environment where little or no attention is paid to external influences or, for that matter, where the individuals within that organisation know little about what is happening in the rest of the organisation. In effect, they operate in a totally enclosed environment where the tasks predominate rather than the purpose. In an open environment, on the other hand, the organisation is more responsive to external factors. However, great care needs to be taken in order to ensure that the individuals are not over-exposed, thus causing confusion.

Other aspects of efficiency and deficiency

Most organisations do not have a single purpose. However, it is useful for an organisation to identify one key objective. When organisations have a multitude of different objectives, then they will find themselves consistently pulled in a number of different directions. Any largely service-based organisation, such as a local council, will find it impossible to cater for all of the various needs of a local community. No matter where it puts its time and resources, other sections of the community will complain that they have been neglected. While the organisation may attempt to balance the various demands upon it, it will inevitably place more emphasis upon one area than another. In this respect, we could identify the organisation as being deficient in this area. Even using some form of ranking system to develop a means by which the various objectives can be prioritised, there will still have to be a temporary shift of emphasis according to need. If the organisation is not sufficiently adaptive to accommodate these short-term requirements then, again, we can identify deficiencies. If, of course, the primary tasks are confused at all times, and the balance is severely impaired, then the organisation will become disrupted and seriously deficient.

An organisation needs to have certain periods in which an *equilibrium* is established in the pursuit of its objectives. This stability can occur even when the external environment is unpredictable or in a state of constant change. By merely establishing an objective, such as the reduction of the workforce, we can find some degree of equilibrium. The organisation is moving towards a clearly defined objective. These milestones which can establish the state of equilibrium are essential in order to ensure that the overall objective is reached. It will be readily apparent, however, that since an organisation will, in practice, be moving towards a number of different objectives in any period of time, they will have several equilibrium points to reach and overcome. Organisations are dynamic by their very nature and it is inevitable that certain equilibrium points will disturb the equilibrium of others. The organisation needs to understand that efficiencies can be gained if they can reach a number of simultaneous equilibrium points, or that deficiencies will come about if they allow one equilibrium point to disturb all of the others.

The establishment of regulations within the organisation will be aimed at fixing the way in which actions and behaviours occur within it. Providing the organisation has a clearly defined set of regulations, then many of the more avoidable deficiencies can be eliminated. Obviously this is dependent upon the fact that all newcomers to the organisation will have to go through a socialisation or induction process.

An organisation may be seen as a series of interconnecting sub-systems. It is the way in which these sub-systems interrelate and co-operate that determines whether the organisation is efficient or deficient. Obviously different parts of the organisation need to be managed in radically different ways. There can be a system-wide approach, yet certain departments or sub-systems may need to be handled in a radically different manner. The structure of the organisation and the division of work within it aims to enlighten the individual as to their position in the overall scheme and the part that they play in achieving the overall objectives. Without some clear delineation between job roles and responsibilities, individuals will either be overcome by the amount of information available, be unable to reconcile the competing demands for their attention or indeed to have a clear focus upon the objectives of the organisation itself.

◆ Manifest and latent functions

Any cursory look at an organisation will reveal that the vast majority of individuals involved are those who do the basic work. We can refer to these as *operatives* or *operators*. All organisations will have some of these individuals within the structure. Patently, a collection of such operators could function perfectly well without managerial control or supervision, provided nobody needed to take control of the strategic direction of the organisation. This heralds the arrival of the manager, whose sole aim is to co-ordinate the work of the operators. Prior to the inclusion of this individual, the only clear differences between the operators was the nature of the work they each undertook. As a direct consequence of the inclusion of a manager, we need to appreciate that some operators will remain responsible for doing the basic work, while others will take more of an administrative role. This essential difference, or division of labour, allows us to identify those who do the work and those who supervise the work. Inevitably, some form of hierarchy will ensue.

If we then assume that the nature of the work undertaken by the organisation becomes ever more complex, encompassing a variety of different processes and patterns of work, there will be a need to enlist the services of analysts. Even the process of standardisation within an organisation means that a number of 'non-productive' individuals are included in the equation. These will all carry out specialist functions aimed at benefiting the organisation as a whole. As the advice of the analyst is incorporated into the processes carried out by the organisation, there will be a sense of institutionalisation of the relationship between those supervising and those carrying out the work.

No matter how complex the organisation becomes, the operators will still make up an operating core. The other individuals within the organisation take on the following roles:

◆ managers at the strategic apex.

◆ middle managers.

◆ analysts dedicated to standardisation.

◆ the support staff.

When we investigate the different forms of organisational structure in Section 2, we will be able to see that all of these roles take on more importance in terms of the hierarchy than the operating core. It is at this stage that careful consideration needs to be given to the relationships and relative power of each group.

Effectively, each of these groups are interdependent. Following the work of James Thompson we can identify three types of interdependency. The first is referred to as *pooled coupling*, where individuals have common resources, but to all intents and purposes are independent of one another. The second form is *reciprocal coupling* meaning that work moves back and forth between the groups. Some will produce inputs which are outputs to the others. *Sequential coupling* is most apparent in assembly-line work, where each group inputs to the whole and contributes towards the finished product.

Operatives at the core of an organisation

The operating core of any organisation includes those responsible directly for the production of products and services. They will include those in a purchasing or acquisition function, those who are involved in transforming the various inputs into outputs, those who distribute the outputs and those who give direct support to the above. The use of the word 'core' to describe these individuals is no mistake, as they are the heart of the organisation. Without these individuals the organisation will have no opportunity or reason to carry out any of its other operations. It is at this core level that the majority of standardisation exercises take place. Providing the outputs remain predictable, the organisation seeks to build around the operating core its administrative support, strategic apex, middle management and techno-structure.

Managers at the strategic apex

It is through the strategic apex that the organisation seeks to transform its mission statements and turn its objectives into reality. Effectively, managers operate as agents for those who control or own the organisation. Although managerial styles are examined in Section 4, it is appropriate to identify some of the key features here. We can say that these managers generally:

◆ are resource allocators.

◆ organise individuals and resources to do specific tasks.

◆ authorise major decisions.

◆ resolve conflict.

◆ monitor and review the employees' activities.

◆ act as an information conduit.

◆ lead.

◆ motivate and reward.

◆ directly supervise and delegate.

◆ attempt to ensure that the organisation operates as a fully integrated entity.

These functions of a manager are illustrated in Fig. 1.14.

Not all individuals, particularly those at the top of the strategic apex, directly supervise. Their responsibilities may differ to the extent that their activities involve:

◆ operating as a spokesperson for the organisation.

◆ liaising with external bodies.

◆ developing contacts.

◆ monitoring information sources.

◆ dealing with important customers.

Fig. 1.14 Main functions of managers

The strategic role of those at the apex of the organisation implies that they have the ability to interpret the environment in which the organisation operates and to develop plans of action to deal with those forces. Essentially, this means that they are charged with seeking a way in which to carry out the mission and objectives of the organisation. They may also have the opportunity to change that mission. Strategies needs to be formulated in relation to the realities of the situation and the apparent strengths and weaknesses of the organisation itself. In some respects their approach is an abstract one, viewed from a very different perspective to that of all other members of the organisation. Decisions need to be taken with a long-term view. They will seek to gradually reconfigure the organisation in order to ensure that co-ordination and efficiency is maintained throughout the transition process.

Middle managers

The majority of those at the strategic apex of the organisation do not have direct supervisory responsibility, as they will delegate this role to the middle managers. The middle managers form an effective link between the strategic objectives and the implementation strategies required to deliver the necessary results. The term 'middle management' is a broad one. We should infer from it that there is a *scalar chain*, each manager being responsible for a number of other managers or supervisors or, perhaps, the workforce directly. This elaborate chain of authority culminates with those at the strategic apex. Those managers fortunate enough to have a limited span of control will find it comparatively easy to directly supervise a number of other managers or subordinates. Inevitably, as we look up the scalar chain towards the strategic apex, we will identify managers who have significantly broad spans of control and limited direct supervisory opportunities to make a real impact on the decision-making processes used by their subordinates.

In more complex organisations a complex hierarchy will be more likely to evolve, placing managers in control of large numbers of operators. Ultimately, of course, all authority will be vested in those in more senior positions. The flow of direct supervision moves up and down the scalar chain: the more complex the hierarchy, the less opportunity senior managers have to meet and co-ordinate their subordinate managers. Senior managers will have to content themselves with making strategic decisions, relying upon their subordinates to interpret these broader instructions in a meaningful and effective way. As we look down the scalar chain, it is apparent that managers will have to take a more realistic and hands-on approach in decision-making and planning, but will have to bear in mind the more generalised instructions received from higher levels in the hierarchy. Decision-making at the lower levels has to be more frequent, less abstract and more to do with solutions than policies.

Analysts

The techno-structure includes the analysts, whose responsibility it is to affect the working practices of others in the organisation. They may be responsible for designing, training, planning and changing work patterns. It is these individuals who will prepare the organisation to withstand and respond to external challenges and adapt the functional parts of the organisation. They will establish the procedures and attempt to standardise as many of the operations as possible. Naturally, the techno-structure analysts operates at all levels in the hierarchy: they will have an input into the operating functions, through the control of work flow by scheduling or quality control; at the mid-point in the hierarchy, by their ability to standardise decision-making; and at the strategic apex, by designing effective strategic planning systems to control the organisation.

Support staff

There is a tendency for many analysts and organisations to consider the position of the support staff as being very similar, if not identical, to those in the techno-structure. Effectively, support staff exist to provide assistance to the organisation in areas unrelated directly to the work of the core. The existence of support staff can be seen either as being an attempt to incorporate many of the peripheral activities and facilities of the organisation, or as an alternative to purchasing these services from an outside contractor. Again, support units can be found at all levels of the hierarchy; the more specialist and complex, the more likely the support unit is to be found nearer to the strategic apex.

As with the majority of work in the complex organisations, support units at lower levels have standardised work patterns. Typically, these would include reprographics, postrooms, reception and canteen facilities. To all intents and purposes, they will operate in a very similar way to that of the operating core, except that they are not directly involved in the central activity. There is a tendency for most larger organisations to cushion themselves at middle management level with support staff. These appear to be almost organic additions, attached to such parts of the structure that appear to be the main users of that support, or areas which have broad similarities. Above all, co-ordination of these support units is reliant upon careful consideration of their relative importance in the hierarchy and their relevance to the operating core.

The flows in an organisation

Regardless of the relative size of the five main parts of the organisation, they are held together by a series of flows. Essentially, these flows are:

◆ authority.

◆ materials.

◆ information.

◆ decision processes.

Flows within the hierarchy

As we will see in Section 2, most individuals envisage an organisation in terms of its organisation chart. No matter how much care and attention has been given to the design of an organisation chart, we are still faced with only an interpretation of the structure of that organisation. The organisation chart does, however, allow us to glimpse at the interrelationships. It also allows us to begin to understand the relative importance of various groupings, but, above all, it seeks to show us the true hierarchy and the potential flows within the structure itself. An organisation chart can never hope to illuminate the informal structures that exist in all organisations. It can also never hope to adequately identify the various divisions of labour that exist.

There will be regulated flows throughout the organisation and for the most part an organisation chart is adequate enough to give us some form of appreciation. The chart is stylised and will only illustrate the regulated or official flows. In other words, these are the approved and regulated flows as suggested or required by the organisation itself.

Materials

If we consider work flow, we may be able to identify the point at which raw materials and components enter the organisation as inputs and go through a series of complex processes and procedures until they are finally released as outputs and leave the organisation. We are looking at a transformation process, but we cannot see the complex flow of information that supports this transition or flows which are generated as a result of this process. We cannot see, for example, an individual employee's timesheet, which has been directly influenced by the level of work passing through the organisation at a given time. Flows are not restricted purely to the operating core; there are innumerable other flows moving up and down the hierarchies, not necessarily related to the production process itself. A flow chart of an order process is shown in Fig. 1.15.

Authority

Most of the formal flows are vertical, passing from one level of authority to another. However, if we consider the support services, we will be able to identify flows passing between groupings that occupy similar levels in the hierarchy. Perhaps, more importantly, the organisation chart gives us an opportunity to appreciate how strategic decisions are transformed into workable realities through the gradual filtration process down the hierarchy. Broad strategic policies need to be implemented and at some point transformed into a workable system that can be implemented at the appropriate level. Each of these flows are interrupted at appropriate points and held in limbo while the necessary decisions are made by a particular manager. Some flows will automatically stop at a particular level and not percolate down to the lower levels of the hierarchy.

The complications which arise out of the differences between line and staff relationships within an organisations add a further level of potential confusion to any form of flow or communication. The support staff may be reliant upon information from the operating core and in other cases, the operating core may be unable to make decisions or carry out actions until the support staff have provided the necessary assistance. This is particularly true of data analysis, requiring the attention of specialists outside the strict line structure. These horizontal flows of information are largely responsible for problems as line instructions may appear to override their need for that information.

Informal flows of information

In addition to the prescribed means by which information flows throughout an organisation, there are innumerable informal systems and relationships that are fluid and outside the direct control of the hierarchy. It is certainly true to say that informal communication systems are of vital importance to the smooth running of any organisation. Informal communication systems, which are largely verbal rather than written, establish a means by which explanations can be given without reference to the normal procedures.

Many organisations have sought to improve their overall communication systems by incorporating as many opportunities as possible to exchange information and ensuring that every individual is informed of any relevant changes. Management information systems, networks and general access to data have been vastly improved with the emergence of new technologies. But, as most organisations would agree, the informal networks of contacts within an organisation, or for that matter, contacts outside the organisation, offer communication

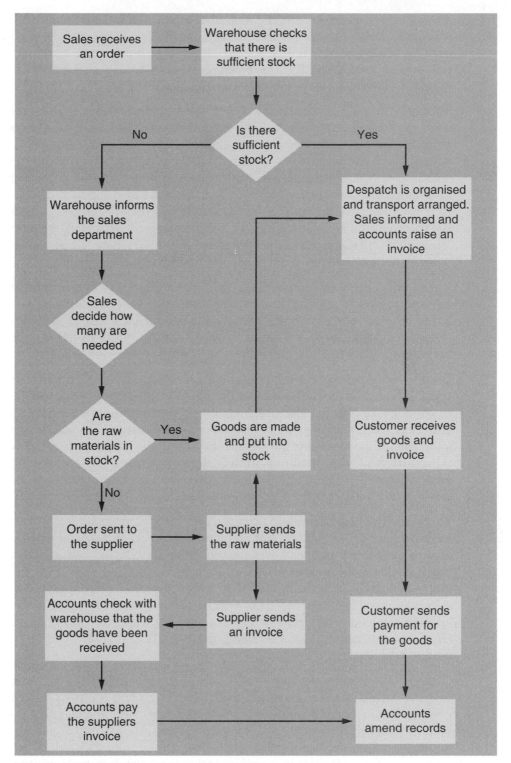

Fig. 1.15 Flow chart of an order process

possibilities that cannot be easily replicated in any regulated manner. The regulation and control of information on the organisation's behalf can serve the purposes of the organisation to the exclusion of the personal needs of individuals within that organisation. Critically, as we will see, the leaking of information can prove to be very damaging to the smooth running of operations.

Informal communication, at its most basic level, operates between peers. However, other channels of communication bypass individuals, particularly when social relationships have been formed between individuals in different areas of the organisation. This may involve some form of diagonal communication from one grouping within the organisational structure to another unrelated grouping. Informal communication may also mean that information flows down the hierarchy, avoiding certain individuals at particular levels. Again, this may result in the distortion of the information, since it has not passed through the regulated channels. The 'grapevine' still remains an important communication network, but it does have a complex nature and is often a web of communication bypass channels.

It may appear that the grapevine is simply a random way in which information can jump across levels of hierarchy, gradually mutating until it bears no relation to the original source or detail. For groupings which are related to functional or specialised work, there is a tendency for 'cliques' to develop which effectively exclude outsiders from the communication net.

Despite the importance of communication and the exercise of authority within an organisation, it is the decisions and the actual production of goods and services that must take priority. Decisions relating to operations are often taken quickly and immediately implemented. Since this particularly affects individuals at the lower end of the hierarchy, the regulated systems may not be very complex. Communications relating to administrative decisions largely involve co-ordination and it is this co-ordination that directly affects the operating decisions. Decisions can be made with reference to routines, schedules and other programmes.

The majority of communication channels may appear to operate within a rather informal network or pattern, but many of these will actually be related in some way to the formal authority system. It is certainly true to say that like-minded individuals or cliques can arise out of close working relationships or shared interests. They will communicate with one another on an informal basis, but the information passed between them will be substantial. This is to say that managers or some other grouping will form a primary grapevine communication system. The information flow will cut across specialised areas and not be based on vertical relationships.

Cliques will certainly develop at all levels of the hierarchy. It is also true to say that the nature of the information that they share will differ according to their position in the hierarchy, reflecting the complexity or completeness of the information with which they are working. This system has often been described in terms of *work constellations* which means that these semi-independent groupings operate in many organisations and are primarily related to their position in the hierarchy. Naturally, some of these work constellations will interchange information between one another. Each constellation will have expertise in a particular area which can be used by another constellation.

Work constellations can be formal or informal, illustrating the fact that they are often encouraged by the organisation itself. This also means that non-functional parts of the organisation, such as the support staff, can form a constellation with one of the work units. It is in the middle management area that the work constellations operate in a rather more informal manner, with the various specialists exchanging work and ideas with one another, particularly when other individuals may be affected by changes that are being considered.

In some organisations these work constellations mirror the work flow, with the administrative support systems operating as a separate constellation. In effect, this means that the organisational structure is mirrored by a series of work constellations which follow the logical progression of the work.

Decisions

In the more flexible adhoc decision-making process, we can see that there are a number of formal and informal aspects related to the flow of information and the communication systems. If we begin by establishing that a decision is a commitment to action, then we must focus on the decisions themselves, rather than the decision-making process, since this is altogether different. In terms of decisions, which will affect the organisation itself, we should concentrate on the *strategic decision*, the *operating decision* and the *administrative decision*.

Obviously, the majority of strategic decisions are made at the apex of the organisation, since these will have an impact on the organisation as a whole. As Mintzberg suggested, there are several stages to this, which are:

♦ the recognition that there are many factors to be taken into account before, during and after the decision.

♦ the diagnosis of the decision as a routine.

♦ the development of solutions.

♦ the selection of the correct decision.

Strategic decisions set in motion a series of other decisions to be made at lower levels of the hierarchy. Decisions which are made at the strategic level need to take account of the probable impacts of these changes at operational and administrative level. It is *because* they have an effect on the operating process that they are strategic decisions.

Operating decisions tend to be typified by the fact that they are routine and implemented immediately. In essence, many of these operating decisions are predetermined by adherence to operating procedures or regulations, but this does mean that individuals, even at the lower end of the hierarchy, need to be aware of the systems and procedures.

Administrative decisions tend to be designed to co-ordinate and guide operating decisions, or to have an exceptional nature and be made on an adhoc basis. Obviously, the latter, being non-routine, may be somewhat more elaborate. It is certainly the case that most administrative decisions cut across a number of functional areas and need to be made with the probable impacts in mind.

Turning to the adhoc decision-making process itself, we can see that there needs to be a mix of different types of decisions. Some will involve more routine decision-making, but others will be far more informal in nature. It is important to realise that only by looking at the flow of authority, work materials, information and decision-making processes can we begin to understand how an organisation actually operates.

 ## Dysfunctions

Broadly speaking, dysfunctions relate to operations or systems within the organisation that appear to be less effective and efficient than other systems which could be readily adopted. A dysfunction is said to be something that actively interferes with the work that has to be done by the organisation. Any cursory examination of an organisation would identify a number of dysfunctions which have operated over a considerable number of years. Many dysfunctions relate to the way in which the organisation has gradually evolved over time. The organisation has simply never had the opportunity or the willingness to address the problems which are inherent in its structure. Naturally, as the dysfunction becomes a part of the organisation, there is a degree of acceptance and the dysfunction becomes the norm. The organisation and the individuals within it will work around the dysfunction, simply accepting that things have always been this way. It is only when the dysfunction becomes acute that the organisation realises that it needs to pay attention to it.

At times, critical decisions, or information that is needed to make these decisions, are impeded by the dysfunction. On a different level, individuals may seek to operate dysfunctionally. This is when managers, in particular, collect information through their informal grapevine communication systems in order to gain real or supposed advantage. Equally, some managers may use a dysfunctional approach to gather information about their subordinates in order to maintain their position of authority.

 ## Synergies and contradictions

Synergies are the benefits which can result by combining different aspects of the organisation, rather than allowing them to act separately. In other words, organisations will seek to group complementary activities in situations where there is a strong possibility of collaboration. This means that a mutual benefit can be enjoyed, particularly when common work or activities form the basis of the alliance.

The organisational structure of a particular business will lag behind the demands placed upon it and while the organisation may desire greater levels of efficiency, its structure may be seen as an insurmountable block to achieving this. In this respect, there will be contradictions between what is expected of the organisation, or, for that matter, the intentions behind the establishment of a particular organisational structure and the needs of the business itself. An organisation which seeks to streamline its communication systems without having due consideration to the flattening out of its structure, will find itself in a position where all reasonable attempts to improve communications are thwarted.

By having a number of levels within the organisational structure which traditionally filter information as it passes down the hierarchy, the organisation will be faced with a number of possible points where the information will be blocked. Any proposed change to the organisation and particularly the structure, must incorporate a radical change in the organisational culture and a clear indication as to the purposes of that change. Without this the organisation will be riddled with contradictions which will be insurmountable and frustrating to all those concerned.

Review questions

1 Identify and describe Mintzberg's five major configurations.

2 Explain the five 'pulls' on an organisation in terms of its configuration decision-making.

3 What is the strategic apex of an organisation and what is its purpose?

4 What are Khandwalla's thoughts on the behaviour which a simple structure exhibits?

5 What are the common features exhibited by a machine bureaucracy?

6 What are standard operating procedures common in professional bureaucracies?

7 What is the logical relationship between divisionalised organisations and diversification?

8 What are the key features of an adhocracy?

9 Describe some ways in which an organisation could assess its efficiency.

10 What are manifest and latent functions?

11 What is the scalar chain?

12 Explain work flow in an organisation using an example of how information is transferred from one part of the organisation to another.

Establishing and designing organisations

In designing an organisation, it is important to consider the conditions in which the organisation will operate, and the extent to which the organisational style is relevant. In addition to this, the design of the organisation will inevitably mirror the preferences of the owners of that organisation. In this way we can begin to recognise some of the parameters which will determine the type, structure, style and complexity of various organisations.

One of the key determining factors is the debate between centralisation and decentralisation. Centralisation, as we will see, means that the majority of decisions are made by a single individual or a small group of individuals. Decentralisation occurs when much of the decision making has been pushed down the hierarchy to lower managers or employees. Certain organisations will be torn between the relative advantages and disadvantages of each approach, and these considerations have been the subject of many research papers and theories.

The complexity of the decision-making process within the organisation is often related to the centralisation/decentralisation debate. Some organisations have adopted a totally decentralised approach, which means that relevant decisions at an appropriate level can be made with the minimum involvement of external influences. In other cases, a decision is made at the strategic apex of the organisation and has to be passed down a multitude of hierarchical levels before it reaches the individuals who will implement it.

The organisational structure will also reflect the degree of autonomy that each individual will have within the business. There are a number of instances when one individual will make a decision which needs to be executed by another. Sometimes this relationship will be on a strictly line basis, while other decisions will be based on staff relationships.

We should not confuse centralisation or decentralisation with structure. You cannot adequately illustrate either of these perspectives by creating an organisation chart. Each organisational unit is interlocked with the other organisational units within the business. Some, of course, will have a purely linear structure, where it is clear that the hierarchy is firmly established and all decisions and authority follow a set pattern. On the other hand, some organisations are designed in such a way as to facilitate groupings. This will either be according to process or product, or some other factor so that greater efficiencies can be enjoyed as a result. The key word here is co-ordination, where various functional activities are grouped; the interlocking units that are related to one another can be controlled by a single individual and a degree of autonomous decision making can be made.

The development of organisational theory and its relevance to the modern context

Organisational design should marry the influences of co-ordination with those of the division of labour. In other words, the organisational structure should reflect how the organisation functions. This means that the structure itself needs to clearly show how materials, authority, information and decisions flow through it. Theorists such as Mintzberg have identified a number of key design parameters which need to be addressed. These are:

◆ job roles

◆ behaviour formalisation and training

◆ horizontal and vertical job specialisation

◆ training and induction

◆ unit grouping

◆ unit size

◆ planning and control systems

◆ liaison devices

◆ control systems

◆ centralisation and decentralisation.

Job roles

The first major cluster of design parameters is related to the positions or job roles within the organisation. Jobs themselves can be specialised, either in terms of their breadth or scope, or their depth. In the first instance, we need to consider how many different tasks are contained in each job role. In the second case, we need to consider the amount of control that an individual has over their own work. There are a number of ways in which the specialisation of each job role can be more clearly determined.

Horizontal and vertical job specialisation

Job specialisation can be achieved horizontally and this is the most predominant form of division of labour. It is common for a work force to be organised in the most productive manner. If an individual specialises in a particular task, then they will probably become more efficient or productive. This means that the job can be standardised, making the outputs more uniform and the system as a whole more efficient. This also means that individuals can be identified who have an aptitude for a particular task or role.

On the other hand, jobs can be vertically specialised in order to allow the individual to have greater control over their work cycle. If an individual has a vertically specialised job role, then they have a degree of decision-making ability over their own goals and standards. There is a tendency for these individuals to become more involved and active as employees. This is as a result of having a different perspective on how the work can be carried out. Those individuals who have horizontal specialisation tend to view their work more narrowly than those who have vertical specialisation. This is not to say that some organisations consider, once they have horizontally specialised a job, that they should not go on to vertically specialise it. There is a strong positive relationship between horizontal and vertical specialisation. In reality, however, most job roles tend to be either both or neither.

Job *enlargement* offers the opportunity for the employee to get involved in a wide variety of tasks which are associated with their main job role. The job may be enlarged vertically so that the individual has more tasks to carry out and has a greater control over them. Horizontal job enlargement allows the employee to be involved in a wide selection of different tasks in the same sequence or at the same level of complexity or production. More generally speaking, the former version of job enlargement is often referred to as *enrichment*. The vast majority of major theorists agree with the contention that both varieties of enlargement considerably improve overall success. However, there are instances when ill-considered job enlargement programmes have led to confusion and loss of production. Motivation, of course, is the key theme here and it would pay any employer to seriously consider the implications of enlargement before embarking upon a wide-scale reorganisation of job roles. There is considerable evidence to suggest that some employees do prefer very specialised, repetitive work. As far as job design goes, those at the lower end of the hierarchy are more interested in job security, as Maslow suggests, while those towards the upper end of the hierarchy have more interest in self-actualisation, and, as a result, respond far more favourably to job enlargement or enrichment schemes.

Most theorists would agree that jobs that have been made complex by horizontal enlargement are not really professional jobs at all. To be considered a professional, there needs to be some degree of vertical enlargement. It is the complexity of the job, coupled with the control over the work itself, that makes an individual motivated. Having said this, there is some truth in the statement that professionalisation increases status as well as reducing the amount of control over the particular job role by administrators.

Straightforward managerial job roles within an organisation are, by their very nature, non-specialist. There has been considerable horizontal enlargement for most managerial roles, although very little vertical enlargement. It is probably true to say that managers nearer the bottom end of the hierarchy suffer from many more overt controls from administrators than those at the upper end of the structure. At the lower end many potential vertical enlargement possibilities have been eliminated by the inclusion of staff posts which are designed to carry out specialist functions. This is not to say, however, that there cannot be a high level of specialisation as a result of both horizontal and vertical enlargement at the bottom end of the hierarchy, but these are more the exception than the rule.

Behaviour formalisation and training

Specifying roles within the organisational structure is something of a preoccupation for many of the management writers, including McGregor, Fayol, Taylor and Argyris. Broadly speaking, we can consider two main features which will determine the role within the structure. The first specific determinant of roles is behaviour formalisation, but equally important is training, including induction.

Specific job roles can be formalised or categorised in three main ways. These are:

1 By *job* – identifying specific tasks and responsibilities, noting them in a job description and ensuring that the individual takes note of this job description, which should prescribe the sequence of responsibilities and tasks.

2 By *work flow* – which looks at the particular specifications of the job and, rather than determining the actual job role itself, relates the tasks carried out by the employee to the job in hand.

3 By *rules* – which are aimed to cover all jobs, work flows and employees, by specifically stating exactly what can and cannot be done. Typically, the organisation would produce a very comprehensive employee manual.

The main point of the exercise, regardless of the background behind this formalisation, is to ensure that behaviour is regulated. But why do organisations seek to do this? Obviously the first major reason is related to co-ordination, through standardising the types of jobs and activities carried out by each individual. In other words, the employee would know precisely what to do in particular circumstances. There is a tendency to think about a very formalised organisation in terms of it requiring a machine-like approach and consistency in all of its operations. There will be considerable horizontal enlargement or specialisation, but this, again, is only related to standardisation through repetition. In many respects formalisation indicates that the organisation wishes to have order.

As we have already seen, and indeed will investigate further in the next section, formalisation and close co-ordination often lead to bureaucracies. Weber described a bureaucracy as being an ideal type of structure, but he was not suggesting that this was perfect. Whether Weber's ideal type of bureaucracy actually exists in reality is not in question; it is rather the case that many organisations exhibit some of the characteristics of a bureaucracy. Writers some years later came to very similar conclusions regarding bureaucracies where they saw specialisation, standardisation and formalisation in many organisations. This is, perhaps, typified by Pugh's investigation into a number of organisations in the Birmingham area.

Organic structures, such as those described by Burns and Stalker, are very much the opposite to Weber's description of a bureaucracy. They do not have a great deal of standardisation. Several theorists have asserted that there are many more organic structures than bureaucratic ones. Perhaps one of the main reasons for this is that the majority of organic structures positively encourage internal competition between different parts of the organisation.

If we assume that highly co-ordinated and repetitive work is bureaucratic in its very nature, then we could also suggest that even work which is not of a uniform nature can, in fact, be standardised or turned into routines by a bureaucracy. For most organisations it is the operating core that tends to have the highest level of behaviour formalisation. Once we leave the more repetitive work and look further up the chain of authority we will see that formalisation becomes less common. In this way, an organisation can successfully embrace aspects of both bureaucratic control and organic freedom. A further complication is that many of the staff functions which would normally be associated with a higher level of the hierarchy actively seek to formalise the lower levels of the organisation while being themselves organic in nature. It is at the points where the organic and bureaucratic meet that there is some degree of uncertainty. As a result, it is far more difficult to draw an organisation chart which adequately describes the hierarchy, power relationships and communication systems in parts of an organisation that have organic tendencies. Many organisations which have evolved rather than been created in the image of some 'master plan' will be organic.

Training and induction

Training and induction are vital in the establishment of specifications and behaviour formalisation. Training refers to the process of teaching the skills and knowledge required to carry out a particular job role. Induction, which derives from the same root as the word indoctrination, refers to the process of passing on and instilling norms to the newcomer.

Most training will attempt to break down comparatively complex operations into a series of simple and easy to learn tasks. There will be some degree of behaviour formalisation in order to achieve consistency in training and co-ordination of the new employees. Titles such as 'apprentice' seek to reinforce this concept, since the implication is that they are still in the process of learning. Regardless of the complexity of the particular job, other titles such as 'trainee' will be adopted as an alternative to apprentice, particularly in the case of non-manual occupations. Whether the job role is manual or non-manual, there is still a standardisation process in operation. What may be different is the length of time that an individual remains an apprentice or a trainee. Once the trainee has adopted the expected or required behaviour and has internalised all of the skills required to carry out the job role, they become fully trained.

Induction or indoctrination begins even before the individual has been interviewed, let alone offered the post. The selection and recruitment procedures will be designed by the organisation to ensure that they are recruiting individuals who either display or are capable of displaying the correct norms and values preferred by the organisation. For most employees, induction is a period of transition or socialisation aimed at instilling the desired behaviour in that individual. Naturally, a number of induction programmes incorporate aspects of training at the same time.

Unit grouping

Having clearly established the nature of each position in the organisation, the exact grouping of each of the positions needs to be identified. In other words, the groupings, whether as units or clusters, have to follow some kind of logic related to the organisation's needs and goals. Given the fact that the organisation has a series of objectives, then the design of this 'super-structure' needs to be carefully considered. Once specialisation and formalisation have been determined, and training and induction carried out, each individual employee has to be slotted into a particular place within the structure itself. Most structural design is initiated by the upper levels of the organisation. However, when we consider changes to the operating core, there is often a pressure to change from the lower end of the hierarchy.

Perhaps the most logical form of grouping is related to co-ordination. In effect, this grouping process has four main effects:

1 Similar jobs can be co-ordinated and supervised more easily.

2 Similar jobs within the groups can share the same resources.

3 By grouping similar jobs performance standards can be established.

4 These groups will facilitate communication between individuals and will encourage gradual but continuous improvement of performance and working practices.

There is a tendency for these groups to have strong co-ordination internally, but they may gradually drift apart from other groups within the organisation. This poses organisation-wide co-ordination problems. As groups become more differentiated in their nature, overriding goals such as efficiency, creativity and responsiveness may mean that each group is inherently distinct. This separation between the different groups has to be closely monitored by the organisation itself to avoid the adoption of these foci.

There are a number of criteria by which groups can be established. These include:

- ◆ knowledge and skill.

- ◆ function or work process.

- ◆ shift pattern or time.

- ◆ output.

- ◆ customer type.

- ◆ location.

Larger organisations will combine a number of these logical groupings. However, the main overriding criteria are the same:

- ◆ to ensure that any work flow interdependencies have been addressed.

- ◆ to ensure that any interdependencies related to function or specialisation are also considered.

- ◆ to ensure that the group itself is viable in terms of the concentration of employees or function against the dispersal of employees and function into smaller non-viable groups.

- ◆ to ensure that any social relationships between the groups are considered, particularly in relation to tasks that are perceived to be repetitive or boring, which would mean that these groups would need social interaction in order to compensate for the tedium.

Centralisation and decentralisation

The issue of centralisation or decentralisation cannot be simply addressed. According to each organisation there will be an optimum level of centralisation or decentralisation. In organisations that have a simple structure, the majority of decisions are inevitably centralised, as there is no middle management in order to filter and disseminate the decisions themselves. On the other hand, in larger organisations, where there is a long scalar chain between the decision-makers and the lower grades, information has to go through a number of links in the scalar chain before it reaches the bottom of the organisation. Each of those managers through which the decision is filtered has to have a share of initiative. An intelligent, experienced and strong manager will be able to couple a wide span of activities and a centralised decision-making process and reduce the influence of any intermediary to that of an information conduit. If, on the other hand, the manager is unsure of their own experience and opinions, then there may be a desire to incorporate the abilities of the subordinate managers, thus effecting a form of decentralisation. Given the fact that managers may find themselves in an environment in which they fluctuate between total control and elements of indecision, it is inevitable that the degree of centralisation and decentralisation will also vary.

Benefits of decentralisation

Good management rests upon reconciling centralisation and decentralisation, or, perhaps more accurately, decentralisation with co-ordinated control. Providing an organisation can achieve co-ordinated decentralisation, then they will be able to enjoy the following benefits:

◆ increased initiative from managers and employees.

◆ the ready acceptance and development of responsibility.

◆ the overall development of managers and employees.

◆ decisions which are related to the reality of the situation and not theoretical constructs.

◆ a flexible management and employee structure.

◆ a higher level of motivation at all levels.

◆ real or apparent opportunities for managers and employees.

Determining the right level of freedom to give each department or division of the organisation requires careful consideration by those at the strategic apex of the organisation. Obviously, there needs to be a series of procedures in place in order to ensure co-ordination. Good co-ordination will mean efficiencies and economies as the organisation is more able to adapt and respond to demands. Those at the strategic apex need to determine which decisions can be made more efficiently and effectively at their level of the organisation and which would be better made at departmental or divisional level. In order to make such decisions, those considering delegation of authority need to be informed and knowledgeable about the workings of the organisation. After considerable discussion, sets of criteria can be identified.

Benefits of centralisation

A number of efficiencies and economies can be enjoyed by all parts of the organisation through the development of a centralised staff operation. Personnel, distribution and other areas can offer a far better service than a division could by purchasing the service outside the organisation, or by providing it for themselves. Providing the centralised operations offer good judgement and skills, then they will also be able to share common objectives with those of the division or department.

Further aspects of centralisation and decentralisation

Centralisation and decentralisation remain topics which are still uppermost in the minds of many management theorists. Each different writer has a peculiar interpretation about what these two considerations actually mean. For the most part, organisations which are controlled by an individual or a very small group are centralised. This fact cannot really be argued with. Decentralisation, however, presents a slightly more difficult problem. Once power is dispersed between a number of different individuals, the process of decentralisation has begun. We should not, however, consider centralisation and decentralisation out of context.

Centralisation is all about co-ordinating decision-making in the hands of the few. But most organisations see that it is impossible to rely on this expert band to make all decisions and this is why many decentralise. Above all, decentralisation offers greater opportunities to motivate individuals.

The delegation of responsibility is in effect decentralisation. This is typified by delegating responsibility down the chain of authority. In other words, it is *vertical decentralisation. Horizontal decentralisation* logically refers to individuals who are not managers having some kind of control over the decision-making process. To add confusion to this debate, decentralisation is also used as a way to describe the dispersal of physical resources or services across a geographical region. Inherent in this will be a degree of true decentralisation in terms of decision-making. However, for the most part, this is purely decentralisation in the strictest sense of the word. Characteristically, centralisation refers to the reversal of this process, where physical resources and services are brought together 'under one roof' in order to make efficiency gains or to enjoy economies of scale. Again, there will be a sense of centralisation in terms of decision making, as fewer individuals are required to make judgements about the allocation of these resources and services.

It would be natural to assume that most bureaucracies are centralised, but in reality there is no strong correlation between these two aspects of organisational design. It is worth remembering that a bureaucracy rests upon the formalisation of behaviour and the standardisation of tasks and outputs. We should not assume that this also means that decision making is necessarily centralised. In parts of the organisation where there is close supervision by managers there will be centralisation of decision making. However, providing there is formalisation of behaviour and most of the tasks have been standardised, centralisation of decision making will be unnecessary.

Decentralisation has come about because of the availability of expert individuals in the middle stratas of the organisational structure. These experts, who have gained a degree of horizontal decentralisation, are able to make a number of decisions on a decentralised basis. Confusion between the roles of line and staff management means that there is often a clash between centralised decision making and decentralised control. The compromise is often selective decentralisation, which is superimposed on to centralised decision-making via the individuals in staff roles.

Questioning management paradigms

Management paradigms are sets of personal values and norms which constitute a stable situation for an individual or organisation. Any major change is said to create a *paradigm shift* which will inevitably mean that the management or organisation needs to consider a reassessment of their values. As Kuhn stated, changes in circumstance are often the reason for a 'risky shift syndrome' which is, in effect, a resistance to change due to fear of the unknown.

Change

If we accept that organisations need to have clearly identifiable values and norms in order to operate in an efficient manner, then we should consider the fact that gradual change rather than radical upheaval is a way in which unnecessary turmoil can be avoided. As we have seen, an organisation will seek to establish a form of socialisation at the beginning of its relationship with any new employee. It may be an inherent feature of this socialisation process that the organisation is in a continuous state of change or flux. Provided that the employee accepts change as an inevitable consequence of being part of an organisation which wishes to be not only competitive, but successful, then many of the potential problems which are often related to changes in the values and norms of the organisation will be perceived as less disruptive.

Structural integration and business functions

Interdependencies

The degree of co-operation and mutual understanding between the different parts of an organisation is often referred to as *structural integration*. Given the fact that the organisation will have established some clear divisions of labour, there will be a number of task interdependencies needed to ensure that the organisation operates in an effective manner. Many organisations will have reciprocal interdependence and will not be able to function efficiently or effectively without the co-operation of one another. If there is a high degree of integration between the different departments or divisions of an organisation, then this may mean that the quality of decision making is impaired, or that too many resources are earmarked to maintain this level of integration.

Integrating or linking roles which are specialist positions, to facilitate the communication and problem-solving process between two or more interdependent groups, provides a means for effective liaison and trouble-shooting.

Linkages

In order to ensure that the organisation addresses the needs of its main operations, it must think beyond the design of jobs and the super-structure in which those jobs exist. There will be a number of vital linkages between the various parts of the organisation or individual job roles. One aspect of this is to express the objectives of the organisation in terms of a series of plans, budgets and schedules, all of which are subject to performance control and planning. However, these planning and control systems need to be formalised in some way in order to ensure that the different groups within the organisation that are jointly responsible act in concert with one another and for the good of the organisation. Naturally, the majority of performance standards and co-ordination systems are imposed upon the organisation by the higher levels in the hierarchy. Each group or unit within the organisation is firstly responsible to itself and then to the more generalised objectives of the organisation. Most organisations would not rely on self-co-ordination by different profit and cost centres as a sole means of ensuring that objectives are reached. To this end, organisations will develop a number of devices by which closer liaison and co-ordination are fostered. These will be incorporated into the structure of the organisation itself. It is important to remember that these liaison or communication systems will bypass most of the more conventional vertical communications and authority channels.

Liaison and integration devices

Specific groups can be established for a finite period of time in order to ensure that a particular project or organisation-wide concern is dealt with. However, interdepartmental standing committees will carry out most of the liaison work. They will be able to discuss and offer solutions on common interest issues.

Many organisations will create a post for a manager whose sole responsibility it is to integrate and to liaise, with the full force of formal authority. They will be able to cut through all of the normal communication and hierarchy levels in order to ensure that particular decision-making processes are adhered to. In many larger organisations the brand or product line manager will have liaison and co-ordination responsibilities. This will encompass the full integration of many specialists within the organisation all working towards a common goal.

As we will see in the next section, the matrix structure offers one of the better opportunities to fully integrate all of the various departments or divisions of an organisation. A fully formed matrix structure takes account of all of the interdependencies, whether they are functional ones related to work flow, market-based ones relying on specialists, or standardisation ones relating to formalisation of behaviour, training or induction. In essence, a true matrix structure will be able to plan and control across the whole organisation by virtue of its configuration. Some matrix structures are permanent, where the interdependencies are more or less stable, while others exist solely for the duration of a particular project.

Since the liaison and integration devices created by the organisation are of paramount importance when there are significant interdependencies, the individual groupings themselves may remain small. This is so that each group does not replicate job roles contained elsewhere in the organisation. They can rely fully on staff functions as they have been integrated within the structure itself. This does, however, mean that there will be a number of managers existing within the organisation with a very limited range of line management responsibility. In effect, they will be solitary or responsible for only a small group, constantly servicing the requirements of other groups. Integration is particularly common in organic structures, where the flexible nature of the organisation encourages relationships.

The vast majority of integration and liaison posts occur at middle management level. Both line and staff managers will have liaison responsibilities as an integral part of their job role.

Review questions

1   How should the design of an organisation reflect the division of labour?

2   Identify six of the key organisational design parameters.

3   What is the nature and purpose of job enlargement?

4   How can job roles be formalised or categorised?

5   What is the role of induction and training in behaviour formalisation?

6   In order to co-ordinate activities within an organisation it is important to group individuals in a logical manner. How can this be achieved?

7   What are management paradigms?

8   How can a long scalar chain affect an organisation's ability to centralise or decentralise?

9   How can an organisation balance co-ordination with the need to offer a degree of freedom to its employees?

10   'Delegation can be defined simply as a form of verbal decentralisation.' Discuss.

11   What is structural integration?

12   Why might it be the case that the majority of co-ordination and liaison roles concentrate at middle management level?

Section 2

CHANGING STRUCTURES

After reading this section you should be able to:

◆ identify different organisational environments.

◆ analyse the relationship between different structures and an organisation's performance and development.

◆ participate in the management of organisational change.

2.1

Different organisational environments

The degree of complexity and dynamism within the organisation will have a marked impact on the prevailing organisational environment. The factors that need to be taken into account before making or taking a decision will give some indication of the complexity of the organisation. It is the interrelationships between the various functional departments that can make the processes more complex, particularly if there is a culture of widespread involvement. Not only do the decision makers have to take into account the probable influences of the different departments or divisions, they may also be heavily influenced by the external environment. The stakeholders (those with a vested interest in the organisation), for example, may further complicate the structure of the organisation. For organisations that have a purely functional basis, there is the ability to maintain a simple internal structure. It is only when the organisation tries to encompass the demands of its different parts and those relevant external influences that the structure becomes somewhat more complex.

Examples of organisational environments

There are four pure types of organisational environment:

◆ simple stable.

◆ complex stable.

◆ simple dynamic.

◆ complex dynamic.

In a *simple stable* environment we encounter the easiest form for management purposes. Most of the work is carried out by following simple routines and procedures which have been well established. The management does not have to be very skilful, well-trained or experienced in order to operate this type of environment.

The *complex stable* environment is somewhat more uncertain. The management will face a number of decision-making problems in conditions of risk. However, since the environment has features of stability, the managers will be able to understand the alternatives. Having said this, they cannot predict future problems but they are probably in a better position to work out what may or may not happen as a result of a particular action. The managers need to be trained to a greater level of competency and the majority of experiences gained in hands-on situations. Normally, an organisation of this type would consider developing new rules and procedures as the situation changes, with a corresponding need to adapt.

In a *simple dynamic* environment both the management and the structure need to be adaptable. Changes will occur rapidly and continuously, but, since the nature of the work involved is still simple, the management is capable of responding relatively easily. Typically, management information systems are able to chart the impact of the changes by simply adapting existing routines to take account of them.

In a *complex dynamic* environment we find the most difficult and complicated management situation. The managers need to have a degree of experience and sophistication beyond that required in all of the other forms of environment. There are a number of decision-making techniques that can go some way to simplifying the management problems, but there can be no substitute for real managerial experience. Since the opportunities and threats facing an organisation of this type are numerous and diverse, managers will have to create unique ways of structuring and managing parts, if not all, of the organisation.

Placid-random and placid-clustered environments

Organisations which operate in environments where there is slow technological change and relatively few competitors have radically different problems to those organisations which are in competitive, growing or changing environments. Obviously, the stability of the organisation has considerable implications for its internal structure. Most businesses will operate in both stable and changing environments. As a direct result of this, some parts of the organisation will be under constant review and probable change, while others will not need to take great note of upheavals in the external environment.

Given the fact that a stable environment is characterised by a low level of change, any changes that do occur will tend to have a minor impact on the organisational structure and the operations of the business. Typically, these organisations will be producing or offering goods and services which have not had to change for a considerable number of years. As we have already said, these organisations will not be faced with constant or radical changes in technology. Further features are that they will have a constant set of known competitors, the ownership of the organisation will be stable and they will not be affected to a great extent by changes in government legislation. In fact, one of the major things which typifies these organisations is that they have constant stakeholders whose identity is constant.

It is for this reason that we can describe these stable structures as being *placid*. Since they have no real reason for making changes, the internal environment is somewhat more easygoing, simple and calm. The top management is perfectly well aware of what is going on within the organisation, but always has an eye on the external environment in case there are issues which need to be taken on board.

The products and services produced by these organisations tend not to fluctuate in quality. As demand changes, they will, of course, adjust the quantity of products and services they supply. But, since the product itself does not change year on year, they do not have to alter the manufacturing process or the way in which they offer their services.

The *random factor* allows the organisation to make minor adjustments in order to compensate for minimal changes in the external environment. This would be typified by an organisation slightly increasing the number of employees in a particular department to cope with added demand, or the gradual upgrading of technological equipment as older machinery becomes inefficient or beyond economic repair.

For more complex or long-term changes in the external environment, the organisation would respond by changing the way in which certain parts of the structure co-operate with one another or relate to one another. In this respect, the *cluster aspect* refers to a series of interrelated activities within the organisation that may have to be changed at the same point in time, or be phased-in over a period of time, to compensate for changes which have been made to a single area of the organisation.

Organisations such as these adapt to fluctuations in demand by changing the size of the work-force and not by changing their products, services or manufacturing processes. Given the stable environment, they are able to predict the level of demand far more accurately, allowing them to plan more successfully and with a degree of certainty.

Disturbed reactive and turbulent environments

With frequent shifts in products, technology, markets, competitors and legal framework, these organisations are characterised by almost continual change. In this respect, they should be viewed as being in constant evolution. Not only will technological innovations mean that their products may become outdated, but also that their manufacturing processes may become obsolete. This organisation is typified by the multinational or large public limited company having to juggle a number of contentious issues and changes in a variety of different markets and environments. With the unpredictability that comes with operations in a variety of different market-places, the organisation has to juggle the needs of various interest groups which exert a constant pressure upon the organisation. Some organisations will react by gradual adaptation; others will have to put themselves in a state of temporary upheaval in order to ensure that their market position is maintained in the short term.

The position of the disturbed reactive organisation

An organisation which could be referred to as *disturbed reactive* is just the kind of organisation that faces an unexpected but serious threat to its operations. If we consider a radical change in legislation, which precludes the production of products to certain specifications, then we can see that what had been a stable environment, or perhaps a placid one, becomes disturbed by this external influence, requiring a reaction. In this respect, we could describe organisations such as these as being purely reactive and only wishing to make changes when they absolutely need to. They would be perfectly happy and capable of continuing to provide products and services as they had always done, without this external pressure having been placed on them.

The position of the turbulent organisation

Turbulent organisations take a radically different view. This may be, on the one hand, because their environment is far too unpredictable and unstable to produce products and services of the same specification for any length of time. Naturally, these organisations would prefer that the situation was otherwise, but they accept the unpredictability of the situation and organise their structure in such a way as to enable it to cope with as much turbulence as may be necessary.

On the other hand, an organisation may actively seek to have a turbulent structure within an unpredictable environment, for example if the products and services it provides are of a temporary and innovative type. The organisation will need to have a structure which is capable of immediate response in markets which are relatively difficult to predict. Only by having an extremely flexible and responsive workforce who are able to gain valuable insights into the probable direction in which the market is moving, can they hope to be successful. While the unpredictability and turbulence of the market and the environment is unsettling, they will have carefully chosen their key employees for their ability to cope with radically changing roles and responsibilities. It would be extremely difficult to create a reliable organisation chart in these cases. The job roles will be blurred and there will be no clear lines of demarcation between responsibilities at the different levels of the organisation. It would be possible to recognise particular roles within the hierarchy, but these would offer just some insight into the decision-making structure and the co-ordination of the organisation as a whole.

 # Types of change

In a rapidly changing market, organisations must be aware of the impact of change upon their operations. Many of the factors which could have been relied upon in the past to be constant are no longer so. Organisations can no longer rely upon a steady level of sales or demand, nor can they continue producing products and services in traditional ways.

One of the major agents of change has been new technology, which has not only affected telecommunications, but has also had a marked impact upon production techniques. The nature of work at all levels of an organisation has changed and will continue to do so as a result of technology. Conventional manufacturing processes require far fewer employees than they have done in the past. The impact of automation leads to a reduction in direct labour.

Markets have also changed significantly, not only with increased competition but as a result of changes in government policy, such as deregulation, which have opened the way for increased competition. Perhaps one of the biggest changes in terms of markets has been the development of the European Union.

Another major change which also relates to the nature and availability of customers is the fact that the UK and most of the developed world has an ageing population. This is known as the *demographic time bomb*. Not only has it had an impact upon the work-force, but it also has increasing influence on the purchasing habits of the consumers.

Response options to change

Response options to change can be more generally categorised in one of the four following ways:

1 *Tuning* – to make the organisation operate more efficiently, perhaps by redesigning job roles. This is usually a proactive approach in anticipation of the need to make changes in the future, and is an example of a tactical change in the organisation.

2 *Adaptation* – usually a reactive move to changes in the external environment often used as a remedy to problems. These changes would focus on selected parts of the organisation. This is also a tactical change in the organisation.

3 *Reorientation* – these are planned strategic changes that anticipate major changes in the external environment. By making these sweeping changes the organisation hopes to maintain or improve its competitive advantage.

4 *Re-creation* – this is the most drastic form of change and would involve significant modification of the organisation. Usually, these changes are made as a result of potential major changes in the external environment, without making corresponding changes the long-term viability of the organisation would be threatened.

These four possible change response options are shown in Fig. 2.1, and each can be triggered to any one of the following changes to the organisation.

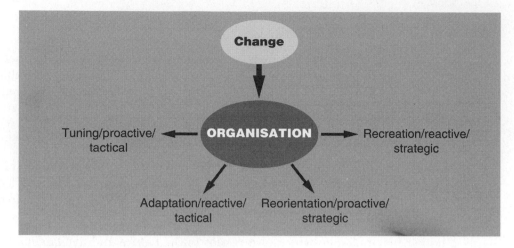

Fig. 2.1 Change response options

Changes in management structure

Major changes in the management structure of an organisation should be as much expected as any other type of change. This is usually driven by the directors of the organisation, the owners or as a result of poor or very good results. Inevitably there will always be winners and losers in such a change. The main point of the exercise will be to improve the overall management structure of the organisation. There are three main goals that can be identified here:

1 The management changes should enable the organisation to better fulfil its vision of the future. Within this, the new management positions should encompass difficult performance targets and encourage enthusiasm.

2 The management changes should revitalise the managers. The key winners of the changes should be held as role models for all, with the expectation that their forms of behaviour should be copied.

3 The management changes should build an effective top layer of management that is able to continue the development of management practices and support the longer-term change processes.

Changes in size

With hundreds of thousands of businesses accounting for many billions of pounds of turnover, the relative sizes of various businesses will differ enormously. Most businesses welcome growth and many organisations specifically aim to achieve it. At the same time many organisations want to remain small. There are obviously a number of different ways in which to assess the current size of a particular business.

These include:

◆ the amount of capital employed.

◆ the level of turnover.

◆ the level of profit.

◆ the number of employees.

Technically, if a business has less than £1.5m turnover, then it is considered to be small. Those with a turnover of around £6m are large. Those that fall in between are considered to be medium-sized. Turnover is used as a more accurate assessment of size since organisations with relatively few employees could be extremely profitable, whereas those with many thousands of employees could be relatively unprofitable. There are a great many reasons for growth and consequent changes in size. These include:

◆ by staying small the organisation may not be able to take advantage of economies of scale, fend off possible takeovers or become more profitable.

◆ the larger the organisation becomes, the greater the economies of scale, leading to lower unit production costs, greater efficiencies and higher profits.

◆ by growing, the organisation should be able to sell more products and services, which would in turn mean a higher level of profitability.

◆ growth means a greater market share and may be able to have an influence on the pricing structure of products and services in particular markets.

◆ by growing larger and diversifying into new areas, the organisation can avoid or at best reduce the level of risks associated with the failure of a particular product or service.

Most growth is *internal growth*. This is also known as *organic growth*. The organisation will gradually grow in size as it sells more products and services to more markets. Organic growth is a slow process, but it does not have many of the associated dangers of faster growth. Alternatively the business may choose *external growth* which would involve a process of acquisition, including takeover or merging with other businesses. By acquiring a controlling interest or complete control of another business the organisation is able to guarantee faster growth in size, although this does not necessarily mean a growth in profitability. It will, however, mean that greater economies of scale may be achieved.

Changes in markets

There need to be considerable changes in the attitudes and approaches of all individuals within an organisation when faced with the prospect of operating overseas. The reasons for the growth may be organic, or perhaps as a result of a merger or a takeover. Without doubt, there are new challenges ahead for the organisation. Some of these are summarised in Fig. 2.2. Many of the potential challenges are no different to those that would be faced by any organisation that is faced with a change in size. Some of the specific concerns related to expansion into the overseas market are:

◆ *cultural factors* – such as language differences, diverse national prices, fragmented and diverse markets, unclear rules and regulations and diverse purchasing habits.

◆ *economic factors* – such as a variety of different financial climates, unstable currencies and a diverse set of different business environments.

◆ *competitive factors* – such as problems in collecting useful and reliable market data, increased numbers of competitors and very little information regarding their strategies and activities.

◆ *legal factors* – such as more, or considerably less, government influence on business decisions, increased political factors and implications regarding the economic plans of the government.

◆ *technological factors* – such as the training of overseas personnel to operate and maintain machinery and equipment, the adaptation of parts and equipment and differences in measuring systems.

If an organisation suffers from changes in market conditions or it perceives that there are troubled times ahead, it may institute some form of *retrenchment*. Essentially this involves the following:

◆ the cutting back on the numbers of those employed.

◆ the cutting back of activities that the organisation is involved in.

This retrenchment strategy is also more commonly known as 'downsizing'. The principal aim of the downsizing is to be able to cut back on expenditure so that it more closely matches the projected income of the organisation. It also allows the organisation to consider the refocusing of operations in order to be in a better position to exploit the situation when (and if) the market conditions improve. In some extreme cases the retrenchment may be the first stage in disposing of the business or closing at least a division, subsidiary or department.

Changes in ownership

Takeovers and mergers

The principal reasons for changes in ownership tend to be related to takeovers and mergers. There are also considerable changes to cope with when the organisation is subject to a management buy-out. In all cases, the organisation will have to adapt quickly and effectively to the demands placed upon it by the new owners. The degree of structural change will obviously depend upon the level of involvement of the new owners. Some changes in ownership may signal significant changes throughout the whole of the organisation and its operations. On the other hand, the change in ownership may not seem to have a serious affect on the business for the short term. Inevitably, changes will be imposed or agreed and this will affect all levels of the management and the workforce.

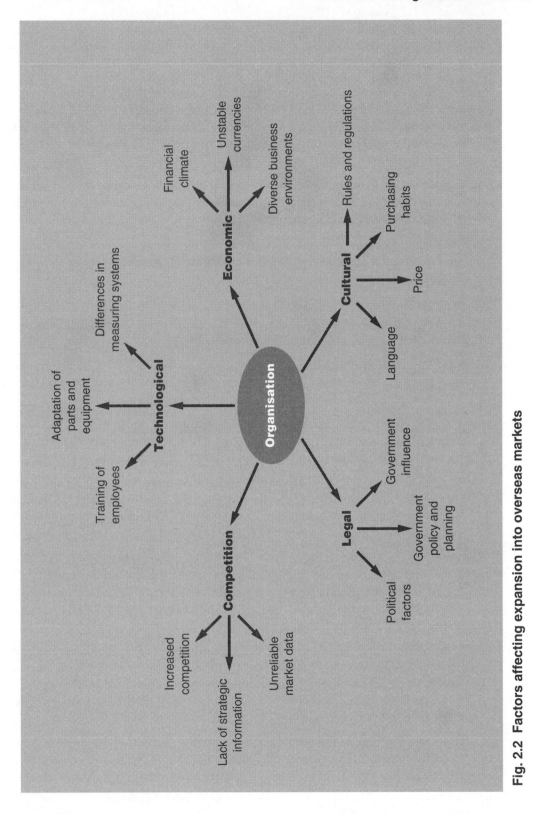

Fig. 2.2 Factors affecting expansion into overseas markets

Takeovers and mergers tend to occur when organisations choose to (or find themselves obliged to) join together and operate as a single business. A takeover is the acquiring of full management control of another business by purchasing over 50 per cent of its share capital. An alternative word for 'takeover' is 'acquisition'. Usually, the buying business is larger than the target business. For this reason, the larger organisation is often described as being a predator. In certain cases, the smaller business may be able to raise enough finance to purchase the shares of a larger organisation. When this happens it is described as being a *reverse takeover*.

A merger is an agreement between two organisations to bring their businesses under the control of a single board of directors. Naturally, this has to be agreed by the management and the shareholders to ensure that the merger is a smooth one.

There are a number of reasons why these activities take place (*see* Fig. 2.3). These include the following:

◆ If an organisation is set upon rapid expansion, then it may be quicker to purchase another business and gradually convert it into their own business (in terms of approach, procedures and name).

◆ If an organisation has calculated that it would be cheaper if they purchased another business than concentrate on growing internally, then it would be a great temptation to consider a takeover rather than gradual growth.

◆ If an organisation is 'cash rich' it may wish to invest some of its profits on the acquisition of another organisation. This may be the ideal move, particularly as it will mean that the cash can be spent before tax liabilities are calculated.

◆ If an organisation believes that another business may be a long-term threat to its position in the market-place, then it may consider acquisition as a purely defensive move. This will mean that at a stroke they have eliminated the potential threat as well as having acquired the skill and expertise of the growing business.

◆ If an organisation wishes to rationalise its operations and streamline them for the future (particularly if it is considering growth into another market), then acquisition is an ideal way of 'buying in' the expertise and know-how, as well as the physical production and distribution needed.

◆ If an organisation wishes to radically expand its operations to achieve greater economies of scale, then it would be a natural reaction to consider an acquisition to achieve this. If the organisation can identify the fact that their costs will be lower by acquiring another business then it is in their best interests to consider this option.

◆ If an organisation recognises that the true value of another business is greater than its selling price, then it may purchase the organisation purely to sell off its assets. This is known as 'asset stripping' (*see* p. 97). The purchasing

Fig. 2.3 Reasons for takeovers and mergers

organisation will systematically sell off any valuable part of the acquired business (either to rationalise it, or simply to acquire a good price for the assets). If the purchasing organisation is not merely interested in asset stripping, then it may be necessary to dispose of duplicated operations and unprofitable areas of the organisation.

Over the last few years, particularly since the 1980s, there has been a marked increase in the number of mergers in the UK. As a direct result of the establishment of the Unlisted Securities Market, smaller businesses found it easier to raise finance. They needed this access to finance in order to pay for their merger activities. At the same time, the government appeared to be more willing to allow takeovers and mergers. This was embodied in the phrase 'the enterprise culture'. Many individuals who had not considered becoming shareholders in the past purchased a number of shares during share issues of the utilities and consequently other organisations. Many people had considered takeovers, in particular, to be unethical and overly aggressive. The feeling was that many victims of such actions found themselves at the mercy of the predators. Consumer groups also felt that organisations, getting larger and more powerful by acquisition, would not provide the same level of service to the consumer.

There are a variety of different merger or takeover operations, and these can best be described overall as an *integration process*. These include the following:

◆ *horizontal integration* – where two organisations in the same area of business activity (particularly at the same stage of production) join together. This allows for greater economies of scale than are evident in larger scale activity. A typical example of this could be two newspapers joining forces.

◆ *forward vertical integration* – this occurs when an organisation merges with another business which is at the next stage of production. A typical example of this would be a food processing business acquiring a chain of restaurants and grocery outlets.

◆ *backward vertical integration* – this happens when an organisation chooses to acquire a business that is at an earlier stage of production. An example of this would be a newspaper acquiring a printing plant, wood mill or forestry operation. This is done to make sure that the original organisation can make the best use of the advantages of not being reliant upon another supplier, so increasing the overall profits.

◆ *lateral integration* – this involves the merging of two organisations that do not have a great deal in common. Perhaps they do have some superficial similarities (such as operating in the same market-place), but beyond that the acquisition is purely designed to achieve a degree of diversification. Diversification means that the organisation can now operate in different market-places that can be designed to be complementary in terms of location, distribution and economies of scale.

A sample vertical and horizontal integration process for a stationery manufacturer is shown in Fig. 2.4. Particularly in the latter case, we can see that the organisation's merger activities aim to diversify and form a conglomerate. The organisation, as a conglomerate, is no longer reliant on a single market and can divert its efforts and resources to other areas of its activities at the appropriate time.

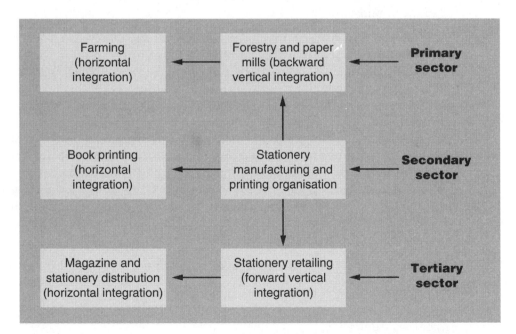

Fig. 2.4 Horizontal and vertical integration for a stationery manufacturer

Predator organisations do not, necessarily, have to acquire 51 per cent of the shares of a victim. Particularly in cases when the share ownership is widespread amongst hundreds of thousands of small investors, the predator may be able to gain control with as little as 15 to 20 per cent.

The organisation that is the subject of a potential takeover can be alerted to the fact that it is a target because the business acquiring the shares has to declare its ownership if the share percentage has reached 3 per cent. This is a legally binding declaration requirement to allow the existing shareholders to be made aware of the situation. If the market knows that there is a potential takeover in the offing, then the share price will increase. Other investors may come in and purchase shares in the anticipation that the share price will increase further. This is particularly true of situations when there are two or more competing predators trying to gain control over the business.

If it is believed that the takeover or merger is not in the public's interests, then the Department of Trade and Industry may require the Monopolies and Mergers Commission to investigate the situation.

As you will have realised, some takeovers are unwanted by the present owners or Board of Directors. These are known as 'hostile takeovers'. The target of the takeover will attempt to mobilise support in order to fight off the takeover. The Board will try to convince the shareholders that it is not in their interest to allow the takeover to succeed. It will then be up to the shareholders to consider the advantages and disadvantages of the takeover and decide whether to support the existing Board or throw their shares in with the predator.

In other situations the takeover may be welcomed by the business. These are called 'friendly takeovers'. Businesses which are encountering difficulties may find themselves in a situation where the only alternative is to look for an external investor. The potential investor would bring much needed capital to the struggling business in return for a share in the ownership.

Some takeovers have an altogether more sinister nature about them. The sole reason for the takeover may simply be to acquire the assets of the business. The predator, once the takeover has been secured, may then dispose of the assets of the acquired business. In many cases, the *book value* or the apparent value of the business, in terms of its trading position, may hide the fact that the organisation has a variety of valuable assets. If these assets are realised, or sold, then they will provide considerable profit for the predator. This is known as *asset stripping*. The predator may have no interest whatsoever in the continued operation of the acquired business. Valuable assets such as buildings, land and machinery can be sold off piecemeal to provide a substantial and rapid return on the investment.

Management buy-outs

Management buy-outs occur when the managers of an organisation purchase the shares from the current owners of that business. By controlling the organisation the managers hope to be able to maximise the profitability of the business as they have a very definite incentive to ensure its success. Many examples of management buy-outs have involved the change in ownership of subsidiaries or divisions of larger organisations. The independence of the subsidiary or division creates a considerable advantage as many tiers of management have been dispensed with and power is concentrated in the hands of the new owners. The managers need to be very sure that they can make a positive impact on the business. A successful buy-out can mean that the managers stand to make a great deal of money. On the other hand, the managers must also take responsibility for the workforce and their future too. Much of the money that is needed to finance a management buy-out will come from loans secured against the personal property of the managers. This will make the gearing (that is the ratio of the organisation's debt capital to its equity capital) of the organisation quite high at the beginning. While the acquisition of a business in which the managers have a significant stake is attractive, they must be prepared to take on a much greater degree of responsibility. They can no longer be wholly concerned with their area of the organisation's operations. They must take an active role in strategic management and the moulding of the business's objectives. In some cases, management buy-outs have either signalled one or the other of the following consequences for the work-force:

◆ manning levels have been significantly reduced and the workforce lives in a much greater fear of redundancy through reorganisation and rationalisation.

◆ the business has become significantly more democratised with the managers actively seeking the co-operation and involvement of the work-force.

Management buy-ins

Management buy-ins operate in a similar way to management buy-outs, but the managers are not involved in the existing set-up. Individuals, who will take the roles of managers in the organisation, buy the shares of the business in the belief that they can manage the business more efficiently and profitably than the existing managers.

Changes in patterns and levels of employment

In order to be leaner and more competitive, some organisations have taken radical steps to significantly reduce their levels of employment. The organisation identifies core workers who will have responsibility for providing a regular and essential level of service at times when demand and business activity is low. However, they will take on a more important role when demand increases. Working around and for these core workers will be a number of peripheral employees. Typically these will be either on short fixed-term contracts or, perhaps, on temporary contracts via employment agencies. Alternatively, some of the peripheral workers could be freelance individuals who can carry out a series of activities for the business at another location. The key advantages to having core and peripheral workers revolve around the organisation's ability to adapt to changes in demand and activity at fairly short notice. The core workers become an extremely important asset for the organisation and the peripheral workers can be dispensed with once busy periods have passed.

The ability and willingness of the employees to adopt different methods of working can play an essential part in the organisation's capacity to cope with change. Many organisations strive to obtain a multiskilled work-force that is responsive rather than resistant to changes in their working practices. This means that, not only do the employees need to be multiskilled, but they need to be willing to dispense with rigid demarcation which separates one job function from another.

As an alternative to this, the employment patterns may have to be changed in order to cope with differences in the need for particular job tasks to be undertaken. This may mean that some jobs will remain permanent and full-time, but others may have to be either temporary or on a part-time basis.

Shift working

Some organisations have used shift working for a considerable number of years. This is often seen as a way to ensure that production and manning remain constant throughout the whole day. The level of manning and consequent production at different times during the day may be related to production patterns and determined by deliveries of components and raw materials or the need to despatch orders at particular times of the day. Other organisations, mindful of the need to ensure that maximum manning levels are achieved at busy times of the day, have introduced flexi-time which go some way to cater for the individual needs of the employee. Under flexi-time, the core periods of the day have optimum manning, while the less vital periods either side of the busy times have a skeleton staff available.

Multiskilling and deskilling

Multiskilling can prove to be extremely useful, particularly in production situations. The ability of an individual employee to stand in for unavailable colleagues may ensure that the production process is not interrupted by their absence. Equally, multiskilling allows the organisation to more flexibly employ the work-force in a variety of different ways according to demands. Multiskilling relates to batch production rather than mass production; *deskilling*, on the other hand, relates to mass production. In the latter case, rather than the job being reliant on particular skills, the employee is required to carry out a series of mundane and repetitive tasks which are predetermined by the speed of the machinery or conveyor belt.

Both approaches have their own advantages in relation to either speed of production or quality of individual products. While it could be argued that mass production requiring deskilled labour is more likely to mean faster production, this is not always the case. Several major organisations, such as Nissan and Volvo have moved across to multiskilled workforces who are equally as capable of producing products quickly and, above all, of a consistently high quality standard. On balance, the multiskilled approach offers greater flexibility in respect of change. Organisations which have a multiskilled workforce will be able to deploy their employees into a variety of different but related work activities, dependent upon the level of demand and the availability of work space and machinery.

Terminology, language, and the impact of IT

Information technology (IT) has made radical changes to the duties and tasks and the speed of output of personnel carrying out administrative jobs. Administrators are now expected to work with computers and a wide range of electronic equipment used for processing and communicating various types of information. Because of this, they can be described as office technologists, rather than clerical assistants. Later in this section we will look in more detail at the way these changes in technology have affected, or will affect, an individual's work load and productivity.

IT has brought with it a brand new language. Knowing and understanding computer terminology is now essential, as it is used so frequently within business today. Obviously, the extent of benefits from computerisation will vary from organisation to organisation, depending on the complexity of their administration systems. The ability to extract information quickly and distribute it immediately is of no use if that information is inaccurate or out of date. For these reasons, the careful selection of hardware and relevant software packages is essential, as is the need for staff training and retraining.

Naturally, it is, for some, becoming increasingly difficult to keep tabs on what is new and what has been around for some time. Many computer suppliers are aware of this and publish the warning that due to the complexities of particular technologies, some upgrades require a certain level of technical expertise. In such cases, they would advise that the installation be carried out at the premises of the purchaser. This, obviously, will add to the expense of upgrading or installing the machine. In addition to changes that affect the performance of the computer, there are some developments which specifically benefit the user on a more personal and comfort-related basis.

Computer networking and multitasking

Networking means microcomputers can be linked together in a network which enables them to share information, centralise the distribution of data and also share the control of the program. For example, a member of staff who is working on some software relevant to accounts information can input the latest data on a customer. Once that information has been entered, then other linked computers can access it. A network is particularly useful when an organisation requires a software application to be accessible by more than one person at the same time. Several people can be inputting different aspects of the same information at the same time and it is also possible for one person to extract information without having to disturb another person in their duties.

The number of machines that can be linked by networking is very flexible and the machines can be upgraded to suit a particular organisation's needs. Obviously, this is an expensive and complicated area. Most organisations seek advice from specialists before embarking on the installation of a network.

A *local area network* (LAN) system consists of a number of terminals which are connected so that information and functions can be shared. Each terminal can be considered to be a workstation. Information should be considered as a resource and the sharing of this information provides benefits to all who are involved. Users do not have to rely on disk-based updates of information, as the simple inputting of information at one terminal instantly fulfils the task. This slightly more sophisticated variety of networking enables terminals to be linked in various remote locations in much the same way as a LAN system. In the UK British Telecom provides the majority of land lines connecting terminals in a *wide area network* (WAN) system. The use of satellites extends WAN systems world-wide. This enables individuals to engage in teleworking as well as providing offices abroad with instant access to the information stored by the parent company.

Major corporations will employ a LAN and a WAN system working together in order to provide a full range of network facilities. Each office will have its own LAN system but be connected with all other offices by a WAN system. They will all have access to the head office's mainframe via the WAN system.

The term *multitasking*, (or multiuser) means very much the same as networking. The difference is that rather than having several microcomputers linked together, one computer has a number of terminals attached to it. This means that each of the terminal keyboards is not actually attached to its own independent software computer, so cannot be termed a computer itself. Any member of staff, even at a remote terminal, (possibly miles away from the computer itself) would need to know how to log in, access information and log out. User names or passwords would also be a security consideration for organisations adopting the multitasking form of computerisation.

Any organisation considering the choice of either a networking or multitasking form of computerisation would need to take account of a number of factors before making a final decision. Issues to be addressed are shown in Fig. 2.5. These will include:

◆ Will the system be sufficient on a long-term basis? It would be ineffective to install a system which could become overloaded too quickly.

◆ Is the system upgradable? Can more micro-computers or additional terminals be added in the future?

◆ Does the master processor have sufficient memory to enable it to function effectively?

◆ Will the system be quick enough? This is important if bottlenecks are to be avoided.

◆ Is staff training or retraining necessary? If so (and it most likely will be), is this a viable proposition, in terms of cost and possible disruption?

◆ the type of work to be carried out.

◆ the complexity of 'loading' the system.

◆ the response times required.

◆ the support available.

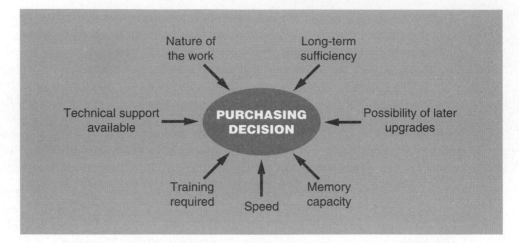

Fig. 2.5 Factors determining the choice between network systems and multitasking

Psychological implications of change

There are psychological approaches to keeping staff motivated in times of organisational restructuring or upheaval. British companies no longer have employees who stay in the same place for years. Change has become a way of life, particularly to IT specialists. These specialists are very often at the heart of many corporate restructuring programmes.

Companies are looking at new ways, such as teleworking, to reduce costs. This move does mean transferring individuals, groups or teams into new structures. Some concern has been voiced over such shifts and it is said that the consequences have not been explored thoroughly. Vyla Lejeune Rollins, an organisational psychologist with KPMG, has said that, 'When you take an organisation through change you have to raise the tolerance threshold of individuals. If people are asked to start working from home, you create problems if you lack the mechanisms to raise their thresholds'. She claims that, provided individuals are worked with creatively and constructively, then they can be helped into new roles.

Workshop sessions and exercises for groups and individuals are advocated, in order to allow individuals to explore their own feelings about the changes they are involved in – what they find enjoyable, exciting and motivating. This process can reveal that organisational change or restructuring is not for everyone. Alternatively, it can be rewarding. Hoskyns, a service supplier organisation used to be structured in divisions determined by the type of service provided. After realising that their clients often had overlapping requirements, Hoskyns decided to implement a three-tier structure – division by industry sector, then five service lines. Hoskyns claim that their staff want to feel they belong to an office and to be locally managed with continuity of their careers and management. They also claim that their staff want technology to be introduced on an ongoing basis.

When the needs of the staff are satisfied, then they feel they are being invested in and can see a number of career options and opportunities. When they are not, there are barriers, either real or imagined, which block the way of progress both for the individual and the organisation.

Obviously, we can see that technology, whether it is related to the production process or to the administration and control systems, will have a marked impact on the stability of the organisation. Before we turn our attention to environmental factors which affect the stability of the organisation, we should, perhaps, consider the impact that Japanese culture, particularly in terms of production process and methods of co-ordination and control, has had on UK and other Western-based organisations.

Japanese management methods

The management methods employed by Japanese manufacturers have had a significant influence on business in the UK and in other Western countries in the last few years. With a number of Japanese organisations operating their own particular styles of production and management in the UK and the rest of Europe, the following has happened:

◆ the Europeans have had the opportunity to observe the Japanese techniques at first hand. Before this there had been few opportunities to visit Japan and see these techniques in action.

◆ the effectiveness and impact of local demonstrations and open days organised by Japanese manufacturers have accelerated this information gathering.

◆ the viewing of a Japanese-style manufacturing plant has allowed European organisations to appreciate the transferability of these techniques to their own particular production needs.

◆ there has been a realisation that the introduction of these techniques is not linked to the peculiarities of the Japanese culture. The setting up of the Nissan plant in Sunderland, for example, has proved that UK employees are capable of adapting and embracing the techniques wholeheartedly.

◆ since the Japanese have led the way in the introduction of these techniques in Europe, the European organisations can learn about the pitfalls and problems that may face them in the adoption of these procedures.

Japanese-style manufacturing has been the centre of much management literature in recent years, although it has been pointed out that the practices are not simply Japanese in their origins. What the Japanese have managed to do is incorporate a number of individual methods into a coherent package of improvements that seem to work. This is something that the UK, the USA and the rest of the Western world have so far failed to achieve.

One of the key aspects of the adoption of new production methods has been the elimination of waste and reduction in stock levels held by the organisation. This factor alone has contributed to higher levels of productivity as it means that there is not so much capital tied up in stock and thereby not contributing to the profitability of the organisation.

Another direct measure of the profitability of an organisation is in terms of the sales per employee, and there are several different ways of assessing this, for example:

◆ annual sales per employee, which is the traditional approach and made purely in monetary terms.

◆ the units of output per unit of direct labour input in which performance is expressed in productivity terms.

Operating profits are further confused by the fact that an organisation may not have addressed the need to cut its overheads and streamline its administration costs. Any failure in this respect would affect profitability but not productivity. This point has to be borne in mind when considering the relative merits of sales per employee and output as methods of assessing performance.

Japanese-style manufacturing and other techniques relating to the management of human resources and suppliers fall into three main categories. These are:

◆ **manufacturing**

total quality control	design for manufacture
statistical process control	cross-disciplinary teams
Just-in-Time production	quality circles
Kanban (materials control)	quality improvement teams
Kaizen (continuous improvement)	set-up time reduction
cellular manufacture	operator responsibility for quality

◆ **human resources**

Theory Z	performance-related pay
single-status facilities	company councils
performance appraisal	profit sharing schemes
the use of temporary workers	managerial rotation
team briefings	

◆ **supplier**

Just-in-Time delivery of supplies	supplier involvement in design
quality assured supplies	reduction of suppliers
single sourcing of supplies	financial involvement in suppliers
supplier development	

Clearly, many of these aspects are interlinked, and not all have been fully embraced by the UK manufacturers at this point. We will now focus on the key manufacturing techniques which have been adopted by UK businesses.

The cellular manufacturing process

The resources in the business are organised around flow lines or product families in order to simplify the work flow and increase accountability. The cellular manufacturing process is quite straightforward. By establishing the nature of the product and its integral parts, the organisation can attempt to work out the most advantageous method of laying out the factory so that the part-finished products can be passed on easily to the next stage of the production process. Similar activities or parts of the production process can be grouped so that they can be carried out in one specific location.

Design for manufacture

Design for manufacture is a process by which the products are designed so that they can be easily manufactured. This concept is fine if the product is new but it would be difficult to adopt in the case of existing products.

Just-in-Time

Just-in-Time production is a manufacturing process which is managed in a very tightly co-ordinated manner. Minimal stocks are held and production is undertaken on an order-by-order basis. This has been adopted by a large number of organisations who can benefit from the reduced level of investment needed to hold large amounts of buffer stock.

The Kanban system

Kanban materials control is a card-signalling system that is used to synchronise the outputs at the various stages of the manufacturing process. This is particularly useful when the production process involves a number of discrete stages that may be undertaken separately.

The Kaizen process

The Kaizen (continuous improvement) is a process which permits the organisation to learn from problems and constantly improve its manufacturing methods. It is characterised by its widespread use of elementary data analysis and problem-solving on the factory floor. This is a very useful technique for an organisation to apply in the early stages of its development when it is not certain which production methods to employ. This method is also very valuable to long-established organisations if they are finding it difficult to identify which alternative available method they can use.

Quality circles

Quality circles involve the establishment of problem solving or process improvement groups. Again, a number of organisations have adopted these but their success relies on the participants being assured that their suggestions are being taken on board and treated with respect.

Ouchi – Theory Z

As you may be aware, Douglas McGregor put forward his Theory X and Theory Y explanation for two radically different management styles. Ouchi introduces a Japanese style: Theory Z. The characteristics of Theory Z are shown in Fig. 2.6.

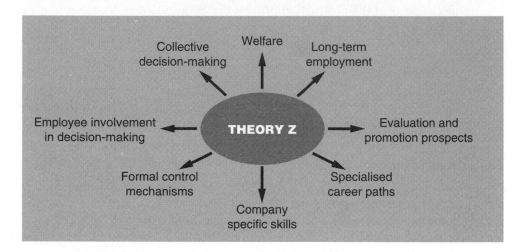

Fig. 2.6 Characteristics of Theory Z

Perhaps the most successful operator of Theory Z in the UK is Marks and Spencer. They have been likened to Japanese companies in their general approach.

Operator responsibility for quality

Operator responsibility for quality focuses the responsibility for levels of quality on the production workers themselves. This is very much in contrast to normal Western practice where the responsibility for quality is in the hands of the manager, supervisor or a specialist.

Set-up time reduction

Set-up time reduction programmes are designed to reduce the time needed to prepare the production line for processing of a particular product. This means that batch sizes can be reduced and the lead time to production can be reduced to a minimum. This requires forward planning and considerable thought in order to ensure that the types of products produced on the production line are similar in all respects. In other words, the order in which the products are made can help ensure the production line need not be completely reorganised before the process can begin.

Statistical process control (SPC)

SPC is a method of monitoring product process performance which uses elementary statistical theory to guide decisions about adjustments to the process. This requires some degree of retraining and involves set-up costs but has been introduced successfully in a number of organisations.

Total quality control

Total quality control is a production philosophy with an emphasis on error prevention, continuous improvement and the concept of quality in terms of the products fitness for use. This is an integral part of total quality management.

The Japanese Nenko system

The large Japanese corporations such as Hitachi, Nissan, Honda, Mitsibushi and Toyota are often cited as excellent examples of organisational communications. Quality circles, for example, have been an integral part of Japanese organisations since the 1950s. There have been a great many studies of Japanese organisations in order to discover the secret behind their economic success. What is certainly true is that employees are committed to Japanese organisations and enjoy considerable degrees of trust, sharing and loyalty. This is not to say, of course, that power does not ultimately rest with the management. Because the Japanese philosophy offers lifetime employment, each of the employees has a strong stake in the organisation and its long-term success. Any degree of participation in the processes of the Japanese organisation are backed up with training, both of group leaders and of employees. It is worth pointing out that when quality circles were introduced in the UK in 1980, they were at an all-time high of 63 per cent of organisations, and this has now dropped to around 10 per cent.

The Nenko system is the basis for managerial practices used in a number of large Japanese organisations. Essentially these cover the following aspects:

◆ employment

◆ salary and promotion

◆ attitude toward work

◆ decision making

◆ relationship with employees

◆ competition.

UK and Western practice compared with Nenko

Before we have a look at the Nenko system in any great detail, let us compare common UK and Western practice with the Nenko system:

◆ *employment* – in the West employment is usually short term and is rather unstable and insecure. In Japan, however, employment is generally long term, relatively secure and stable.

◆ *salary and promotion* – in the West this is based on an individual's contribution and promotion can be rapid. In Japan, however, there is an emphasis on seniority and only when the individual has been with the organisation for any length of time do they receive pay based on merit.

◆ *attitudes towards work* – in the West the focus is on an individual's responsibility, whereas in Japan this is a collective responsibility with group loyalty and very duty-orientated.

◆ *decision making* – in the West, again, this is very individually-orientated with a top-down process. In Japan decision making tends to be consensus or group-orientated with a bottom-up approach.

◆ *relationship with employees* – generally in the West this is depersonalised with formal contact. The organisation is most definitely seen by the majority of employees as interfering with their own personal life. In Japan, however, individual employees are seen as members of the family. Although there is a paternalistic approach involved, the employee certainly expects the organisation to show concern for their personal affairs.

◆ *competition* – in the West competing within the organisation is relatively free and positively encouraged. In Japan this has very low priority among individuals within the same group but becomes high between groups and certainly between organisations.

A summary of this comparison is shown in Fig. 2.7.

Now let us turn our attention to some of the principal details of the Nenko system as we have outlined above. The Nenko system is certainly borne out of the Japanese culture and the economy. The West has found it very difficult to take many of the basic concepts on board. In Japan after completing formal education an individual would join a Japanese organisation and fully expect to stay there for the rest of their lives. This has changed to some extent in recent years, with increasing uncertainties in the Japanese economy and performance.

The Japanese firmly believe that job knowledge and skills improve with seniority. This means that lower level managers are often paid on the basis of seniority. The Nenko system also encourages group loyalty and the sharing of obligations. Employees are encouraged to think of themselves in terms of the organisation to which they belong. This means that individuals have a strong sense of loyalty to an organisation. The employer places great emphasis on flexibility and group support and their loyalty is borne out by the long-term training and development of their employees.

The managers in Japanese organisations make extensive use of group decision-making practices. This consensus approach begins with defining the problem and then turns to how to reach the solution. As we have said earlier, ideas

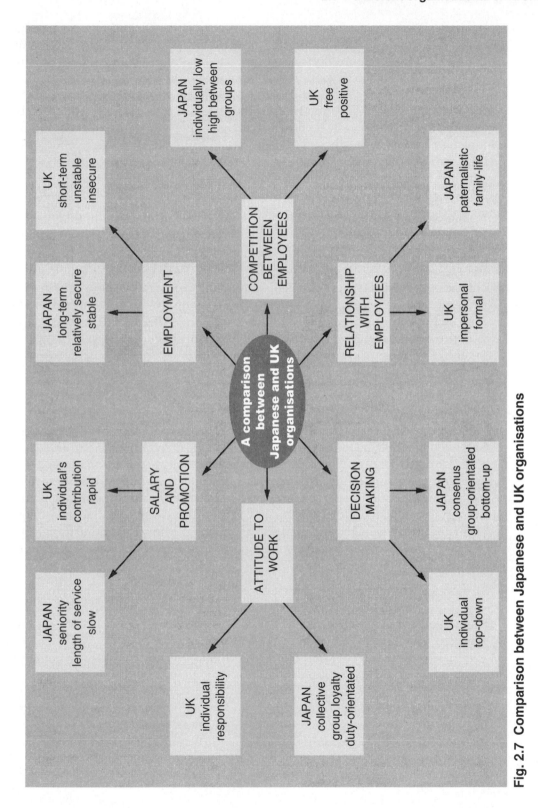

Fig. 2.7 Comparison between Japanese and UK organisations

tend to be bottom-up rather than top-down. In this respect Japanese management will actually consult any employee who will be affected by a major decision. This bottom-up decision making is know as the *Ringi* system. It is not decentralised as the management still retains the right to reject recommendations. The system has been heavily criticised because it does encourage management to make decisions on a situation-by-situation basis, so it is probably better to consider it for short-term decisions rather than long-term strategic ones. Some Japanese multinationals have now abandoned the system as they feel it is slow and laborious. They have now adopted a more dynamic approach.

Japanese workers are not now as hard-working as in previous generations, when in fact they had the appearance of being workaholics. The new generation of Japanese are beginning to realise that some of the western ideologies and systems of work are in fact more preferable. To this end many have adopted something known as 'flexible individualism'. This means that they are interested in self-expression, lifestyle and possessions. Indeed, the paternal system characterised by the Japanese is also breaking down, with household duties being shared by both husband and wife. Women have finally entered the job market and are more able to attain higher levels of education through the colleges. This, perhaps, should not be a great shock to the West since the Japanese are the masters of modifying their culture to suit new situations.

Configuration

As we have seen, there are many different forms of configuration. Specific types will be discussed in the next part of this section. Whether the organisation exhibits features of a tall or flat structure, we will often find some form of symmetry where there is a degree of stability in the environment. However, once an organisation begins to grow or is affected by upheavals in the environment, we will see distortions in the configuration or structure with bulges occurring in parts of the organisation as the proportion of administrative staff increases. There will be, in effect, disproportionate growth in various parts of the organisation.

Given the fact that there are a number of different shapes which an organisation can adopt in order to reflect the scale, size and complexity of their operations, there are very few overriding theories or approaches that can be generally accepted as adequate explanations of why configurations change as a result of external influences. Providing the organisation is in full control of its environment, it can gradually, or rapidly, as it sees fit, change the configuration to suit its own purposes. However, the majority of organisations cannot enjoy this luxury, they are often forced to make radical and fundamental changes to their organisational structure or configuration. Above all, the organisation needs to have a degree of flexibility. Providing the organisation can understand the nature of the change or changes that are relevant to them, they may be capable of making configuration changes which mirror the impacts upon them. They must be flexible on a continual basis. While some organisations do not perceive or accept that change is either inevitable or desirable, a great many more will only consider the pertinent changes. At the same time, a significant minority of organisations will openly embrace change and we can see that their configurations are capable of adaptation and response.

This illustrates key differences between various organisations and although we can investigate their configuration through their organisation charts, we may not readily understand the continual developments going on within their structure or, perhaps, the reasons why they have configured themselves in a particular manner. The best we can hope for is to understand how the organisation has structured itself in the light of existing criteria and what contingency plans have been put into operation in order to accommodate future change.

 # Contingency

Contingency and the internal and external environment

As we have mentioned previously, contingency factors are a number of independent variables that have to be taken into account alongside the more dependent design variables. Typically, we can identify the following contingency factors which arise out of the different situations in which the organisation may find itself:

◆ the age of the organisation.

◆ the size of the organisation.

◆ the technical systems used and the complexities of those systems.

◆ the stability of the organisational environment and the complexity of that environment.

◆ the apparent and presumed levels of hostility within the organisational environment.

◆ the ownership of the organisation.

◆ the relative power of the members of the organisation (e.g. managers, subordinates).

Problems arising from these contingency variables can be solved by structural changes to the organisation. Issues that relate to the age and the size of the organisation can be best addressed by job specialisation, training and induction. The technical complexity of the organisation can be dealt with by behaviour formalisation, the grouping of similar tasks, and linkages between departments and divisions. The stability of the organisational environment can be controlled by installing adequate planning and control systems, as well as integration or liaison devices. Issues of hostility, ownership and the relative power of individuals within the organisation can be handled by careful vertical or horizontal decentralisation.

Other contingency variables

It is appropriate that we investigate the remaining contingency variables that may be present in an organisation beyond that of the environment at this point, before turning our attention to the different structures and the ways in which organisations can respond to change.

Structural issues and organisational philosophies

Most organisations face a variety of contingencies simultaneously. One of the most common problems to face an organisation is when a bureaucratic structure is needed to address the requirements of technical systems, while the age of the organisation indicates that it should have an organic structure.

A fundamental question that needs to be asked is whether organisations actually differ from one another on account of their age, size or rate of growth. All of these are probable contingencies. Mintzberg suggests that a number of theories or propositions could be put forward to try to come up with some answers to these imponderable questions. Are we right to assume that, as an organisation ages, it demands more formalised behaviour from its employees? To some extent there is a predictability about a stable organisational structure and consistent operations that would lead to a more formalised atmosphere. Organisations in this situation would tend to try to replicate solutions that have worked in the past.

Whether the structure of an organisation is related to its age is one question that may be answered by asking when the organisation was established, rather than how long it has been in existence. It is certainly true to say that the prevailing philosophies at the time of the organisation's inception will have a marked influence on the way in which it was structured, at least in the first few years of its existence. Given the fact that organisations will gradually evolve and absorb the prevailing philosophies in the external environment, there will still be a residue of the original structure and philosophy. The younger the organisation, the more likely it is that it has not passed through a series of evolutionary changes. Most organisations would avoid revolution or immediate and funda-mental change; they would gradually evolve over a period of years. Given the limitations of technology in the past, the majority of organisations would have been unable to create anything other than a bureaucracy to control their opera-tions, with formalised behaviour as an integral part of all of this. As technology changed and became more applicable in the business context, the organisation would have been able to step up its evolution and make a series of fundamental changes over a relatively short period of time. Yet, despite any structural change, real or apparent, there will still be a surviving core of values and norms which were in existence in the earliest stage of the organisation's life.

Size and complexity

It would be easy to assume that the larger the organisation, the more complex the structure. Each particular part of the organisation would be involved in a specialised area of activity, exemplified by a number of differentiated departments or divisions, but held together by a strong co-ordinating administration. In practice, job specialisation does divide up the labour force and larger organisations with more employees increase their outputs. This means that co-ordination is vital in order to control these more elaborate organisations. As we have seen, liaison and integration roles have proliferated, particularly in these larger organisations. While a smaller organisation will have less clearly defined divisions of labour, the larger organisation will have very clearly marked lines of demarcation. With diversification, additional levels and areas of complexity will arise. However, this poses a number of co-ordination problems for the larger organisation. They will have to juggle the complexities of functional requirements, product differences and the need to cater for a number of different geographical markets. As we have mentioned already, and will return to later in this section, the matrix structure offers some solutions to these problems. The matrix is, of course, a complex and elaborate structure. It relies on having functional operations controlled by line managers, as well as administrative and specialised functions carried out by staff employees.

Spans of control

Allied to the increasing size of an organisation, we should also consider the fact that each interdependent department or division will be larger. This will mean that the administration has to grow in size and complexity in order to control the variety of different functions carried out by these departments and divisions. As the size of an organisation grows, so too does the span of control for each of the managers. More specialisation leads to greater differentiation between the departments or divisions, but within these management becomes simpler. Working in specialised areas, the manager is able to control and co-ordinate in a far more meaningful manner than when having to deal with a wide variety of different job roles and functions.

A growing work-force

As an organisation grows, it may choose to incorporate new employees within existing departments or divisions. However, if an organisation is interested in diversification, for example, whole new sub-structures will need to be incorporated within the overall structure itself. Whether the incorporation of new employees is in existing departments and divisions or new ones, an increased management structure will also have to be considered. This may simply mean extending the span of control of existing managers, or recruiting new ones. Coupled with this is the need to make the administrative structure more elaborate. It would be impossible for an administrative structure designed to cater for the present needs of the existing workforce to be expected to handle all of the additional requirements that are associated with an increased work-force.

Specialisation of job roles

As the individual job roles within an organisation become more specialised, it may no longer be appropriate for general managers or supervisors to control these functions. This, again, leads to a more complicated management structure and, perhaps, the separation of existing departments and divisions into wholly new working units which enjoy a greater degree of independence. Standardisation, which, as we have seen, enables the organisation to formalise behaviour and plan more effectively, should reduce the work-load on specific managers. However, at some point or level of the hierarchy, another individual will find that they are responsible for these standardisation plans.

It is certainly true that the rate of growth of an organisation will affect the size of the individual units that can be identified on an organisation chart. Perhaps at departmental or divisional level these changes will be far more radical. The administrative aspects, as well as the chain of authority, will probably lag behind the changes at departmental and divisional level, and this will lead to some inconsistencies in co-ordination and control for the short term.

Behavioural issues

It is a commonly held view that the age of an organisation also reflects how formalised the behaviour is within it. Providing the activities and operations of the organisation are fairly constant, they will be able to predict the ways in which they can respond to challenges. Given that size is a determinant of the degree of control and co-ordination within the organisation, we could suggest that a large organisation exerts less formalisation upon its employees than a smaller one. This, of course, ignores the concepts of tradition and routine. With an organisation that relies on generalists rather than specialists, there will be less formalised behaviour, since it is the very nature of these generalists and their ability to react in different sets of circumstances that makes the organisation work. It is inappropriate to try to standardise behaviour or approach in these circumstances. If the organisation relies on strict planning and control at all levels of operations, then there will be a need to formalise the behaviour. This will avoid unnecessary complications.

Rapid growth does disrupt the structure of any organisation and for the most part the organisation needs to rely on the flexibility of its key employees to cope with the upheavals, rather than trying to exert formalised behaviour upon them which may be inappropriate given the new circumstances. Bureaucracies find it very difficult to cope with change. A bureaucracy's strength is in the formalisation of behaviour along with a strict adherence to rules and regulations. Given new sets of circumstances, employees will find it very difficult to operate in a different manner, needing to circumvent existing codes of practice and behaviour that have been instilled in them since their induction to the organisation.

Review questions

1 What are the four phase types of different organisational environments? Briefly describe each one.

2 What are the characteristics of a stable environment?

3 What are the typical features of disturbed reactive and turbulent environments?

4 What are the four major options open to an organisation facing change?

5 Can most organisational growth be categorised as internal or as organic?

6 Explain the terms 'retrenchment' and 'down sizing'.

7 Identify and describe four reasons for mergers or takeovers.

8 Distinguish between management buy-outs and management buy-ins.

9 Explain multiskilling using examples.

10 How have Japanese management techniques influenced UK businesses?

11 What is the 'Kaizen' process?

12 What are Ouchi and Theory Z?

13 With reference to the Nenko system, how do Japanese techniques and approaches differ from those of the UK?

14 Identify the key differences between Japanese and UK organisations.

2.2

Different organisational structures

There are many factors which may determine the nature of the organisational structure. We have identified some of them already, but now let us consider them in a slightly different way.

Essentially, all the factors fall into two categories:

1 *Internal* – caused by factors within the organisation itself.

2 *External* – caused by factors which may not be in the control of the organisation.

Internal factors affecting organisational structure

Having made this distinction, we cannot really say that the internal factors are 'self-inflicted' as the organisation may need to restructure to gain greater efficiencies or 'iron out' certain problems. The internal factors may have been brought about by actions initiated by the organisation in the past. An example of this may be the development of a new product or service that radically changes (over a period of time) the requirements of the customer, the source of raw materials or the need to obtain alternative sources of finance. Having established that there are numerous forms of business structure, we can now confuse the issue by saying that organisations are never static and are always evolving and changing. First, in this section, we will look at the various criteria which determine the changes themselves.

Changes in the size and scope of an organisation's objectives can often mean a radical rethink in the structure of the business. Some organisations may opt for a new and more flexible structure as they diversify and expand. Simply 'tacking on' new parts to an existing structure does not always work. The chain of command and the exercise of authority can become difficult if the organisation experiences organic growth, with structural 'add ons', and does not really address the need to restructure. Perhaps the organisation is growing too fast to contemplate a radical change and needs to wait until the 'growth spurt' has slowed down. The danger with this philosophy is that the organisation may have outgrown the structure and be experiencing severe difficulties as a result.

In terms of size itself, the organisation does need to adopt a structure which not only best suits the nature of its operations, but takes into account the fact that perhaps not all operations will be carried out at a single site. Equally, the organisation needs to consider whether it is advisable to maintain a hierarchical structure or a more formal structure if it has diversified into a number of different product areas or markets.

It is often the case that the senior management, while striving to continue to control the organisation, does not even understand what some parts of the organisation are doing. If they lack understanding, how can they truly improve the structure or method of decision making? This is perhaps the most likely reason for making changes in the organisational structure. Simpler forms of organisational structure are more relevant in smaller businesses, but as the organisation grows it needs to adapt to ever more complex requirements.

Most organisational structures are based on the assumption that the business will expand. This is not the only form of growth however. Diversification and structural changes are often advisable instead of simply growing bigger while maintaining the same general structure. As businesses grow, they may need to consider relocation in order to achieve sustained and permanent growth. Moving closer to the source of raw materials, skilled labour, or better distribution points may be key considerations. Clearly, a move may also be brought on by growth itself, if the organisation simply needs larger premises in order to continue its operations successfully.

An organisation which has a variety of sites needs to adopt a slightly different structure to accommodate the problems of communication and overall control. Within a single site operation, the organisation must also consider the most appropriate structure for its business. Again, this may depend upon the nature of the business. In service industries, for example, the organisation would be structured towards providing customer service as a priority. For manufacturing organisations, the bulk of the structural considerations would be related to the production process itself, with other departments supporting and servicing the production unit. Organisational structure may, of course, be related to the premises in which the organisation is located. An inappropriate building may preclude the restructuring of the business since the physical location of each part of the organisation remains fixed. This state of affairs is particularly true of organisations which add on new extensions and buildings to their site without really considering the implications of their placement or location. In these cases, the organisation may not have had the time to spend considering the future when faced with immediate demands for expansion and new accommodation.

Changes in structure may be brought about by the nature of the business itself. If the organisation has a variety of diversified products or services it may be logical to separate the management and production in order to establish specific profit centres. Equally, this organisation (often product-based) revolves around the need to attract expertise in a particular area so that the individuals can identify with a particular product or service rather than a whole organisation. As with the type of product the organisation produces, the specific function of the organisation may bring about changes in structure. As we have already said, businesses have a wide variety of different goals. These differing goals and objectives will determine the historical structure of the organisation, as well as the structure best suited to taking that organisation into future successful years.

Formal and informal organisations

Formal organisations can be defined as those that have established the express purpose of achieving a particular goal or set of aims or objectives. These sorts of organisations have clearly defined rules and instructions as well as quite highly developed channels of communication. Good examples include most businesses, governments and international institutions. Because there are so many different forms of formal organisation, we need to clarify this large group a little more carefully. One of the easiest ways is to separate them into productive and non-productive categories (i.e. those that manufacture and those that provide a service).

Informal organisations are also known as social organisations. These do not tend to have clearly defined goals and examples include families or communities.

The relationship between function and structure

The function of the organisation (the reason why it is in operation and the objectives set at the beginning) will strongly determine the type of organisational structure in place. Should these objectives not be met, or should they have to be amended during the course of time, then radical changes to the organisational structure may have to be made. As we have mentioned earlier, organisations tend to change their type as they mature or grow.

A sole trader may begin a business career with no intention of changing the type of business at all. Growth, changes in legislation or tax incentives may encourage the sole trader to become a limited company. With this change, the organisation will probably need to take on a different structure in order to cope with the new demands placed upon it. Individuals who were employed on a casual and 'when needed' basis may become permanent members of the workforce. Specialists, such as accountants, who had been paid and retained when required, may have to be permanently incorporated into the structure.

With this structural type of business change may come a change in ownership itself. If a sole trader enters into a partnership, the ownership will now be split between the original owner and any new partners. Equally, a sole trader or partnership that becomes a limited company (particularly a plc) will have to cope with structural and control changes demanded by the shareholders. Another form of ownership change is the disposal of an organisation to another party.

The new owners will be likely to institute changes merely because they wish to stamp their own authority and presence on the organisation. Many of these changes will be seen by the employees in particular as being brought about purely for the sake of change and they will have little support for them.

Technology and the changing structure

Technology has a part to play in the changing structure relating to working arrangements. Generally, new demands on the organisation can force changes which may include:

◆ change in hours worked (e.g. shift working).

◆ level of manning (due to technological development).

◆ greater supervision (quality control).

◆ total hours worked.

◆ relocation to new premises.

◆ multiskilling (undertaking new and varied tasks).

◆ redesigning of job tasks.

There is, quite rightly, a greater emphasis on the customer and meeting the customers' needs. Traditional concerns with internal problems and the running of the organisation, and, indeed, office politics, have slowly given way to other concerns.

Customers require and demand greater levels of service, advice and after-sales service. To this end, the restructuring of the organisation will be needed to provide support for these services, not to mention the training of all staff to cover these considerations.

External factors affecting organisational structure

Competition can have a direct impact on the organisational structure. Any organisation which ignores what the competition is doing may be doomed to failure. Structural changes are often copied within a business sector, particularly if the first organisation to restructure is clearly more competitive and successful.

Apart from the obvious effects on the internal functions and activities of the organisation, competition may force the organisation to consider restructuring in order to stay competitive. A competitive edge, or the ability to stay ahead, can mean the difference between success or failure. All aspects and parts of an organisation can have a role to play in maintaining this advantage over the opposition. Here are some examples of how the structure of the organisation can contribute:

◆ *administration* – by streamlining procedures and cutting down on wastage.

◆ *sales* – by following up sales leads, providing high standards of customer service and ensuring that key customers are especially well provided for in all respects.

◆ *marketing* – ensuring that products and services are fully researched and supported with appropriate advertising and promotion.

◆ *distribution* – providing swift, efficient and reliable delivery at all times to all customers.

◆ *accounts* – ensuring that all invoicing, statement and other financial documents are correct at all times.

The organisation must always be aware that a currently stable situation will not always remain so. The organisational structure may need to radically change if there is a sudden or unexpected market change. We need to address how the structure of an organisation may be affected by change. Principally, the organisation may:

◆ ensure that employee levels are sufficient to take up extra work, or be capable of redeployment.

◆ ensure that employees are multiskilled and require minimum retraining to undertake new duties.

◆ ensure that production facilities are flexible enough to respond to changes in production at short notice.

◆ ensure that the management is aware of the necessity to keep an eye on the market, including regular checks on the competition and market trends.

◆ ensure that the product or service is not wholly reliant on a single market.

The nature of a market can depend upon your interpretation. Market can mean:

◆ the volume of sales in total for a product or service.

◆ the demand within a specific region for a product or service.

The availability of suitable employees and the proximity to a large market (in population terms) can have an influence on the structure of the organisation. In the first instance, the structure may have to be adaptable and include more part-time or casual employees than the organisation would prefer. This means that such employees cannot be fully integrated into the organisational structure since they are not full-time or permanent.

Closeness to markets (in demographic terms) may be a problem for certain organisations. If the organisation produces goods which are inappropriate for the immediate market, or the population density is not that great, then they must consider having more employees located in various places around the country and closer to the market concentrations. In this sense, conventional organisational structures may not be appropriate since the level of autonomy at these remote sites will need to be developed and accepted. In this respect, the organisation must be willing to allow decision making to take place (within set guidelines). Teleworking, or working from home via a computer link, is becoming a useful solution to the availability of labour and the high costs of business premises.

Gradually, computerised management information systems are making it possible to streamline management and structures. On a higher level, the use of computers allows much greater flexibility in structural terms. It is no longer necessary to locate all employees in one large building or a connecting series of premises. Outlying units can be directly 'plugged in' to the organisation regardless of their location. Technology also changes the nature of the structure relating to production itself. Automation means fewer employees on the shop-floor and more in management and supervisory positions. Technology, particularly in the field of information and telecommunications, has radically changed the structure of organisations.

Factors underlying structural differences

Many organisations have been traditionally organised in a form of a *pyramid structure*. Individuals at each level of the pyramid (or hierarchy) are fully aware of their role, rank and position in the organisation. As we will see, this formalised *chain of command* is suited to allowing orders and instructions to be passed down the pyramid and information to be readily transmitted up the pyramid. The structure depends on many factors. These include:

◆ the size and nature of the market in which it operates.

◆ the type of business it is involved in (e.g. if the organisation is in the primary sector, it is likely to be organised in such a way as to allow as efficient processing of the raw materials as possible, and may be based around a single mine, forest or quarry).

◆ the maintenance of good communications.

◆ the size of the organisation (the number of employees).

◆ the number of branches/outlets/sites (a multi- or split-site organisation would need to be organised in a radically different manner from an organisation which is housed in a single building).

◆ the type and number of clients.

◆ how much it is affected by government legislation.

◆ impact of new technologies.

◆ nature and extent of responsibilities and obligations.

◆ past and current structure.

◆ future plans.

◆ complexity of business activity.

Different market sectors

A manufacturing organisation may either carry out all of its processing procedures on a single site, or it may need to transport partly finished goods to other specialist sites. Organisation in this case may be based on the single factory unit, or a cluster of factories which contribute towards the finished product.

Distribution organisations tend to be organised in a regional, national or international framework. Depending on the bulk of goods being distributed, the organisational structure will be complex in certain geographical areas and simpler in others. In other words, if the organisation is busy in one area, the size and complexity will reflect this. As with many organisations, good communications between the regions are vital and a separate part of the organisational structure may concentrate on dealing with communications.

In the retailing sector the obvious organisational structure is that of the branch. However, many functions of the business are carried out centrally. These services tend to be of a managerial, financial or buying nature, and this allows the individual branches to concentrate on the selling process.

Professional services tend to operate on the basis of a number of specialist individuals who are assisted by a variety of support staff. Often these support staff are drawn from a pool of clerical and secretarial employees.

The number, type and size of the clients may have a bearing on the organisational structure. If the organisation deals with only a handful of clients, then the structure need not be overly complex. On the other hand, if it is dealing with literally millions of retail customers, then the demands on the structure may be much greater.

Past history and future needs

The past structure of the organisation and its history may be a good or bad influence on how it is structured. An old-fashioned organisation which has successfully managed to survive for many years may not see the need to change its structure. It may not appreciate the benefits of reorganisation and may be structured in such a way as to prevent the possibility of growth or adaptation to new demands. The current structure of an organisation can again be a positive or negative influence on the day-to-day running of the business. If the organisation has recently undergone changes, it will be unlikely to adapt to further changes without encountering considerable problems.

The future needs of an organisation should directly influence its structure. The need to constantly react to changing demands, diversify into new areas and respond to changes in legislation, are all strong reasons to consider how the organisation is structured.

At this point we shall look at all of the different varieties of organisational structure and later try to assess their appropriateness in different situations.

Simple structures

The simplest organisational structure is that of the person who works on their own. This person would obviously be responsible for everything that the organisation does. Someone, for example, who set up a mail order business would be responsible for buying in products, designing the catalogue, getting it printed, carrying out market research to find the kind of person who would buy the products, researching a mailing list, sending out catalogues, taking orders, despatching goods, dealing with any correspondence, paying bills, banking cheques, doing the accounts and a hundred other things. In this situation the individual who is running the business is at the centre of everything.

The larger the organisation, the more need there is for people who specialise in a particular area. Good examples of these are bank managers, solicitors, accountants. All of these people have specialist skills and can take some of the responsibility off an individual business person's shoulders.

Division of labour and specialisation

As a business expands it needs to employ people; some part time, some full time. The person who set up the company needs to think about what has to be done. The business needs to be organised in the best possible way to meet the objectives that have been set. The owner of the business needs to define individual and departmental responsibilities. Who will supervise the employees? Who should tell them what to do? Where does everyone fit into the organisation? And who is ultimately responsible? This is known as the *division of labour* and *specialisation*.

The division of labour involves breaking down the process of producing things or providing services into clearly defined specialist tasks. If the process is broken down into these separate tasks then production can be increased. Instead of one person trying to do everything, everybody who works as part of the production process of goods or services specialises. Specialisation means being more efficient. What kind of advantages are there in specialisation?

◆ Resources can be concentrated where they are needed the most.

◆ If the worker becomes more skilled at doing a particular job, he becomes more efficient.

◆ Specialisation allows greater output. This means that each item produced is made more cheaply because the labour involved in producing it is less for each unit.

◆ If people specialise then they can pass on their skills and experience to others and help them become more efficient.

◆ If people specialise then hopefully they can get a better standard of living. By specialising, people can develop their own talents and are able to trade what they can do with other people.

◆ By specialising in one job a person can do that job well rather than doing lots of jobs not so well.

There are some disadvantages of specialisation:

◆ Specialisation can often lead to jobs becoming very boring. Simple repetition of the same task day in day out demoralises people and they can become less efficient.

◆ Specialisation is always dependent on how good or efficient the specialists in the previous tasks were. If they are not as efficient or as fast at every stage of production this can cause bottlenecks.

◆ There is a tendency in specialisation for workers to become little more than machines. This, in turn, could lead to loss of skill.

◆ Specialising actually reduces a worker's ability to adapt to change.

◆ Those who specialise have only a narrow view of the product or service which they are actually producing. Someone who makes an article from start to finish has a better overview and can help to make things more efficient in the long run.

Bureaucratic structures

The bureaucratic structure relies on a system of rules and regulations, a set hierarchy, clear divisions of labour and predetermined procedures. In effect, these organisations have created a blueprint for all operations. Essentially, a bureaucratic system has seven specific characteristics. These are:

1 a formal system of rules.

2 an impersonal approach.

3 clear divisions of labour.

4 distinct authority and hierarchical structure.

5 a clear and detailed authority structure.

6 the requirement for employees to give long-term career commitment.

7 rationality in terms of pursuing the organisation's objectives.

Rules and regulations

Above all, a bureaucratic organisation offers the opportunity to enjoy consistency and predictability. Given that the rules and regulations are formal, this means that all employees are expected to have particular codes of behaviour. While this provides a clear disciplinary structure and conformity of procedures, it also helps to maintain the stability of the organisation, which overrides the personal wishes or desires of the managers and employees.

The impersonal nature of bureaucracies

The impersonal nature of a bureaucracy means that all employees are judged on their adherence to the policies and procedures of the organisation, rather than their personal characteristics. This should mean that a fair and objective method of evaluation for all employees is an integral part of the organisation's approach. There is no room for subjective personal considerations when evaluating or appraising subordinates.

Division of labour

The division of labour, as we have seen, clearly identifies the specific duties of each employee. It allows the organisation to accurately target each employee in terms of their training and development needs. All tasks and duties are performed on the basis of an individual's specialisation and expertise, rather than expecting them to cope with tasks which do not normally fall under their remit. To this extent, the unskilled employees can be deployed according to their specific tasks without having to train or develop them beyond what is needed for the immediate job.

The bureaucratic hierarchy

We should visualise a bureaucracy in terms of a pyramid shaped hierarchical structure. All job roles are organised according to their power and authority. Naturally, the power and authority is greater at the apex of the organisational structure, where control and decision making occur. Bureaucracies would claim that this clear and unequivocal structure allows all employees to understand exactly where they are within the structure and within relation to one another.

Authority structures

As an integral part of the hierarchical nature of the organisation, the rules, impersonality and division of labour reinforce the authority structure. All employees readily understand who holds the authority to make particular decisions and, as we will see when we consider organisational culture, there are three major types of authority structures, all of which can exist within a bureaucratic organisation. Briefly, these are:

1 Traditional authority – which is based on tradition and custom.

2 Charismatic authority – where subordinates comply with the wishes of an individual because they have special qualities or abilities.

3   Rational/legal authority – where the impersonal rules and regulations apply to all employees, and managers are obeyed by virtue of their position within the hierarchical structure.

Obviously, the most common types of authority are those of tradition and rational/legal within a bureaucratic structure. However, there may be instances of charismatic authority in particular divisions or departments.

Positive qualities of bureaucracies

A positive aspect of a bureaucratic structure is that both employees and employers consider their relationship to be long term. They are, in effect, committed to one another and wish to form a long-term bond. Job security is, of course, extremely important for most employees, and a bureaucratic structure is as likely to offer this as any other. Providing the employee shows similar commitment, the ability to carry out the job satisfactorily and has the necessary qualifications, then the organisation will likewise commit themselves to that individual. Most bureaucracies operate a gatekeeping system which requires minimum entry qualifications or experience in order to ensure that new recruits have a basic level of competence. This also serves to avoid any possibility of patronage as all employees are offered positions on the same basis. Providing the individual satisfactorily performs the duties which they have been assigned by the organisation, there will be a clear progression route available to them. This is typified by gradual year-on-year salary increases, pension schemes and, of course, job security.

Bureaucratic organisations encourage managers to take a rational view in order to achieve the proclaimed objectives of the business. In other words, their managers should be logical and scientific when considering all of the options before taking a decision. Most of the activities within a bureaucratic organisation are, or tend to be, goal-related, so it is relatively easy to identify the steps which need to be taken in order to achieve these. A rational and logical manager will only need to ensure that the correct deployment of financial and human resources is made in order to reach successful accomplishment.

Complications and drawbacks of bureaucracies

The bureaucracy obviously functions most perfectly when there are a set number of standardised routines to be undertaken. At the lower levels of the organisation, all an employee needs to know is that, providing they follow the set procedures, they will successfully complete the task. The major complication arises when the organisation does not have sufficient control over the quantity or quality of output in relation to their organisational goals.

While bureaucracies are designed in order to improve the efficiency of the organisation, there are a number of drawbacks. These include:

◆ rigid rules and regulations.

◆ the protection of authority.

◆ slowness in decision making.

◆ inability to cope with technological change.

◆ incompatibility with professional approaches.

'Red tape', rules and response rates

The existence of 'red tape' which requires strict adherence to rules and procedures, is a major source of problems within a bureaucratic structure. Naturally these rules and regulations stifle creativity and innovation. There is a tendency for them also to lead to a reduction in motivation, the real or perceived inability of employees to gain promotion and a high turnover of employees. In addition to this, an unyielding bureaucracy will often be faced with severe problems in terms of quality output. The other major concern related to rules and regulations is the fact that there may be a high degree of duplication and consequent waste of resources, simply to follow the set procedures.

There is a tendency in the vast majority of bureaucracies for managers and employees to work towards the basic minimum productivity levels. They are more concerned with following the rules and procedures, protecting their own authority and, of course, expanding it as much as possible.

One of the principal criticisms of bureaucratic organisations is that they have an inability to react effectively and rapidly when the need arises. By following set procedures which have, in effect, become rituals, when each level of management has to have an input into the decision-making process, they find themselves responding far too slowly. It is worth remembering that bureaucracies may not recognise this problem. Providing they are following the procedures, it is the task that is important and not the outcome. Bureaucracies will not adapt or radically change their procedures without extensive experimentation and testing.

Problems faced by managers

Most bureaucratic organisations encounter severe difficulties when managers have been appointed on the basis of their professional ability to understand specific areas of operation. It would be in the nature of these individuals to innovate and find solutions to problems. They find themselves in the position where they are blocked by policies and procedures which have existed far longer than their tenure in their job. Against innovation are pitched the seemingly incompatible qualities of consistency, order and efficiency. For the most part, managers will have been appointed on the basis of their hierarchical position, whereas the professional will have attained authority stemming from competence or technical ability and knowledge.

Some final plus points about bureaucracies

Most of what has been said regarding bureaucratic structures may seem negative. However, not all bureaucratic structures are unprofitable and inherently inefficient. Bureaucratic structures are very good at processing routine information and in circumstances when the needs of the customer are unlikely to change. Coupled with this, bureaucracies flourish when the technological development of the market is slow or non-existent. To this end, the bureaucratic system is very good at training employees to carry out simple tasks of a routine nature. Standardisation of procedures, along with the formalised behaviour systems, suit many business functions, particularly when consistent products or services are required.

Functional structures

A functionally based organisational structure is usually designed around the specific parts of the organisation that produce, market and sell the product or service. The actual sub-structure of the organisation may take a variety of forms, either hierarchical or flat, for example. Typically, a structure adopting the functional system will be controlled by a managing director who is supported by a range of senior managers. Each of the managers has responsibility for the direction of a specific function of the organisation. Examples of these functions are shown in Fig. 2.8 and could include:

◆ advertising

◆ finance and accounting

◆ personnel

◆ production

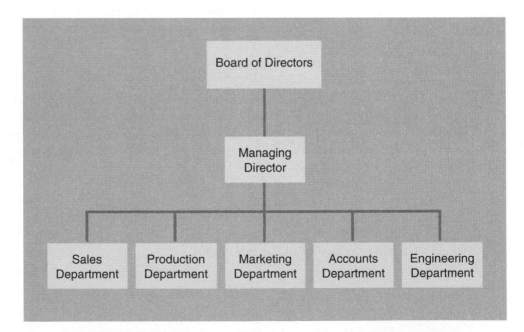

Fig. 2.8 Functional organisation chart

◆ purchasing

◆ sales.

Departmentalisation around functions

The creation of positions and departments around specialised functions is an integral part of the functional structure. Departmentalisation according to function is, perhaps, the most obvious and common manifestation of this structure. There will be a common theme in terms of function or process within each department. This enables management to concentrate on specific issues which are within their technical experience and ability.

There will, of course, be line functions relating to most of these departments. However, as we have seen, the staff functions which provide a variety of different services and advice to the departments will be relatively common. The scalar chain of command which determines the authority and responsibility of named individuals within the organisation will be based on a hierarchy. There will be clear flows of authority from the strategic apex of the organisation to the lower levels of the hierarchy. There will be a unity of command which enables subordinates to clearly understand to whom they are accountable and from whom they should receive instruction. This is a common feature of many organisations and not just functional structures.

Advantages of functional structures

The functional structure does promote skills specialisation, while at the same time it reduces the duplication of scarce resources. Within each of the large departments in such an organisation there will be clear career progression. As the organisation is structured on a functional basis, this will lead to clearer lines of communication and, hopefully, greater productivity and performance, since managers responsible for each functional area will have a degree of expertise.

Possible disadvantages of functional structures

Since the functional structure has an emphasis on routine tasks, there is a tendency for these organisations to have relatively short time horizons. Within each functional department there will be a tendency towards managers adopting a parochial perspective and this will limit their capacities for career enhancement to top-level management.

One of the principle concerns regarding a functional structure is that there will be a reduced level of communication and co-operation between departments and divisions. While each department or division is reliant, to some extent, on the operations of others, the co-ordination and scheduling will be extremely difficult. Providing each department can reach its objectives or targets, the functional structure operates fairly well. However, it is when one or more department fails to meet expectations that the accountability problems arise. The blame for failure can either rest upon the departmental manager, who should have realised that the objectives were unattainable, or top-level management, who should likewise have realised that the objectives were unreasonable.

Divisional structures

Larger organisations often need to take a radically different approach to their structure, particularly in the case of organisations whose operations are complex and span several different countries. They may find it impossible to adopt more traditional forms of organisational structure. As we will see, there are three major methods (which are all essentially divisional in nature) that can be used to facilitate *control*, *efficiency* and *communications*. These are:

1 *Division by function*. In this form of structure the organisation has identified its key functions and has either an individual (or in the case of larger organisations, a department) who oversees this function throughout all sub-divisions of the organisation.

2 *Division by product*. As we will shortly see, Philip Morris, a multinational organisation, has identified not only trade name sub-divisions but also, below this, product sub-divisions. Each sub-division is semi-autonomous but has clearly stated goals, objectives and profits to achieve.

3 *Divisions of multinationals*. Again, using the Philip Morris example, and bearing in mind that the organisation operates in a variety of different countries throughout the world, it is logical that the organisational structure reflects this diversity and potential control headache. As we will see, an organisation such as this can choose to invest, examine or sell off a sub-division as it sees fit.

Division by function

Division by function, or departmentalisation is the process by which an organisation has certain functions which it carries out, grouped logically under a particular manager. There are usually five ways of grouping employees or the things an organisation does. These are:

1 By what they produce, known as the product.

2 By their function, in other words what they do for the organisation.

3 By process, which means how they do it.

4 By geographical area, which may be various regional offices or separate companies.

5 By type of customer, for example they may deal with other business organisations, or they may deal with retail.

Product divisions

An alternative to basing the organisational structure on function is to base it around one or more products or ranges of products. As we will see when we consider the divisions of multinationals, it is easy to identify how an organisation has grown organically by acquiring other organisations and incorporating them into the larger organisation, but maintaining their individual identity. The other feature that a study of multinationals might reveal is how the organisation values its individual brand names or product names (particularly in cases where the same product is known under various different names across the world). An example of this is the Snickers bar which was known by this name in all countries except the UK. In order to establish its name worldwide, Nestlé decided to give up the name Marathon for ease of marketing, distribution and promotion.

If a multinational organisation acquires another organisation in a different country, it is probably not a good idea to instantly change any household names which may have been trading very well for a number of years. Again, for this reason, we will find divisions by product,.

Another reason for dividing an organisation by product is to establish a series of cost or profit centres. Essentially, this means that specific spending related to a particular product can be identified, as can any profits generated by that product.

Divisions of multinationals

Large multinationals may have literally dozens of separate companies or divisions being directed, to some extent, by a head office or *holding company* (*see* p.136). Typically, in real terms, the head office is comparatively small. This is always dependent upon the degree to which they involve themselves in the day-to-day running of the subsidiaries.

Each of the individual companies or divisions has relative autonomy, being free to make their own decisions on general matters. It is only at corporate level that the head office exerts its influence. General guidelines, of course, have been created by the head office relating to most decisions that have to be made.

Unilever, the multinational chemicals giant, is divided into some 500 separate companies, 50 of which operate in the UK alone. All of the 500 operate under guidelines issued by the parent company. In each country there is a national manager who has responsibility for all facets of the organisation's activities. The role of co-ordinating the efforts of the different national managers is undertaken by a director in the parent company. The director assists in setting the policies for each country grouping. In this way, the organisation as a whole and in any particular country especially, can respond to developments whether related to the competition, consumers or government.

Mechanistic structures

These are functionally divided with clearly identifiable chains of command. Each task carried out by the individuals making up the organisation is clearly defined. In this way, orders filtering through from the top of the organisation are carried out to the letter. Because of this accountability and rigid structure, organisations like this seem to take on the qualities of a machine, hence the name.

Organic structures

In these organisations, many of the job roles have been somewhat blurred, as the definitions of tasks and duties change according to the needs of the organisation. Individuals work as part of a network, where communication is easy and the authority to make decisions is readily available. Although there are roles within the organisation that relate to the direction of the work, the actual carrying out of the tasks can differ according to the nature of the work in hand.

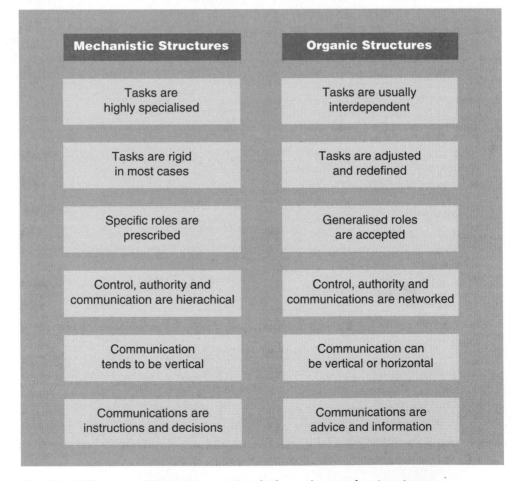

Mechanistic Structures	Organic Structures
Tasks are highly specialised	Tasks are usually interdependent
Tasks are rigid in most cases	Tasks are adjusted and redefined
Specific roles are prescribed	Generalised roles are accepted
Control, authority and communication are hierachical	Control, authority and communications are networked
Communication tends to be vertical	Communication can be vertical or horizontal
Communications are instructions and decisions	Communications are advice and information

Fig. 2.9 Differences between mechanistic and organic structures

Figure 2.9 highlights a number of differences between mechanistic and organic business structures.

Matrix structures

In this form of organisational structure there exists the opportunity to dispose of the more normal departmental boundaries. Typically used in Japan, the matrix system allows for teams to be created that consist of a number of individuals from various parts of the organisation, brought together to undertake a particular task. This can mean that individuals may have to report to their regular manager as well as a project leader.

Features of the matrix

The system appears to work quite well, offering the team members the advantage of being able to meet without direct reference to their departments. Also, it allows individual expertise to be utilised when and where needed. Unfortunately, it is often the case that both the departmental and the project managers make too great a demand on the time and effort of the team members. There is also a blurring of the lines of accountability, particularly if the project flounders or fails.

Task forces

There is a tendency for matrix structures to evolve in stages, with the first stage being the establishment of temporary task forces composed of individuals and representatives from different parts of the organisation. At the end of its life span the task force will be expected to have comprehensively studied a particular problem and suggested a number of recommendations. It should be noted that task force members may still retain their departmental affiliations alongside their duties within the task force itself. If it is felt that these task forces have contributed significantly to the operations of the organisation, then a more permanent form will be considered. Teams and committees organised on a permanent basis will be responsible for considering specific needs or problems. Once again, these will probably consist of a variety of individuals from product or functional areas, representating their particular departments or divisions.

Project managers

Project managers can be appointed to operate and integrate the activities of teams and committees on a full-time basis. The project manager will be able to ask for competent representatives from each of the major areas of the organisation in order to carry out a specific task. Once this system has been established, incorporated and accepted by the organisation as a whole, the business is well on its way to accepting the concept of a matrix structure as shown in Fig. 2.10. In other words, individuals within the organisation and the organisation as a whole have successfully accommodated the difficulties and benefits of multi-authority relationships.

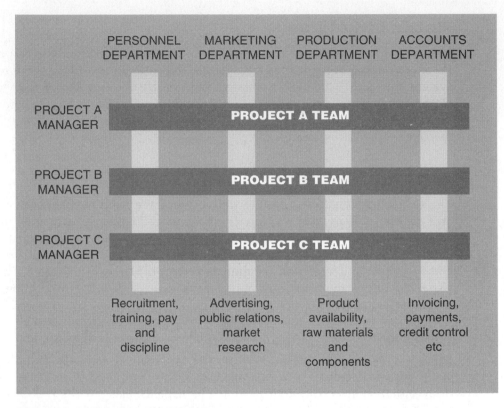

Fig. 2.10 Matrix structure chart

Multi-authority relationships

Multi-authority relationships replace the more formal or traditional chains of command within the organisation and operate by negotiation. Traditional rewards in relation to relative position in the hierarchical structure are no longer of great relevance.

Flexibility and responsiveness

The matrix structure is able to make use of specialised and functional knowledge from specific departments within the organisation. As a direct result of this, the matrix structure facilitates enhanced communication between departments and encourages a greater level of consistency in terms of the policies adopted by different departments within the organisation. Given the fact that there are multiple sources of power within the organisation under a matrix structure, recognised mechanisms will need to be established to deal with this different form of culture. Finally, the most positive aspect of the matrix structure is that it enables the organisation to adapt to environmental changes by simply shifting emphasis from functional to project aspects.

Possible disadvantages of the matrix

Most organisations operate with clear lines of command and authority, but the matrix structure does not enjoy the same kind of clarity and this may affect management's ability to understand what is required and what changes need to be made. When their roles become more ambiguous, there is a tendency for employees' stress levels to increase, as they try to compensate or adjust to the competing demands of their functional responsibilities and their matrix assignments. There may also be inconsistent demands made upon individuals, as well as departments, arising out of the suggestions and needs of project teams. This may result in limited involvement of some departments, while others will be in a constant state of crisis management in order to cope with demand.

Above all, one of the major criticisms of the matrix structure is that it encourages those who are politically adept to flourish far more than those who have technical ability. There will be constant competition between individuals to try and gain control of the more influential project teams at the expense of individuals who just see their role as being advisers within these teams.

Centralised structures

There are two different ways of looking at centralised structures, both of which contain features of many of the other types of organisational structures. Indeed, they may be actually organised in another form, but will have centralised features.

1 Centralised services. This version of a centralised structure involves the re-organisation of key services to provide for the organisation as a whole. In this respect, it would be common to find, for example, the reprographics (printing) functions centralised and controlled in such a manner as to provide cross-organisational services. Central control means that the service should be more efficient in terms of work throughput and output, as well as attempting to keep costs down (e.g. by the non-duplication of staff roles).

2 Centralised decision-making. In larger organisations that do not favour a decentralised approach to decision-making, there may be a preference to restrict command and decision functions to a few individuals. They will be supported by a variety of employees and will be responsible for cross-organisational decision-making. This may be the case with those organisations that are more traditional, or that rely on the expert knowledge of a handful of individual specialists.

Advantages and disadvantages of centralised structures

The main advantages of a centralised organisational structure are:

◆ decisions can be made quickly.

◆ specialist staff can be used.

◆ larger discounts can be obtained by centralising purchasing.

The main disadvantages are:

◆ there is little opportunity for total decision-making.

◆ individuals lack the opportunity to learn about the decision-making process.

◆ centralised power can be misused.

Decentralised structures

In recent years, some major organisations have recognised that a pyramid structure can prevent quick and necessary decision-making and be resistant to change. A new form of structure has developed, known commonly as *decentralisation*. This is the exact opposite to the centralised services structure which assists individual branches or sites. Each part of the decentralised organisation that carries out a distinctly different function is given a level of autonomy. This means that they are allowed, up to a point, to make decisions for themselves without the permission or consent of the directors or the central office. Each sub-organisation can be more flexible and responsive to its own needs and those of its customers without having to wait for a decision from a central office.

Most typically the structure consists of a central holding company (these are the owners of several companies who, while they are interested in the profits and decisions made by their companies, do not meddle in the day-to-day business) which has devolved (passed down power and authority) responsibility to each company forming part of the group.

Advantages and disadvantages of decentralised structures

The main advantages are:

◆ local decisions can be made by local managers.

◆ individuals can learn about the management process.

◆ head office managers can concentrate on the strategic decisions.

◆ there is a greater overall freedom of decision-making.

The main disadvantages are:

◆ the organisation can be difficult to supervise and control.

conflict often occurs between different parts of the organisation.

◆ unless the policies are clear, then decisions made can be in conflict with corporate strategy.

Flat structures

The flat structure is essentially a version of the hierarchical structure, but it has a number of different features. It should be remembered, however, that this is still a pyramid style structure, but one with fewer layers (*see* Fig. 2.11).

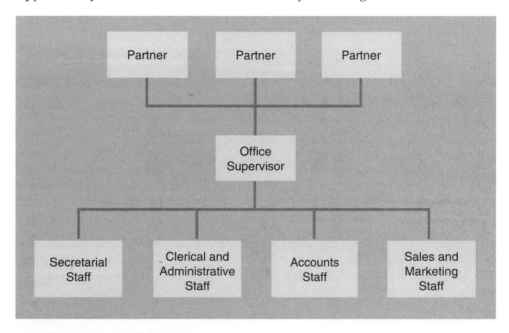

Fig. 2.11 Flat structure chart

The theory behind having fewer layers in the pyramid is that decisions can be made quickly and efficiently. Each layer is able to communicate easily with other layers and the organisation avoids the danger of becoming 'bureaucratic'. This simpler structure is generally found in organisations operating from a single site where directors and other decision makers are readily available for consultation and guidance. Employees find it easier to understand the reasoning behind the directors' decisions and therefore feel more a part of the organisation and less isolated. Equally, junior managers and other employees are more motivated as they are often given more responsibility through delegation.

Hierarchical structures

The best way to understand what a hierarchical structure looks like is to imagine a pyramid. At the top of the pyramid are the owners or major decision makers of the organisation. As we look further down the pyramid, the shape of the organisation broadens as more employees are involved at lower levels. At the base of the pyramid are the majority of the employees and below them are the customers.

Responsibility, power and authority are more highly concentrated at the top of the pyramid than at the bottom. Decisions flow down the pyramid affecting a succession of layers of employees. This explains why this form of structure is also referred to as a 'pecking order' since the higher up the pyramid you are as an employee, the more power and authority you have. Equally, we can see that the lower down the pyramid you are, the less influence you have in the organisation as a whole.

The reason for this hierarchical structure is that important decisions need to be made by those who have expertise and experience combined with sufficient authority to make sure that the decision is implemented. Those at the top of the pyramid take all the credit for success, but also bear the consequences of failure.

Typically, hierarchical structures begin with directors at the top of the pyramid making decisions for heads of department below to pass on to middle managers who then tell the junior members of staff to implement them. The higher an individual is in the pyramid, the less likely they are to understand precisely how decisions are implemented at the lower levels. These individuals may just have an idea of overall strategy and base their decisions on information received via the various layers below them. Each time information passes from layer to layer, the relative importance of what has been said may change. It is therefore likely that those at the top of the pyramid will have a distorted view of the organisation and how it really works. Conversely to those at the bottom of the pyramid, the directors will seem remote, unable to understand the organisation's needs and unwilling to change decisions which may adversely affect the day-to-day running of the business.

The main feature of this structure is that each layer sees the organisation in its own peculiar way. Each layer will have different opinions, priorities and interpretation of overall organisational policy.

The most common version of the hierarchical structure is the steep pyramid where there are many layers of management. The reason for this may be that the organisation operates in several different locations and needs to duplicate the administration in order to function efficiently. Alternatively, the nature of the business may be very complex, requiring the processing of many orders, messages, pieces of information or complaints.

Because the structure is multilayered and complicated, those further down the pyramid find it difficult to understand how and why decisions are made and the organisation may find it impossible to make sure that the employees follow through 'corporate decisions' (general statements of policy and procedures). The organisation may also suffer from being 'bureaucratic' in that decisions take a very long time to put into operation, and the systems designed to help implement them become more complicated than they need to be because they have to pass through so many layers of the hierarchy.

◆ Co-operative alliances

The co-operative alliance is run by a group of individuals with a financial interest in its success and a say in how the organisation is managed. It is probably best to think of co-operative alliances as being rather like the divisions of a multinational. In other words, each member (or independent business) in the alliance is free to make their own day-to-day business decisions. They are not, unlike the divisions of a multinational, accountable to a head office in respect of their profits or decisions. It is only when we consider the purchasing function of the organisation that we can more readily draw parallels with a multinational. In this respect, we should consider the purchasing function as being centralised. Each independent business does not order directly from the supplier; rather, they order via a central office or buying group.

The cost of having a central office or buying group are off-set by an extra few per cent of discount offered by the suppliers but not passed on to the independent businesses. In other words, the viability of this central purchasing unit is reliant upon the business fortunes of the members of the alliance. In times when the independent businesses are purchasing relatively large quantities (collectively), the purchasing unit can make a reasonable profit. In difficult times, when the purchase levels are lower, they may find it difficult to cover costs.

Normally, the independent businesses will be visited by the suppliers direct in order to inform them of new product availability or ideas. However, the independent businesses will not (necessarily) buy direct from that supplier. Suppliers are well aware of this situation and although they would prefer the independent business to buy direct (since they would not have to offer such large discounts), the buying group alliance is honoured.

The central purchasing unit, in whichever form it takes, will probably have regional representatives who can inform the independent businesses of special offers, trends and promotions. They will also co-ordinate marketing and advertising which is usually paid by subscription by the independent businesses. Through pooling the advertising and marketing budgets, the members of the organisation can acquire far better deals from the media and printers.

◆ Other organisational structures

Among the variety of other possible structures and configurations there are:

◆ *Geographically-based structures* – retail businesses generally use this form of structure as it best fits with the demands that will be made of regional and local managers. Using a traditional hierarchical structure, in the main, the organisation will take the form of a relatively small head office, which supports a number of regional offices. These regional offices have various support functions to assist the outlets within that area. In other cases, manufacturing organisations may have a similar structure, particularly when they have widely dispersed factories throughout the country.

◆ *Market-based structures* – some organisations are structured to cater for each of their major markets. If an organisation produces a wide range of different products, it may well be advised to have separate companies or subsidiaries to exploit each market.

◆ *Product-based structures* – in many respects this is a similar structure to the market-based organisation. Each company/division or unit will be responsible for all of the activities related to a particular product. The product divisions will also have their own manufacturing, accounting, sales and purchasing departments.

◆ *Autocratic structures* – again, usually a hierarchical structure, in which the decisions are made by a single individual who requires unquestioning support and reaction to their directives.

Stages of development

Structural transitions

As organisations grow, they will go through a number of structural transitions. For the most part, these transitions will be gradual and predictable rather than radical. In this respect, we should expect that the organisation moves from one form to another as a continuous process, which is smooth rather than abrupt. In other words, the changes are discrete and may, at the time, seem unidentifiable.

Many theorists have suggested that there is a clear pattern of transition; perhaps from craft to entrepreneurial; into bureaucratic and then to matrix. However, this presupposes that all organisations follow the same path and that all stages occur, when in practice many organisations will miss out one or more of the transitional stages.

Sole trader as starting point

The most basic form of organisational structure is the sole trader or relatively small business organisation that is typified by the production of craft-based products. There will be a degree of standardisation in terms of process, which rests upon the apprenticeship system. All gradual changes within the organisation will be embraced by each craftsperson. The management will have an integral part to play in the production process, with responsibility for very similar operations to those of other employees.

Informal division of labour

Assuming that this craft structure grows, there may be a need to divert the energies and expertise of one or more individuals towards innovation and sales.

Equally, one individual may have to take responsibility for co-ordination through supervision. It is certainly true that this stage has a greater degree of labour division, but it is still rather informal and organic in nature. There will be a strong reaction by both management and employees to any attempt at formalising or standardising operations. The organisation's success will depend upon flexibility and innovation rather than an elaborate structure. In reality, the majority of organisations begin at this stage of development.

Moving into bureaucracy

It is said that the bureaucratic structure is the next logical step in the development of an organisation. As we have seen, these organisations attempt to maintain centralised control within an environment that has not only grown in size, but also in complexity. The once informal procedures and policies become formalised into a set of codes and behaviour. At the same time each individual within the organisation will have a clearer job description, thus facilitating more efficient co-ordination. The proliferation of the administrative function is significant, as the organisation moves from an organic structure to a bureaucratic one. There will also be an attempt to standardise as much of the organisation as possible, in order to further increase the co-ordination. This is when a techno-structure is superimposed upon the organisation. There will be a clear division between those who supervise and those whose work is supervised.

Divisionalisation

The divisionalised structure, which we have already investigated, still retains many of the features of a bureaucracy. These organisations are typified by those who have diversified into broadly similar areas of operation. The bureaucracy is unable to efficiently co-ordinate the radically different requirements of each of the divisions, therefore, the central headquarters' size and impact upon the overall organisation is reduced.

Adoption of the matrix

For many of the theorists, the divisionalised structure is simply a temporary point which some organisations stop at *en route* to the matrix structure. Many organisations that have diversified and reconfigured themselves along divisional lines, further expand and diversify into different geographical markets. Not only that, they may find themselves producing radically different products which bear no relation to other activities. While, to some extent, co-ordination could be continued along a divisional basis, the matrix structure is far more efficient. There is a natural tendency for a divisionalised structure to begin adopting features of a matrix structure at a very early stage.

The co-ordination factor

As we said at the beginning of this section, we should not assume that organisations develop along strictly linear lines. They will go through a number of transitions which may be fundamental, but are all aimed at maintaining co-ordination. While loose co-ordination may be appropriate for smaller, less complex organisations, direct supervision may be required for larger and more complex operations. It may be more useful to consider the stages of development more in terms of changes in the hierarchy, adoption of co-ordination sub-systems and gradual adjustment, rather than any radical notion of structural change.

Chaos theory and organisations

Chaos theory was originally developed in the natural sciences, but it has been applied to help us to understand the activities of organisations. Central to the theory is the notion that the environment in which organisations operate is becoming increasingly unpredictable and chaotic. As a result, the ability of an organisation to make any kind of long-term plan in response to the constantly changing environment, is seriously curtailed. Consequently, the best that the organisation can hope for is merely to make necessary changes that offer it some sort of short-term advantage. Chaos theorists believe that change can be categorised in two different ways:

◆ *closed and contained changes*, where the response of the organisation should be structured in order to be effective; or

◆ *open-ended changes*, where the response of the organisation needs to be far more flexible because the more structured approach will flounder and fail as events overtake it. The goal, in these instances, is to try to create some form of order out of the chaos.

R. Stacey in *Managing Chaos* suggested that the only way an organisation could respond effectively to external chaos was to create internal chaos. In order for an organisation to succeed in such circumstances, he recommended that it should adopt the following steps:

◆ that the organisation tries to focus on particular strategic issues or challenges;

◆ that it then tries to develop a specific solution to that individual issue or challenge;

◆ while doing this, it also needs to focus the attention of all members of the organisation (at various levels) on considering the impact of the issue or challenge, as well as on the solution;

◆ resources and attention then need to be allocated to assist in the implementation of the solution.

The outcome of following these steps will be the gradual development of the organisation. It will grow and respond in a dynamic and organic manner to each of the challenges and issues facing it, as they arise. Chaos theory also helps us to understand the importance of creativity in framing solutions to commonly occurring problems. It is certainly true to say that organisations will have to be innovative in their attempts to cope with the stresses and strains exerted upon them as a result of a continually changing environment. At some level, the organisation needs to try to reach an equilibrium state where the operation and activities that are necessary for continued existence in the market can be achieved. Given the fact that the organisation will never be in a position to stand still, it nevertheless needs to be as effective as possible. The organisation cannot hope to address all of the demands which change (or chaos) place upon it, rather it is only by systematically tackling the most important challenges that it can hope to have any real effect. Organisations will fluctuate between stability and instability. This can be considered in relative terms, since the degree of stability or instability may affect the organisation in different ways. The key strategy needs to be flexibility and a willingness to respond to change. Organisations which hang on to structures, policies and procedures in spite of the changes being wrought in the external environment, will ultimately fail.

Phases of growth and decline

As we have seen, we can clearly identify the probable stages in development between the early life of an organisation and its more developed and mature form. These stages are listed in Fig. 2.12. It will be readily apparent from what has already been said that not all transitions in structure necessarily occur at a steady and predictable pace. There may be situations when the organisation does not have time to carefully consider all of the implications that can be associated with

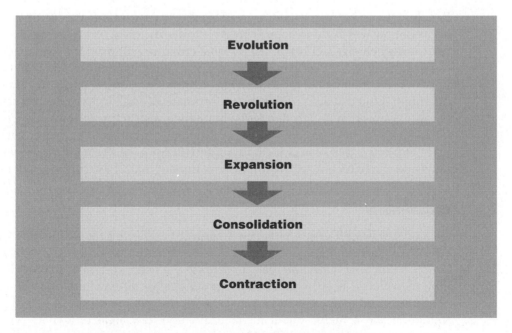

Fig. 2.12 Phases of organisational growth and decline

a particular structural change before it actually has to implement it. This is even more the case when an organisation is forced to contract as a result of the reduction in demand for its products or services. An organisation may have to consider a radical restructuring as a result of operating in a vastly different manner, such as outsourcing or subcontracting. We will address each of these principal concerns in turn.

Evolution

Evolution is the most gentle and potentially least disruptive form of transition from one structural type to another. If we assume that organisations will grow at a consistent rate, with the ability to take on board the features of each progressive structural type, then we can accept that evolution is a common occurrence. However, given that the majority of organisations operate in environments where they can neither predict nor prepare for probable changes in either demand or technology, then perhaps evolution is not an option open to most of them. Evolution can be viewed as a matter of degree: on the one hand, a metamorphosis is considered to be an evolutionary change, but at the same time it means very radical change; on the other hand, more gradual changes taken together may mean that radical change has occurred without the organisation necessarily realising it. Evolution for one organisation may be seen as radical, whereas in others it may be seen as gradual.

Revolution

Revolution can be seen as a drastic alternative to evolution. This means that the organisation will have to cope with a radically different structure as a result of widespread changes, either in the external environment or in the management of the organisation. As we have seen, mergers, takeovers and management buy-outs can all mean that radical or revolutionary change needs to take place overnight. Organisations which are unfortunate enough to have been taken over by an organisation which demands immediate restructuring may also be faced with the prospect of having to shed or rationalise significant parts of their structure. Typically, this would include a rationalisation of the administrative functions and the reduction of any duplicated areas of manufacturing operations.

Expansion

As an organisation grows either in a natural manner by the acquisition of new customers and products or by the acquisition of another organisation in a horizontal, vertical or lateral merger, it will face the need to radically reconsider the way in which it is structured. This may mean an all-encompassing review of operations and management processes, with the need to consider merging, consolidating and bringing under the co-ordination new areas of activity. We have seen that there is a natural tendency for organisations to shift from simpler informal structures to more bureaucratic and co-ordinated ones. There may, however, be the need to retain innovative qualities and flexibility that have perhaps contributed to the organisation's ability to grow in the first place. Growth is not necessarily expected within an organisation. Certainly, we should not always expect growth in terms of the number of employees or the complexity of the organisational structure. It is perfectly possible for an organisation to grow in terms of turnover and profitability, without radically growing in size or number of employees. These two factors may follow, but are not necessarily to be assumed.

Consolidation

In situations when an organisation has diversified into areas that were not necessarily related to its core operations, they may find a need to retrench or consolidate before they proceed to the next stage of organisational development. This may mean a radical restructuring of the organisation, incorporating the shedding of departments and divisions which are felt not to reflect the importance of the core operations. Naturally this would be accompanied by a restructuring of the administrative functions, as well as a reconsideration of the levels of management and hierarchy.

Consolidation may mean that an organisation contracts in certain areas, while it simultaneously expands in others. This may be true of organisations that have prematurely expanded into markets which their structure was not really ready to cope with. They may have acquired the expertise and processes in order to cope with this new market and may now have to consider realigning these to give them a better competitive advantage in their core operational areas.

Contraction

Organisations which have expanded too quickly, or find themselves in situations where certain operations have become uneconomical, may be forced to consider contraction. For most organisations in this position, contraction is the only alternative to business failure. Assuming that the organisation can step back and view the situation dispassionately, it will be able to make logical savings in a variety of different areas within the organisation, without unduly affecting the overall operations.

For the most part, a leaner organisation will mean that selected individuals have been made redundant or have been offered early retirement. Unfortunately, as is often the case, the more senior and experienced individuals within the organisation are those which fall into the category of early retirees, and it is those who are more capable of finding alternative sources of income that will offer themselves up for voluntary redundancy. In both cases, the organisation is all the poorer for the loss of these employees. Assuming that retirements and redundancies cannot be made on a voluntary basis, the organisation will have to make a series of decisions which may put the whole structure of the organisation in jeopardy and reduce morale and motivation to an all-time low. Again, individuals will have to be selected at particular points within the organisational structure to reflect the necessary savings that will have to be made. If we assume that the organisation is not considering the wholesale closure of specific departments and divisions, then the management will have to look across the whole of the organisation to identify individuals.

Franchising

The franchise is a form of organisation which has been imported into the UK and the rest of the world from America, where over a third of all retail businesses are operating on what has become a franchise basis. This is becoming a very popular form of business organisation in the UK. The main features of franchising are as follows:

◆ Franchising really amounts to hiring out or licensing the use of product lines to other companies. A franchise agreement allows another company to trade under a particular name in a particular area. The firm which sells the franchise is known as the franchisor.

◆ The person who takes out the franchise needs a sum of money for capital and is issued with a certificate from the franchising company. This person is known as the franchisee. The franchisee usually has the sole right of operating in a particular area. Some examples of franchises can be seen in many of our high streets – Pizza Hut, Prontaprint, The Body Shop and Spud-U-Like, to name a few.

◆ Another important feature of the franchise agreement is that the franchisee agrees to buy all of its supplies from the franchisor and the latter makes a profit on these supplies.

◆ The franchisor takes a share of the profits made by the franchisee's business, without having to risk any capital or be involved in the day-to-day management of the business.

◆ The franchisee benefits from trading under a well-known name and enjoys a local monopoly. In other words, each franchisee is the only business to operate under that name in a particular area.

◆ The franchise agreement allows people to become their own boss without the normal kinds of risks of setting up a business from scratch.

The main characteristics of franchise operations are summarised in Fig. 2.13.

McDonalds' franchised restaurants

By the turn of the century McDonalds aim to have 1000 outlets in the UK, and of that total it is expected some 300 will be franchised restaurants. McDonalds joined the franchising business relatively late (1986), and favour granting additional franchises to existing franchise holders. The franchise deal, in the first

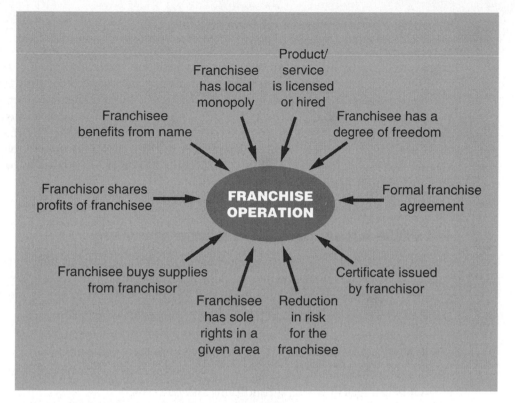

Fig. 2.13 Features of a franchise operation

instance, runs for some 20 years. McDonalds are very careful in choosing their potential franchise holders. They can pick and choose as the enquiry numbers are large. They look for outgoing people, with a good financial mind, who are enthusiastic and quite aggressive in business terms. They also favour individuals setting up franchises in their own town or area. Training lasts for some nine months. There is a 'Hamburger University' in north London and the total cost of the training is around £40 000 per franchise.

A typical franchisee would need to find some £124 000 (around 40 per cent of the cost of setting up the restaurant). If an individual wanted to franchise an existing McDonalds restaurant then the cost would be between £100 000 and £1m. If a potential franchisee is particularly good, but does not have the full 40 per cent investment capital, then with £40 000 a deal could be struck. The balance is paid over a three-year period by putting the restaurant's profits back into the business.

The McDonalds franchise operation has been extremely successful, with only one franchisee having dropped out so far, although some have not made it through the training period. Even with the McDonald's name and reputation, there is no guarantee of success.

Special requirements of franchising

Franchising is seen as a viable alternative to that of increasing the number of employees directly involved in the main structure and operations of an organisation. Obviously, these franchises need to be closely monitored and administered in order to ensure that the policies and procedures of the franchisor are complied with at all times. Equally, there is a need to ensure that the returns on turnover and profit levels are correctly and accurately given to the franchisor by the franchise holders. This will involve an increase in the number of administrative staff and the inclusion of new roles within the organisation that encompass some form of franchise management and co-ordination.

Flexible structures and home working

One of the implications of changing working conditions is that employees are expected to be far more flexible in their approach and availability for work. Principal areas included in this are hours worked, location of the work, work space available, multiskilling needs and job sharing opportunities.

Hours

There are innumerable variations in the hours worked by employees when one considers changes in working conditions and patterns:

Shift working

The working of non-standard hours, has long been an accepted method of ensuring that either the production process is in operation at all times, or that individuals are available to provide essential services on a 24-hour basis. Shift working is absolutely essential in such occupations as the emergency services. Clearly, the fire brigade, police force or ambulance service, for example, could not operate on a 9–5 basis.

In manufacturing, where shift work is again an accepted norm, the production process often requires this form of working. If the manufacturer employs flow production, for example, then it is essential that the production line is staffed at all times. While there may be additional payments made to employees working unsociable hours, this cost is insignificant compared to that of constantly stopping and starting the flow production process.

In some cases, employees may be required to work days for a period then, after a short break, a period of nights. Alternatively, the contract may require the employee to work a mixture of days and nights.

Flexible working arrangements

Systems such as flexitime, allow some 2.5 million people to take advantage of the opportunity to arrange the hours to suit both themselves and their employers. Normally, employees will be expected to work during the core time – usually

10 a.m. to 4 p.m. – but can then choose to make up the balance of the hours at some point between say 8 a.m. and 6 p.m. Alternatively, employees may choose to work longer hours for short periods of time and thus build up days off.

Compressed working weeks

These operate in certain organisations which choose to close early on Fridays, or perhaps close on Fridays altogether. This means that employees work longer hours between Monday and Thursday. It can prove to be a suitable arrangement since the organisation can concentrate its business activities on four full working days which are fully staffed by all employees who have the advantage of enjoying an extended weekend.

Compressed annual hours

These are stipulated for certain employees who find that their contracts simply specify the number of hours they will be expected to work throughout the year. With such arrangements, they may work extremely long hours for short periods of time (providing this does not breach legislation) and then have long breaks at the end of these work periods.

Location

It is now possible, due to technological advances, for an individual to undertake certain job tasks at home, via a computer linked to their employers premises. There are, however, more traditional forms of *home working* which are largely related to the clothing industry. A form of 'piece work' which allows an individual to work at their own rate, providing that certain quotas are reached, has been common for decades. Employers using this form of production or processing of garments, for example, or for a similar skilled or semi-skilled function, will be able, very quickly, to respond to changes in demand. They will have a pool of 'outworkers' to whom they will deliver part-finished products and simply inform the employee of the piece rate and the date by which the finished goods should be ready.

An individual may, within certain limitations, be able to undertake other employment in addition to this home working commitment. Indeed, in terms of computer access and the cost of enhanced telephone lines, employers may positively encourage home workers to do this.

Structurally speaking, the inclusion of remote workers in its labour force does involve a radical change to the way in which the organisation manages and co-ordinates its activities. Many organisations have experienced a steep learning curve, but one that they are in control of and are developing with at a rapid rate.

Many organisations have tried to use home working, but have discovered that it is unsuitable, since it may result in the individual becoming isolated through lack of social contact throughout the day, and thus becoming unmotivated.

There are control problems associated with the widespread use of home working as a primary method of carrying out core activities, since there will be a reliance on the various 'outworkers' completing the series of necessary tasks at precisely the right point. At the same time, the organisational structure needs to be able to accommodate the requirement of continuous communication and supervision on a remote basis. There can be no substitute for meeting with colleagues and sorting out an agreed policy or set of procedures. The technology exists to do this on a remote basis, through the use of video-conferencing, but this may be seen as an unnecessary expense by the organisation.

As an alternative to home working, but still in relation to the location of the work, an employee may be expected to be *geographically mobile* as an essential part of their job. Individuals, particularly those who are involved in maintenance, will be expected to carry out their duties in a variety of different locations. This may mean that the working location may differ every day, or at the very least the individual may have to work for short periods of time in a variety of different locations. In some cases this may even mean working in different countries at various times during the year. This flexibility requires the willingness on the part of the employee to travel to different locations (and, of course, an ability to handle any domestic problems which may arise from this mode of work), but also that the employer rewards the employee for the disturbances to their life.

Work space

Increasingly, organisations have recognised the positive benefits which may be accrued from making their working environments open plan. A series of *work stations* are established within a fairly 'free form' environment, where the exact delineation between different sections or departments of the organisation are much more blurred.

Some organisations have taken the work space revolution to its most logical conclusion. In such organisations the desk has been abolished altogether. *Communal working areas* are available and all individuals are issued with a portable computer which may be plugged into the main network at a variety of points in the building. Also, these organisations have addressed the problem of filing and storage and positively discourage their employees from collecting paperwork and attempting to store it anywhere. In the electronic office of the next century it is envisaged that paper will become redundant and all transactions, documents and information will be available via a computer screen.

There is a statutory minimum requirement in terms of work space per employee. However, this is openly ignored by the majority of employers. Indeed, it is rare to find anyone who actually knows what the statutory minimum requirement is.

Many organisations also have a *clear desk policy*. Essentially, this means that at the end of each working day the employee must remove all paperwork from their desks. There are two main reasons for this:

◆ much of the information may be of a sensitive or confidential nature and it would be unwise to allow unauthorised individuals to have access to it.

◆ that the organisation values the appearance of a clean and tidy office environment and, indeed, the clear desk policy assists operatives to carry out thorough cleaning duties.

Multiskilling

Since the introduction of trade union legislation aimed at reducing the power of employees in relation to employers, *demarcation* has all but disappeared. In the past, demarcation was a common reason for industrial disputes. Demarcation is essentially to do with the clear definition of job descriptions, tasks and roles. Trade unions fought against the blurring of these definitions. Multiskilling requires individuals to perform a broader range of activities within the work place. It is now common for a machine operative to undertake most basic forms of machine maintenance. Previously, demarcation demanded that any maintenance work should be carried out by an individual employed specifically for that task. While multiskilling offers greater job satisfaction in terms of giving greater job variety, it has meant the loss of many jobs. A fringe benefit of multiskilling has been, in some cases, higher rates of pay. Multiskilling has also given organisations the following benefits:

◆ since machine operatives carry out most maintenance, there will be less 'down time' while machines are being serviced or repaired.

◆ machinery, as a result of this, will be more productive.

◆ following on from these two points, the organisation should be more competitive.

◆ a natural result of all of the above is that the organisation should be able to offer better pay and conditions to its work-force.

Job sharing

Job sharing has become increasingly popular in recent years. Employers have discovered that job sharers are very beneficial to the organisation since they approach the job in a fresh and positive manner, only having had to work for part of the week. Employers also benefit from the fact that there are two individuals with different ideas to solve particular problems.

Individuals involved in job sharing will normally be able to choose their working hours, but most commonly they will either work for two-and-a-half days per week each, or mornings only, or one week on, one week off. This type of arrangement ideally suits individuals with commitments outside the work place, such as child care.

◆ Contractual responses to changing needs

Non-standard and short-term contracts

The use of non-standard contracts has come about largely as a result of the economic recession experienced in recent years. In addition, organisations have had to cope with an increasingly competitive international market, and as a result, a level of uncertainty regarding the demand for their products and services. To this end, fixed short-term contracts have become quite common. In this way, the employer is able to increase or decrease employee numbers as a quick response to changes in demand.

Early termination of a fixed short-term contract is normally regarded as dismissal in legal terms. However, provided that both parties agree to exclude the employee's right to redundancy payment (assuming that the contract is for two years or more), and also to waive the right for compensation for unfair dismissal (providing the contract was for over one year), fixed short-term contracts are flexible and attractive to both employer and employee.

In essence, fixed short-term contracts not only provide the employer with the opportunity to respond to fluctuations in demand, but also to deal with projects or tasks on a one-off basis, or to bring in specialists to carry out a particular function. Areas which have significantly increased their use of fixed short-term contracts are:

◆ health

◆ education

◆ distribution.

In fact, most public sector organisations find that the fixed short-term contract allows them to reduce their long-term commitments in the knowledge that their future budgets may not be wholly predictable.

Pay implications of short-term contracts

The changing nature of contracts obviously has an impact upon the pay received by the employee. One of the more obvious impacts is that the employee is only paid for hours worked. While this arrangement may be beneficial to the employer, it does mean that the employee cannot predict their income beyond the short term. The nature of these new contracts may mean that the employee has only guaranteed work for limited periods of time. These work periods may be punctuated with considerable amounts of unemployment. While flexible working conditions and their relationship to pay may allow the organisation to more accurately budget for particular contracts or projects, the employee is faced with the prospect of having to seek work elsewhere. For the employee's part, this makes it very difficult to make any long-term financial commitments, for example on a mortgage or a loan. Without guaranteed work and the pay associated with it, financial institutions would be unwilling to risk significant loans.

Short-term staff implications of new technology

The introduction of new technology does present some short-term problems for an organisation. They may find themselves in a position where they are unable to find or attract sufficiently experienced staff. Indeed, if the technology is sufficiently new, these new staff may not exist. In this situation, a forward looking organisation will have appreciated this concern and have taken steps to institute retraining programmes. New skills can also be identified as being opportunities for individuals to embrace a new occupation, providing they are aware of the technological advances. In some respects, this proactive approach can ensure that the individual is well placed to take advantage of short-term skill shortages. An organisation will be only too happy to acquire the services of such individuals, albeit for a relatively short time.

Even in the most mundane forms of occupation, technological advances may not be the only reason for new skills development. Simple changes in procedure may not appear to require significant reskilling of employees. However, in practice new implementation of a procedure will involve a certain level of retraining. In these cases, both the organisation and the employee needs to be flexible. The organisation should be patient and allow the employee to 'catch up' with new developments and the employee should be prepared to spend time and effort in acquiring these new skills and knowledge of procedures.

Increasingly, as we have mentioned earlier, the multiskilling of employees can be a solution to short-term skill shortages. Adaptable and flexible employees should, at least in practice, be able and willing to adopt new procedures and learn to use new technology.

Controlling labour turnover

Controlling the labour turnover of the organisation can be a time-consuming operation. Basically, for some organisations, it can mean the difference between profit and loss. If the organisation is unable to keep their trained employees for a great length of time then they will have to consistently train and retrain their staff. This will have a net impact on the level of production and the quality of the products or services offered or produced. The formula for working out the labour turnover is:

$$\text{labour turnover} = \frac{\text{number of employees leaving each year}}{\text{average number of employees}} \times 100$$

The main reasons behind a high labour turnover may be some of the following:

◆ wage and salary levels in the organisation are lower than other comparable rates in organisations in the locality.

◆ the managerial structure and approach is either ineffective or unnecessarily strict.

◆ employees are suffering from low morale and poor motivation.

◆ there are better job opportunities in terms of non-pay considerations elsewhere (e.g. better promotion prospects and more interesting work).

As previously stated the development of technological systems that are geared towards the improvement of communications within the organisation can make it possible for employees to operate in remote locations. These networking systems allow the employees to spend far more productive time at the terminal even in their own homes. Work can then be fitted around other work commitments or personal ones, enabling the individual to devote the specified number of hours at the terminal on a full or part-time basis. The completion of the work in a relaxed environment has been shown to provide greater motivation, increased effort and a higher output which in turn leads to a lower level of labour turnover.

Certainly, the careful selection of individuals can do much to alleviate the problems associated with having to cater for a variety of different demands and other commitments by employees. Careful selection also means that the organisation does not have to go to the expense of reorganising or expanding their working environment as they grow.

Review questions

1 Identify five changes in working arrangements that could be forced upon an organisation.

2 Identify three advantages and three disadvantages of specialisation.

3 Explain the chief characteristics of a bureaucratic structure.

4 Outline the main disadvantages of a bureaucracy.

5 What are the key features of a functional organisation?

6 Describe the key features of a divisional organisation?

7 Distinguish between mechanistic and organic organisations.

8 Why might an organisation choose to centralise its functions?

9 Outline the key features of a hierarchical structure.

10 Describe the probable stages in the development and growth of a typical organisation.

11 Describe the main stages of growth and decline.

12 Describe the main features of a franchise operation.

13 Identify the main features of flexible working arrangements.

14 Explain why non-standard contracts have increased in popularity as far as the employer is concerned.

15 How might technology influence the structure of the workforce in an organisation?

Responding to change

Managing change is only one of the many functions carried out by a manager. By simply looking at the job descriptions attached to various management roles, we can only just begin to understand the complexities of the job. As we will see in this chapter and in Section 4, when we consider the different managerial styles, there is a wide gulf between the manager's point of view and that of other employees. Not only do managers have to have sufficient experience in order to understand the operational nature of the organisation, but they also need to be sufficiently aware of the impact that various new policies will have on their subordinates.

Taking a simplistic view, we can see that most work needs to be managed, and someone has to make the decisions about how that work will be carried out. This is the basis of any attempt to look at change in terms of structural modification. There will always be a degree of conflict between current working practices and structural arrangements and that of any proposed change. It is perfectly possible that management's best intentions will be misunderstood by the workforce and any changes in working practices or job roles will only seek to reinforce this mis-understanding. Organisations inevitably operate in an environment which is constantly changing, as we have already seen. However, constant change can be seen by some as being the norm, while others will attempt to resist it.

Although in this chapter we need to address the ways in which an organisation responds to change, we still need to realise that this is essentially to do with people and their responses, rather than the organisation as an organism or entity in its own right. All organisations are made up of a number of individuals, each with their own viewpoint, status and position. Any attempt to alter this will inevitably mean a certain degree of resistance. What modern management attempts to do is to incorporate and respond to this resistance and move forward in a spirit of co-operation and understanding.

As we will see in the final section of this book, the culture of the organisation will have a marked effect upon the individual's ability to accept and respond to change. The prevailing culture may be responsive to gradual technological change, but there will be some who are unable or unwilling to accept even this form of change. Some individuals will consequently be left behind. Whether the organisation can incorporate these into the newly reconstituted restructure is a question that can only be answered by the business itself. It may be prepared to only make subtle changes in certain areas where individuals have undertaken a particular mode of work for a long period of time. The management will take a longer-term view of these individuals, but expect those who are perhaps younger, and have had less experience within the organisation, to adapt more rapidly.

Since all change inevitably means a shift in the working patterns of every individual within the organisation, there will be a need to reconfigure the structure to cope with the new working conditions. While changes can be imposed by the management, it may take years for the employees to come to terms with the change and the long-term implications of it. In the short term, this may lead to demotivation, with key members of staff seeking to leave the organisation, and a general feeling of disorganisation and confusion. At this point the organisation will be vulnerable, not only in terms of its ability to cope with routine operations, but also in its ability to respond to changes or threats from competitors or the external environment in general. If the organisation can impress upon the employees that the reasons for the structural change lie as a primary response to a perceived external threat, then they may be able to impose the reconfiguration and maintain the support of the employees.

Reasons for change

Perhaps a more apt heading would be 'the forces of change', since not all reasons for change result from the organisation itself realising that it needs to make structural adjustments to its internal strengths and weaknesses. While it is true to say that some change may come about as a result of an innovative idea, derived perhaps from a manager or a project team, the vast majority of structural changes are reactive rather than proactive.

The reactive approach

When an organisation is faced with the possibility of having to make a structural change, it will need to begin by investigating the nature of that change and the probable impact upon the business if it does not respond. Obviously, it is in no one's interest to continually be in a state of flux between one structural identity and another. Not only is this extremely wasteful and disorganised, but it also means that the organisation may not be in a position to carry out its normal operations. For this reason, the organisation needs to consider any potential change from its existing viewpoint or culture, and to try to minimise the effects of change as much as possible. This may mean that the organisation will simply amend or partially reconfigure some aspects of its operations rather than taking the more drastic step of a total reconfiguration. At the very least, someone will have to take responsibility for quantifying the changes required and the implementation strategy. It may simply be a case of having to draw in the reins of control and make minor adjustments to operating procedures. The organisation will have to consider more drastic action if this does not work.

One of the major criticisms of adopting this approach is that on the one hand the organisation is accepting that change is inevitable, but on the other it is stating that the majority of its policies and procedures are adequate to cope with the dangers that may exist in the future. Cost implications are paramount in this approach. Providing the organisation has the correct policies and procedures in place, it may not have to incur excessive expenditure in order to radically reconfigure the structure. It will simply make do.

Turbulent times

Many theorists will suggest that organisations often encounter change as a result of turbulence. This means that changing political or economic sets of circumstances will impact upon the organisation in a haphazard manner. For organisations which operate in essentially stable political and economic environments, turbulence may not be as drastic a problem as it is for others that are operating in emerging or developing economies, with an inconsistent record of political stability and order. Having said this, even the most stable economy with a generally accepted political democracy may face turbulence as a result of activities beyond the borders of that country.

Many of the woes which befell the UK economy have been firmly blamed upon the European Union or on fluctuations in the economy of the USA. Without question, not only are economies interdependent of one another but, more seriously, organisations in different countries or markets, which are geographically remote, will have a marked impact in terms of turbulence. The relative misfortune of a subsidiary or joint venture in a country which is suffering a grave economic or political crisis may mean that the parent company, while itself in a stable economic and political environment, will have to seek ways in which it can respond.

The vast changes in the structural configuration of Lloyds of London amply illustrate the impact of turbulence upon operations as a result of factors abroad. In this respect, the turbulence is both theoretical and literal. The vast insurance claims that hit Lloyds were as a result of underwriting insurances in other countries. The underwriters could not and did not take account of the risks that they were exposing themselves to when they snapped up foreign business. At the end of the day, after massive losses, the net losers were Lloyds themselves. Not only did they have to radically reconfigure their structure, driving many hundreds into unemployment, but also many of the stakeholders in each of the syndicates were forced into bankruptcy.

The proactive approach

By adopting a more forward-looking stance, the organisation will gradually change as the external environment or the reasons for change develop. They will have done this before the situation becomes so serious that it necessitates a more radical set of changes. This means that the senior management within an organisation have to keep a close eye on developments in the market-place or in the activities of their competitors. It would be difficult to predict the probable outcomes of a change in policy, ownership or market spread of a competitor, and this may have to be dealt with on a more adhoc basis. Any competent manager in a strategic position will be fully aware of the probable changes and it is on these that the organisation will have to act. This may mean that the organisation will have to make changes which are only short term in order to accommodate a temporary change in circumstances. Others are of a more fundamental nature and will ultimately mean a radical overhaul of the operations of the organisation and the adoption of a new organisational culture.

Returning to equilibrium

As we said earlier, organisations can either begin structural change as a result of internal innovation or recognition that changes need to be made, or as a result of anticipated changes in the external environment. In either case, the organisation will aim to return as quickly as possible to a state of equilibrium. This means that any source of change needs to be met with an appropriate set of actions. On the one hand, some of the policies and procedures of the organisation will actively support the stability of the organisation, while, on the other hand, there will be some that positively disadvantage the organisation in terms of its ability to respond to the varying forces of change.

In order to return to a state of stability, the organisation needs to match the threats or opportunities which change produces with an appropriate set of policies and procedures that are either in place or are in the process of being developed. While this juggling act is extremely difficult, it means that if the organisation is sufficiently aware of the probable causes of change, then it will be more likely to be in a position to respond to them in a less radical manner.

Minimising disruption

As we have said, radical change leads to destabilisation, or, at the very least, an extremely strong reaction from management and other employees. The minimisation of disruption to the organisation is obviously in the best interests of all concerned, and it will only be exceptional sets of circumstances, such as the total collapse of a market or product, that will trigger massive disruption.

The most effective way of minimising the disruption to the organisation is to have a rolling programme of planned changes. These will be supported by the various policies and procedures which have been set up by the organisation in order to cope with the various dangers of change and to combat those which would seek to maintain the status quo. Obviously, any organisation can reconfigure itself rapidly, but, this may be at the expense of performance.

Improving performance

The current levels of performance within an organisation may be acceptable to the management. However, in most cases, it is natural for the management to wish to improve performance, regardless of any internal or external changes. This is an integral part of the organisation's ability to make planned changes and goes a long way to establishing an organisational culture which accepts and expects gradual and planned changes. All organisations will hope that, as a result of a reconfiguration, or as a result of their planned changes, performance is improved. We can thus see that change is only one aspect of most organisations' long-term planning strategies.

We have already mentioned that time, which can be expressed in terms of the response time or the age of an organisation, has an impact on the structural type which the business adopts. Most changes have a particular *time span*. This refers to the period in which the organisation has the opportunity to bring itself into a position of parity with other organisations reacting to that change. We can see that an organisation which misses this window of opportunity will need to either consider more drastic change in the future or suffer the long-term consequences of not having responded when it had the chance.

Efficient and effective means of communication are needed throughout the length and breadth of the business. All changes to policies and procedures have to be cascaded to all parts of the organisation. This is essential, since if the organisation intends to retain its level of productivity and performance, all relevant areas of the organisation need to move in concert with one another, otherwise there may be blocks which will have a marked effect upon the organisation's overall ability to respond and react.

Further aspects of change and innovation

As we have already mentioned, most organisations which have developed their operations over a period of time rest very firmly on specialisation. This means that any structural changes will affect far more employees and parts of the organisation than would have been expected had the organisation configured itself in such a way as to have developed broadly autonomous sub-units or divisions. Probably the most common response from organisations has been to subcontract or outsource a variety of sub-operations and systems to contractors. This means that in times of change they can simply renegotiate the deals that have been struck with the subcontractors, rather than having to reconfigure their whole organisation to accommodate rather superficial changes.

As we have seen and will return to in the next section, technology has radically altered not only the way in which people work, but the way in which the organisation structures itself. On the one hand organisations may have adopted production line processes or automation, or may have passed through this phase and have reconfigured along the lines of semi-autonomous work groups. At the same time, other organisations have been slow to respond to the long-term benefits of incorporating information technology within their structure. Over the past few decades we have seen entire departments or at least offices, disappear as copy typists have been replaced by photocopiers and secretaries have been supplanted by word processors. It is certainly true to say that in many organisations there has been a move away from specialisation in the non-manual areas of the organisation to a more multiskilled approach. Not only does this make the individual employee far more valuable to the organisation, but it means that they can be moved from one division or department to another with only a change in type rather than nature of work. Whether this can be fully implemented as far as the manual workers are concerned may very much depend upon the nature of the work involved.

Traditional or static cultures which form an effective short-term resistance to change are becoming less common. Most organisations are dynamic in their very nature, but whether this is as a result of management's viewpoints or intentions or whether it is a reality across the organisation as a whole is the subject of some conjecture. Organisations need to be able to respond to change instantly without causing massive disruption to their operations. Many are able to do this, and as a result can exploit the opportunities which are presented to them. Above all, there needs to be a culture within the organisation which embraces change as an inevitable and welcome aspect of its existence.

Classification of change control systems

The management of change cannot be approached in a rigid or systematic manner. The very nature of change means that there are blurred boundaries in relation to the change itself and to the parts of the organisation which it may affect. To this end, theorists have tended to borrow from a number of different disciplines and traditions in their attempts to classify and explain the theoretical nature of the management of change.

Schools of thought on learning and change

Individual perspectives

The first major approach that we should investigate is the *individual perspective school*, which is further sub-divided into the *behaviourists* and the *psychologists*. The behaviourists consider the management of change from the perspective of an individual's interaction with the environment. The psychologists, on the other hand, or more precisely the *Gestalt–Field* psychologists, state that the environment is merely a reflection of an individual's behaviour. Perhaps the most well-known behaviourist was Pavlov, who you may know did much experimentation which involved bells and dogs. Following his suggestions, behaviourists state that individuals are conditioned by the expected consequences of particular actions or sets of circumstances. By behaving in a particular way, the employee receives a reward. They will have a tendency to repeat this behaviour in order to receive the reward again. Any actions which do not receive the reward are avoided. Following this line of thought, we can then see that from the behaviourist's perspective, if the organisation changes the conditions under which rewards are given, the employees will accept and respond positively to the change. There is a suggestion that rewards need to be immediate and this will simply reinforce the preferred behaviour patterns.

The Gestalt–Field theorists see learning as a process of gaining or changing the way in which people behave. Behaviour arises out of an individual's ability to interpret a range of stimuli, therefore organisations which adopt this approach will strive to assist their employees to understand the reasons behind change and the circumstances which have forced the change.

Human relations

We can see that by combining both the behaviourist and Gestalt–Field approaches, we reach the *human relations school* perspective. This is typified by the work of Maslow, who stresses the importance of both internal and external motivators in adapting human behaviour and motivation.

Group dynamics

Schein, Bernstein and Lewin are all members of the *group dynamics school*, who believe that organisational change is best achieved through teamwork and groups. They stress that it is important for an individual employee to see and take on board the way in which their peers are responding to change in order to adopt a common set of norms. The group will exert pressures on each individual member and will attempt to normalise behaviour and approach. Groups are in a continual state of adaptation and never reach a stage or state of equilibrium. It is norms that form the backbone of this approach, by adopting either implicit or explicit norms, the individual becomes aware of their role within the organisation.

As far as roles themselves are concerned, they are seen as patterns of behaviour to which each individual is expected to conform. These are normally defined in terms of targets or, perhaps, job descriptions. Roles need to be very clearly defined and also compatible in terms of their relationship to the rest of the group and to the broader organisation. The organisation will espouse certain values, perhaps from their mission statement, or less implicitly as part of the corporate culture. These, in effect, tell the individual what is right and what is wrong. If for no other reason than the fact that this school offers organisations the opportunity to realise that their employees are not just individuals but are members of a variety of different groups, we can find that this approach to theory and practice is fairly useful and applicable in a number of circumstances.

Open systems

The *open systems school* sees most organisations as being a collection of inter-connected and interdependent sub-systems. In this way we can see that any change in a particular sub-system will have an impact on the rest of the system. The focus of the open systems school is on how these sub-systems work, what needs to be changed in order to improve performance and what net effect change will have on the overall operations of the organisation.

Broadly speaking, organisations are seen as open systems. Naturally they react to the external environment, but also, more crucially, they react and interact with each of the sub-systems that make up their constituent parts. These sub-systems need to be co-ordinated as they are interdependent. Without this the organisation will find it impossible to reach its business objectives. As a result, the organisation strives for synergy and is not overly concerned with the specific performance of each and every sub-system.

Models for the management of change

Just as there are a number of different theoretical approaches to the management of change, there are likewise many more models which can be adopted to manage change. *Organisation development*, which is a system-wide application of behavioural science to the development of an organisation, is the wellspring of many of these different models. Effectively, there are three main approaches, these are:

1 The action research model.

2 The three-step model.

3 The planned phase change model.

Action research

Action research proposes that the most effective way of solving an organisational problem is to make a systematic and rational analysis of all of the criteria and circumstances involved. This means that all information and ideas from each and every group or stakeholder are taken into account and used to propose a solution to the problem. In effect, any attempt to make a change in the organisation is a learning process. By involving itself in change, and investigating it as changes are made, means that the organisation has been carrying out action research.

In any action research project there are usually three main groups:

1 The *organisation* itself, usually in the guise of a senior manager.

2 The *subject of the change*, being the individuals in relation to whom the change is to take place.

3 The *change agent*, who is usually not a member of the organisation but has probably been brought in as a consultant.

The main point of the exercise initially is to enable all three groups to agree common terms of reference before any of the processes can begin. Once this has been achieved, data is gathered and analysed on a participative basis. Each group will have their own viewpoint and stance which needs to be taken into consideration. Once the data has been analysed, a proposal can be created and then implemented and evaluated. The process very much depends upon correctly analysing the situation, as well as identifying all of the possible alternatives which may be adopted under the circumstances. One of the major problems with this approach is that over-analysis can mean a lack of response and considerable amount of time wasted on attempting to judge and evaluate each probable alternative. There needs to be considerable co-operation throughout the whole process and although this is essentially a top-down process, close relationships need to be established between each of the three groups. Action research is still considered to be one of the primary means by which effective change can be imposed upon an organisation.

The three-step model

The three-step model begins with the assumption that most changes are short-lived. In other words, any changes which are made to the organisation which are not subsequently reinforced will tend to slip back into previous modes of behaviour and levels of performance. This means that it is essential for the organisation to firmly establish the new conditions of change in such a way that they are fully incorporated into the policies, procedures and operations of the organisation. The three-step model specifically refers to the following:

◆ *Step 1* – the need to *unfreeze* the present way in which things are done

◆ *Step 2* – the need to then *move on to a new level* or set of policies and procedures

◆ *Step 3* – the need to *refreeze* so that all of the changes have been incorporated into the system.

Any change from one set of behaviour to another will involve the development of new values, behaviours and attitudes, both within the organisational structure and in the business's processes. If these have not been developed then there will be a tendency for the organisation to revert to its previous form. This new state of equilibrium incorporating all of the changes should stop the organisation from regressing back to the former status quo.

Planned phases of change

These models may appear to be rather basic and obvious in their attempts to establish a logical way in which we can approach change and the process of change management. Perhaps one of the more useful developments is that of Bullock and Batten who suggested that there are four main planned change phases:

1 The *exploration* phase, which is, in effect, an opportunity for the organisation to decide what changes need to be made and what level of resources they are

going to give to these changes. This also means that the organisation has to be aware that change needs to happen, that it needs to look for assistance to help with the change, and to establish a series of criteria which relate to the relationship between the organisation and any external consultant that may become involved.

2 The *planning* phase, which involves the organisation in the careful consideration of the nature of the problem. This means that the organisation has to begin the gradual process of collecting data and then diagnosing the problem itself. They will also have to establish goals and actions attributable to named decision-makers who can not only support but approve the proposed changes.

3 The *action* phase, which involves the organisation in actually implementing the change itself. This will enable the organisation to move away from its current status quo to a new structure which takes into account all of the necessary support mechanisms that need to be in place to achieve this. In addition, the organisation will begin to evaluate the impact of the change so that it can make the necessary amendments.

4 The *integration* phase, which occurs directly after the changes have been implemented. This phase is primarily concerned with stabilising the new changes so that they become part of the organisation's accepted set of norms and values. This will inevitably entail the retraining or redeployment of individuals in order to compensate for the changes.

The management of organisational change through structures

Organisational states

It may seem readily apparent that an organisation can be in any one of three structural states – the *current* state, the *future* or *proposed* state or the *transition* state. It is this transition state that can often determine whether the organisation is capable of making the changes required in order to reach its desired future structure. Given that the organisation will need to determine all major tasks and activities during the transition period, it will also have to clearly identify the proposed structures and management mechanisms required to carry out those tasks and activities.

The organisation will be able to identify clear structural objectives, such as the full integration of new technology, a change in the production process or the physical move to new premises. All of these will involve considerable structural change. Whether the organisation can actually identify the management structure or style required to adequately control the new structure is one thing, but it also needs to have structures and approaches in place to manage that transition to the new state.

Planning for transition

Activity planning is a key way in which operations can be handled, or at least considered, during the transition period. To begin with, individuals will have to be given specific roles and responsibilities in relation to the transition. In addition to this, there will have to be clear lines of communication established which facilitate all necessary information being passed down to those who need to be kept in touch with developments. As with any form of change, a number of criteria need to be addressed and met:

◆ all activities must be clearly linked to the change, goals and priorities. In other words, someone must identify anything relevant that is happening.

◆ all activities need to be clearly identified and specifically defined rather than looking at broad generalisations.

◆ all activities need to be considered as being integrated with one another, as decisions or changes in one area will affect other parts of the organisation and these effects need to be taken into account.

◆ all activities need to be prioritised and placed in a clear chronological order so that the organisation can make the changes in a logical set of sequences.

◆ all activities need to be adaptable so that contingency plans can be brought into operation if there is some need for adjustment as a result of unexpected resistance or problems within the predetermined sequence of events.

In order to ensure that the management of change is carried out in an efficient and effective manner, there needs to be a number or series of sub-systems in place to manage and monitor the impact of change as it happens. These relate to:

◆ the senior management being fully aware of the implications of each stage of the change.

◆ specific managers being given responsibility of co-ordinating certain aspects of the change.

◆ coping immediately with the negative effects of change and perhaps the implementation of a contingency plan in order to compensate.

◆ retraining or redeployment of individuals so that old operating procedures are adapted or eliminated at the correct point.

◆ staff functions to support the implementation of the change, with some kind of understanding of future adaptation plans.

◆ the establishment of specific project teams and systems whose existence is temporary and related directly to particular aspects of phases of the change.

For the change process to move forward at a steady pace, the organisation will have to have established either a totally new structure or at least an effective change management system. There are a number of ways in which the change process can begin, which do not necessarily affect all parts of the organisation simultaneously. These include:

◆ intervention across the board where individuals from each part of the organisation have an input into the planning process and implementation of management systems.

◆ the establishment of a pilot system in one specific area of the organisation which is then closely examined to see and assess probable impacts on the organisation in general.

◆ a series of short-term experiments to see whether the impact of change has a positive or negative affect on a particular area of the organisation over a short period of time.

◆ the creation of temporary management structures to see how particular individuals fit into new proposed roles.

The more stable an organisation is, the more likely it is to find change difficult. To this end, it is common for these organisations to establish temporary systems for the implementation of change. The vast majority of successful transitions from one organisational structure to another involves the organisation in finding new ways in which to handle problems and radically overhauling existing mechanisms which are used for handling day-to-day activities.

Perhaps one of the first things that most organisations will need to do is to carry out a planning exercise, or to institute a comprehensive management training programme. While both of these are perfectly acceptable in terms of preparing the organisation for proposed changes, they are only really addressing small parts of the organisation and are relatively ineffective.

During the transition state from past structure to future structure, we will find certain individuals within the organisation who are operating in all three states. This may cause considerable confusion as different parts of the organisation begin to adopt new working practices or adapt to new structures. The working relationships between individuals who are at different stages of change will be strained and they will not be as capable of coping with immediate problems as they would have been in a stable set of circumstances. The organisation needs to identify a change management system and, indeed, a transition state that will cause the least amount of tension as it moves between ongoing systems and structures; from the past to the future .

Management skills

In order to have an effective transition between one structure, which is still operating, a temporary structure, which is capable of coping with operations and change, and a future structure, which is beginning to operate in its new configuration, the organisation will need to have capable managers who have at least the following skills:

◆ power and authority to keep the changes moving and allocate resources as and when necessary.

◆ respect as leader from the majority of people in the organisation so that decisions made can be seen in the light of more broad requirements than strictly those related to a particular area.

◆ the ability to communicate with all levels of the hierarchy on a persuasive basis rather than using their formal authority derived from their position.

Changing attitudes

There has certainly been considerable movement away from organisational structures which are typified by multi-tiers of hierarchy. Since organisations are striving to become customer-centred, they need to be responsive to a number of different markets and customer types, rather than relying on the more traditional functional approach. This has meant that organisations have tended to become flatter with considerable interdependence between their various parts. Coupled with this, there has been a period of devolvement in terms of power and authority, enabling middle managers in particular to make important decisions without having to seek permission or authority from those higher up in the hierarchy.

Organisations have also begun to realise that they need to consider different parts of themselves as 'customers'. In response to this, many have adopted a network approach, where the organisation is really just a loose confederation of operations, who co-operate with one another and support each others' activities. This has meant that all bureaucratic structures have been swept away and replaced with something far more flexible. In addition, there have been the challenges of moving into new markets, with radically different needs. Rather than replicating existing structures, they have had to create new structures which specifically address the needs of these new markets. If we add the further complication of coping with the implementation of technological change, we can see that most revised organisational structures mirror the need to be far more adaptable, rather than relying on direction from the upper tiers of the hierarchy. Given the fact that the majority of organisations now are driven from the bottom of the hierarchy, rather than the top, we can see that those at the sharp end of the operations are appreciated for having as much to offer the organisation as those who have a strategic perspective.

Review questions

1 Explain why, when responding to change, it is a distinct advantage to be 'forward looking'.

2 What is 'turbulence' and what impact does it have on organisations?

3 Describe the approach of the individual perspective school to the management of change.

4 What is the 'open systems' school?

5 Describe the following:

(a) the action research model

(b) the three-step model

(c) the planned phase change model

6 What is meant by the term 'transition structure'?

7 List the criteria which should be considered when an organisation is activity planning.

8 Identify four subsystems that should be in place to help manage and monitor the impact of change on an organisation.

9 What skills would a manager need to possess to ensure an effective transition from one structure to another?

10 How could the realisation that individuals and departments within the organisation are customers affect an organisation?

11 'Technological change has had a dramatic affect on the way organisations structure themselves'. Discuss.

12 Identify and explain the probable sources of change that would face an independent high street retailer.

Section 3

COMMUNICATING IN ORGANISATIONS

After reading this section you should be able to:

◆ evaluate the effectiveness of different communication systems.

◆ identify and evaluate relationships between organisation type and communication systems.

◆ examine and evaluate the impact and implications of technology on communication and administrative systems.

◆ communicate through formal and informal channels using a variety of appropriate media.

◆ make recommendations for improved organisational communication.

Models, forms and channels of communication

One of the key objectives of all organisations is successful communication both within the business and with customers and clients. Sometimes people may consider themselves to be good communicators when they are not. In any organisation with a large number of employees, communication problems will be encountered if the correct systems are not in place to monitor the information provided. Should these systems prove to be inefficient, then gaps occur between instruction and action which can be costly. With this in mind, much research has been carried out to try to analyse the problems that can be encountered if poor communication systems are in place, and to identify how they can be improved.

In this section we look at the objectives of communication, both internal and external. We will also consider a number of common measures to evaluate the impact that communication systems have on specific businesses:

◆ accuracy of the system

◆ whether the system creates efficiency

◆ whether, in relation to alternative methods of communication, the system used is cost effective

◆ whether the system is secure against unauthorised access.

 ## Models of communication

In order for effective communication to take place, the sender must be able to transmit the various facts, opinions, feelings and attitudes to the receiver in such a way that they can be understood and interpreted appropriately. The various stages of transmitting a message are shown in Fig. 3.1. There are a great many factors that can lead individuals to receive inaccurate information or have the wrong perceptions.

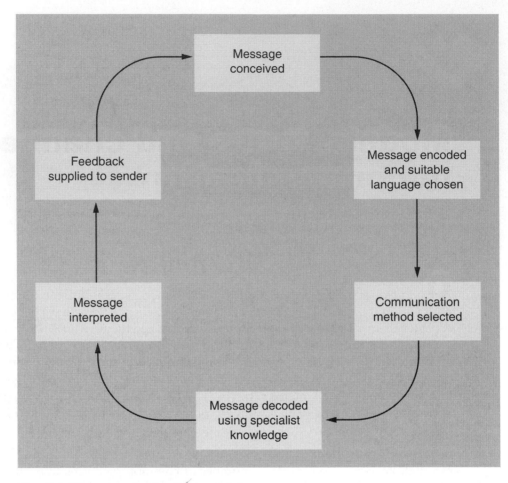

Fig. 3.1 The communication model

Interplay of sender and receiver

Any form of interpersonal communication involves an exchange between a sender and a receiver. These roles change and shift according to the nature of the communication process and the number of individuals involved. The characteristics of the sender and the receiver will have a marked impact on the communication process. The sender, for example, may have certain goals in mind as they communicate with the receiver. They may change the meaning and the balance of a message that they have received before passing it on to another individual. This is very likely if the sender has a particular opinion or attitude that they wish to express as an integral part of the communication. On the other hand, the receiver may have their own agenda which will cause them to misinterpret the message or place a different emphasis upon it. Both of these sets of circumstances may mean that the communication is distorted in some way and it is only when there are no vested interests that truly accurate communication can take place.

In the vast majority of models there will be references to transmitters and receptors, which refer to the means available for sending and receiving the messages. In effect, these are the *media* available to the individuals involved in the communication. Given the fact that all communications are restricted to a combination of the senses (see, hear, touch, smell and taste) there are only a limited number of possibilities.

What's in a message?

Messages include the data that is transmitted, and the coded symbols that are an integral part of the message are designed to give particular meaning to the message. The sender will hope that any message sent will be understood by the receiver in as close a possible way to the original (or intended) meaning. The channels, as we shall see, are simply the means by which the messages are transmitted. These would include common business methods such as the telephone, the memorandum and the report.

The other key aspect is 'noise'. This refers to the probable interference that may inhibit the message getting to the receiver in a clear manner. The normal response to this would be to either try to cut out as much of the noise as possible, to communicate in such a way as to make the noise less intrusive, or simply to repeat the message until it gets through. This noise can refer to any number of circumstances or sets of conditions that can interfere with the message.

The sender attempts to transmit the message through a selected channel to the receiver's receptors. As we have already noted, these are the senses: the only way that the receiver can accept and respond to the message. The sender will need to encode the message in such a way that it can be readily understood by the receiver or, perhaps, in a specialised manner so that only a selected number of receivers can understand it. This may be particularly useful if the sender only intends that a specific number or type of individuals understand the message.

Once an individual has received the message, it may need to be decoded. Through a shared language individuals are able to decode messages more accurately, leaving less chance for misunderstandings. The accuracy of interpersonal communication is evaluated in relation to the ideal state, the sender's intended meanings are the same as the interpreted meanings of the receiver.

As we will see, the initial communication between a sender and a receiver is only the first stage of the process. The receiver may then become the sender, giving feedback in response to the original message. Feedback enables the sender to double-check that the message was fully understood and the receiver's response is in line with what was expected. The communication system should be considered as a dynamic, two-way process.

Management models of communication

The role of any manager within an organisation will inevitably involve many communication responsibilities. These often take the form of more personal qualities, as communicating well is one quality that can make or break a manager. A manager who is a good communicator will be far more likely to achieve set objectives than one who does not communicate so well.

Providing information, either to their own line manager or to their subordinates will be a key function of a manager within any organisation, regardless of its size or function.

A manager may need to provide information in order to:

◆ assist their team to make a decision.

◆ help their team solve a problem.

◆ delegate some responsibility to another member of their team.

◆ motivate their team.

◆ inform their line manager of developments.

◆ supply feedback to a group of managers at their regular meeting.

In some of these situations a manager may not experience any communication problems. Alternatively, others may lead to a degree of stress or tension. With regard to the provision of information in *external* communications, then, the content of the communication will differ, but the same standards apply.

Whether the communication is internal or external to the organisation, there are some common factors to consider, including:

◆ What is the best means of getting the message across?

◆ Is this the best time to put this information over?

◆ Think about the way the information is going to be provided – it may be that verbal communication would be the best channel, but with this method there is no record of what has been said. Alternatively, lots of graphs and numbers can be boring and the impact can be lost.

◆ Is information technology necessary to provide the information? Before the information is passed on it should be remembered that electronic technology is very quick. Once the message has been sent, then it is almost always irretrievable.

◆ Is there a requirement to give any feedback from the provision of this information? If so, how and what is the best way of requesting this?

Another objective of communication is to give instruction to subordinates or fellow team members. Several methods of communication can be used here, but we will specifically deal with the *verbal* method. When talking to another member of staff in order to give their instructions relating to a specific project or task, it is important to remember the following (*see also* Fig. 3.2):

◆ ensure that the instructions are clear.

◆ take each stage step-by-step.

◆ make sure that any relevant written documentation relating to the instruction is to hand as this will be useful to clarify relatively complex points.

◆ give clear instruction regarding any deadlines involved.

◆ give the recipient the opportunity to ask questions about the instruction.

◆ ensure that the recipient knows that they can come back for further information if necessary.

◆ ensure that the recipient knows who else to contact should they require additional help or information.

◆ try to make the recipient aware of the reason for the task or project so that they know why they have been asked to do something.

◆ allow the recipient to provide some form of feedback about the carrying out of the instruction.

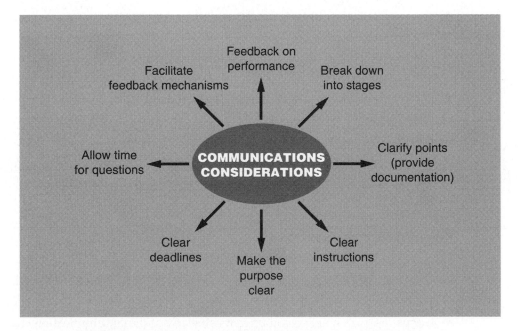

Fig. 3.2 Communications considerations within an organisation

Keeping employees up-to-date on the objectives and activities of the business is vital if they are to remain well motivated and informed. Without access to this important information, employees themselves become poor communicators. It has been proved that if people lack knowledge about the organisation as a whole they may lack effective communication skills.

Over a period of 50 years, all types of organisation have grown enormously. This, in part, has been due to the technological developments that have taken place simultaneously. Some organisations have up to 10 000 employees working on one site. In such a situation there is a particular need for effective communications so that people feel they are being kept fully up to date with the objectives and aims of the organisation; otherwise individuals may lack a sense of belonging, commitment and fulfilment.

Quality checks on communication systems

Making regular checks on the standard and quality of the communication channels open to the organisation should be of prime importance. In addition to checking the success or otherwise of the communication processes themselves, the organisation can use communication methods to ensure that:

◆ employees are receiving correct information and instructions.

◆ employees are being kept up-to-date.

◆ employees are being given the opportunity to give feedback.

◆ the administrative systems in place within the organisation are working successfully.

◆ any possible changes to the administrative systems are carried out quickly and efficiently to the best effect.

◆ customers are happy with the quality, standard, delivery and transportation of the goods or services.

◆ the after-sales service is being provided to its best effect.

Such checks on communication processes and administrative systems should not be carried out on a one-off basis; they should be systematically approached on a regular basis.

Feedback mechanisms

One of the main objectives of any communication system in an organisation should be to facilitate feedback from employees and customers. Feedback comes in several forms:

◆ from a message which could be sent using any of the communication channels.

◆ from instructions given or information provided.

◆ from customers as to the service being provided or the goods being produced.

Unless feedback is provided promptly and unambiguously, then the communication process is likely to be frustrated and inefficient. When a message is sent, the recipient, however busy they may be at the time, should take steps to provide feedback to the sender of the message. This feedback may simply be a reply to say that the message has been received and is being dealt with. Alternatively, when written communication is involved, this may take the form of a written acknowledgement to say that their letter, memorandum or complaint is being dealt with.

In, say, the giving of oral instructions or the provision of information, some kind of feedback is necessary to ensure that the recipient has understood what is being said or asked of them. This feedback can sometimes be just a 'yes' or a nod of the head. For the speaker, it is important to ensure that they do not feel they are talking to an empty room.

Feedback from any form of communication helps to cement the understanding of the recipient and to allow the sender of the message to feel secure that they have provided the correct information and that it will be dealt with.

Negotiation and communication

Negotiation, whatever the topic of conversation, is a very important element of the communication system for all organisations and is a crucial management skill. Good skills in negotiation require the manager to secure the desired outcomes for the organisation by ensuring that the others within the organisation accept what is being said.

If negotiations have been successful, then both parties in the process will feel they have achieved what they set out to do. It is fair to say that negotiation processes tend to work through the same stages, regardless of the topic of negotiation. These stages are:

◆ *Stage one* – when both parties in the negotiation process prepare themselves for what they consider to be the ideal outcome.

◆ *Stage two* – when both parties tend to 'test one another' with their proposed outcomes.

◆ *Stage three* – when the non-contentious parts of the negotiation are decided. This helps to establish goodwill.

◆ *Stage four* – some 'trading-off' takes place. By this we mean that either party may concede on small points that are not really important to them in order to gain some advantage over the other party.

◆ *Stage five* – when, due to the comments and decisions made by the other party, the good negotiator will spot a favourable balance.

Good negotiation skills include:

◆ the ability to decide in advance what is the worst acceptance point and when negotiations should be called off.

◆ knowing what parts of the package they are prepared to give up.

◆ having good knowledge of the views of the other party.

◆ knowing when they have asked for enough and should stop.

◆ ensuring that all agreed conditions, concessions and undertakings have been taken note of and recorded (this may be in the form of minutes of meeting).

◆ trying to ensure that the other party does not feel they have lost face.

The role of confirmation

Confirmation in verbal communication can literally just mean a nod of the head or saying the word 'yes'. Alternatively, it can mean a telephone call to confirm receipt of a message or goods. In written communication, it can mean a letter sent to an organisation to confirm an order or the receipt of goods. It can also mean a letter to a hotel to confirm accommodation arrangements made over the telephone, or to a travel agent confirming flight bookings.

It is always good practice to respond to any communication. The recipient is more likely to then go on to deal with the communication and it gives the sender peace of mind that the communication is being acted upon.

Personal communication skills

Central to the efficient running of any organisation is the clear and effective channelling of all communications. It is a fundamental requirement of all those in a position of authority, and some who are not, to be able to communicate in a clear and effective manner. To be a good manager or administrator, an individual will need to spend a great deal of time communicating with others, as communication is, of course, a two-way process.

To be a good communicator takes practice and experience. It does not matter who you communicate with – it could be colleagues, customers or suppliers, they will judge you by what you say and how you say it, so it is important to be aware of the following points about what the communicator should and should not do:

◆ the communicator should always speak clearly.

◆ the communicator should try not to speak too quickly or too slowly.

◆ the communicator should demonstrate an awareness of their audience by using appropriate words for different situations and not be either too complicated or simplistic.

◆ the communicator should be able to listen to what the other person is saying so that they can respond accordingly.

◆ the communicator should show confidence; both in themselves and in what they say.

◆ the communicator should try to put the other person at ease.

◆ the communicator should think about what they say and try to make their responses logical and easy to follow.

◆ the communicator should try to use the right tone for the situation and not be too aggressive or passive, or allow their feelings to confuse what it is they have to say.

◆ if the communicator has a regional accent, while this is fine in most situations, if it is particularly strong or broad they may find it helpful to talk slightly more slowly than usual.

◆ if the communicator thinks that their voice is not pleasant to listen to, being perhaps too high, they should try to lower the pitch a little.

◆ the communicator should never interrupt someone who is speaking and should wait until they have finished.

◆ the communicator should take care to use the right tone of voice, as this can affect how the other person receives what is said. The same statement may be either acceptable or unacceptable, depending on the tone.

It is important to identify the main channels of communication and look at their purposes within the organisation.

◆ Internal communication channels

The way in which an organisation is structured will determine the channels through which communication is made. There is a definite relationship to be identified in terms of an individual's position, authority and status within an organisation. Depending on these factors, an individual will be more receptive and accessible by the establishment of an effective communications system. Information needs to flow freely around the organisation. In a small business, it is easy for everyone to know exactly what is going on, but in larger organisations the flow of information may be awkward and disrupted at various points. Indeed, certain individuals within the organisation will impose barriers to communication to avoid information overload. They will not be interested in or able to handle the sheer volume of information and will have nominated other individuals to perform monitoring tasks on their behalf.

In order to determine how effective the channels of communication are within an organisation, we must look at whether the right information has reached the right person at the right time. If there are any barriers that prevent this from happening then they must be overcome in order to increase the effectiveness of that individual. The way in which an organisation is structured will often determine how hard or easy it is to get the information through to the right person. Organisations may consider fundamental changes in their structure if these barriers appear to be insurmountable.

Once the information has reached the correct person, it must be in such a format as to allow that individual immediate understanding. If the information is unclear, misleading or ambiguous in any way, then the channels of communication, however good they are, have been wasted.

Many basic forms of communication are applicable to both internal and external situations. The skills of communication are similar whether one is dealing with colleagues or customers. The different needs of these two groups may determine the exact style of the communication. Internal communications can very often be dealt with in an informal manner. We shall look at the various forms of internal communication in turn a little later in this section, but first let us look in more detail at communication in general.

Different ways of communicating

The five main modes of communication are:

1 Listening.

2 Speaking.

3 Reading.

4 Writing.

5 Information technology.

In addition, we must also consider communication that is carried out using none of the above. This is known as non-verbal communication or body language. Let us look at these methods in a little more detail.

Listening

During the course of a day we may listen to a number of different people, but it is a rare person who will remember everything that has been said to them. This is particularly the case if the way in which conversation is listened to is unstructured and confused. In order to use listening as effectively as possible, the individual must:

◆ actually hear the message itself.

◆ interpret the message.

◆ evaluate the message.

◆ act upon the message and make use of the information it contains.

It is often a good idea to take notes during a conversation. Some people find it very helpful to use a tape recorder.

Speaking

Speaking need not necessarily take place face to face. It may also take the form of a telephone conversation. The use of questioning techniques is important in clarifying the exact nature of the message. To be effective the individual should have the following qualities:

◆ clearly know their own role in the conversation.

◆ be aware of the receptiveness and interest of those listening.

◆ in some cases, be aware of the listener's own knowledge of the subject of the conversation.

Being an effective communicator means making sure that the listener is always attentive and that any points raised within the conversation are not ambiguous.

Reading and writing

We have chosen to take these two skills together since the writer of the message must be acutely aware of how the message will be received by the reader. To be an effective writer an individual must take the following points into account:

◆ the information will be read by a variety of people in different situations.

◆ complex information needs to have sufficient background description in order to make it clear.

◆ information should be capable of having a long life, in the sense that it may be referred to many times in the future.

As with many other forms of communication, the written word may suffer from being ambiguous. Even the most informal of messages needs to be clear. Organisations will often use standard formats for written communication, which have been designed to avoid ambiguity. Certain forms of written communication can be easier to understand than others, but the writer should ensure that the reader always has sufficient information in order to form an opinion if required. The presentation of data, for example, should be carefully considered since financial information in particular can often be misleading or unclear.

Information technology

Information technology has transformed the way in which much information is processed, handled and distributed. The availability of computer facilities throughout organisations has meant that information can be relayed quickly and effectively. This is, of course, vital to the success of a business, but does require that individuals within the organisation be sufficiently trained on many different computer software packages.

Non-verbal communication

As we will see, not all messages rely on the spoken or written word. We can 'read' a great deal into the way in which someone uses their body to convey information. Each gesture or facial expression may have its own particular meaning. Being able to read these gestures and expressions is a skill in itself, not to mention being able to use these gestures and expressions yourself. An individual may use non-verbal communication (NVC) or body language in order to support or clarify the message they are giving or receiving.

We all send and receive non-verbal communication. It is important to know how you can read other people's non-verbal communication. Let's start with the face and what that can give away about what you are really saying:

◆ raising the eyebrows *could* show surprise or disbelief.

◆ if your pupils dilate, this *could* mean either anger or love.

◆ opening your eyes wide *might* show hostility.

◆ grinning *could* show that you accept what is being said or are simply friendly.

Gestures, on the other hand, can also give interesting clues as to what the speaker really means:

◆ pointing, to identify someone or something directly when referring to it.

◆ giving a thumbs-up sign, to signify agreement or acceptance.

◆ shaking your head, to show disagreement.

◆ fiddling with something, such as jewellery, a tie or the strap of a bag may indicate nervousness.

◆ pacing up and down may show impatience or boredom.

◆ looking at your hands, or fiddling with something, may show disinterest.

Posture shows some interesting things too:

◆ standing upright may be a sign of alertness.

◆ sitting in a hunched position indicates nervousness.

◆ lounging in a chair, on the other hand, shows ease – or possibly tiredness.

◆ standing with your shoulders hunched shows that you may be miserable or depressed.

Whether you stand or sit, in relation to the person you are talking to, can show some important things:

◆ you are likely to stand closer to a person whom you know well.

◆ where you stand, and how close to a person, may depend upon your nationality or upbringing.

◆ the nature of the circumstances in which you met the person to whom you are talking will have an effect on how close you stand to that person.

Common forms of internal communication

It is appropriate that we briefly consider some of the more common forms of communication, although these will be covered in more detail as an integral part of one of the communication-based modules that you will be studying.

Internal memoranda

Internal memoranda are used for communicating between different departments within the same organisation. These are often called *memos*. They are normally shorter than a business letter and usually deal with one particular subject. When more than one point is being made it is normal to number them. Memos are not signed in the same way as a business letter, but the person issuing the memo would normally initial it at the end.

Reports

Although reports issued or received by an organisation can be either informal or very formal, both types contain certain common elements, although not necessarily in the same format.

A report may contain research findings and recommendations, or it may be an account of something which has taken place.

A report may contain the following headings or sections:

◆ *terms of reference* – what the report is about, for example it may be about research on a particular topic.

◆ *procedures* – how the information has been gathered.

◆ *findings* – a statement of facts.

◆ *conclusion* – a general statement summarising the findings.

◆ *recommendations* – for future research or projects, based on the findings and conclusion.

◆ *appendices and bibliography* – listing further helpful sources of information.

It is usual to sign and date a report. Sometimes it is helpful to break down the headings used in a report. This could be done by using a series of numbers, for example:

1   Establishment of company catering facilities

    (a)   Lunch period arrangements

        (i)   Arrangements of seating

Summarising

It may be that during the course of your work you will be asked to use the written form of communication called *summarising*. This means that you are given a long article or report and have to read it and present the information more briefly. The original document may be long and complicated, so it is necessary that you understand the information you read before you start. You would then identify the most important aspects and write a shorter piece. The following are guidelines for carrying out this task:

◆ Read through the whole document first, rather than trying to understand everything as you go through.

◆ Read the document again, more thoroughly. You could highlight the areas of importance at this stage, or cross out the unnecessary information.

◆ Make a list of the items you have to use and that are important to include.

◆ Compare your list with the main document to make sure you have not forgotten anything important.

◆ Write a draft summary. It may be that a manager should check this for you at this stage. Once you are happy with this draft, you may want to write a final draft.

◆ Once the draft has been agreed, you can write the final summary.

Projects

Just as you write up projects for your course, so you may be asked by your employer to write up a project for them. If this task is new to you, it may be useful to look at some of the guidelines for completing projects:

◆ Find out the date for completion of the project. Allow yourself plenty of time to research and write up the information.

◆ Find out exactly what is required of you. How long does the project have to be? How many pages of typing or writing are expected? Is there a limit to the number of words submitted?

◆ Do you have to submit the project in a certain format? Are there set headings you are expected to use?

◆ Where will you find the information you need? Make a list of the sources of information you will need to use. Many other organisations offer assistance in project work. It will obviously depend on the type of research you are carrying out.

Papers and briefs

Papers and briefs take the form of additional information provided by individuals to assist decision makers. In other words, their key function is to enable others to make the right decision. These documents will include essential background information on a subject, usually written by an individual with a particular interest or experience in this area. A discussion document also gives essential background material, but in addition offers advice as to the decision which should be made. These documents will usually include a series of arguments for and against a particular course of action and these must be considered in the process of arriving at a preferred conclusion.

Notes

Notes are short, often informal, forms of communication which may be hand-written. Under this heading, we may include telephone messages, informal arrangements and details of informal short meetings.

Messages

If an organisation wishes to pass a message on to a number of employees, it may place information on its staff noticeboards. These messages may be formal or informal. Perhaps there is a change to normal organisational procedures, or maybe a social event is being planned by the organisation's personnel department.

Notices

Notices allow the quick and easy sending of information to a large number of people, although there is no guarantee that the information will be read. Notice-boards can also be used by individuals wishing to inform employees of items for sale or events planned.

Newsletters

Another way that an organisation can inform all its employees about matters of interest is by issuing a newsletter. Several larger organisations use newsletters to contact all members of staff, particularly where they have branches in different places. These newsletters can include both formal and informal information. They may state that a director is retiring, or that one of the sales assistants has recently given birth to a baby.

Meetings

The success of a meeting will be largely determined by the way in which it has been organised in advance. The document that is used to inform those who are to attend a meeting about the nature of that meeting is known as an *agenda*.

Essentially, an agenda has the following format:

◆ apologies for absence

◆ minutes of the last meeting

◆ matters arising from the minutes

◆ reports

◆ motions

◆ any other business

◆ date of next meeting.

A sample agenda is shown in Fig. 3.3.

CHEDISTON SOUTH SAFETY REPRESENTATIVES MEETING

A meeting of Safety Representatives will be held in the Conference Centre on Friday 23 June, 19XX at 09.30 am.

AGENDA

1   Apologies for absence.

2   Minutes of the last meeting.

3   Matters arising from the minutes.

4   Report from the Chief Safety Officer on recent legislation received on Health and Safety at Work procedures.

5   Consider implications of possible new extension to the office block.

6   Feedback report from those who recently attended the training sessions at Head Office

7   Any other business.

8   Date of next meeting.

SARAH BROWN
Secretary

Fig. 3.3 A sample agenda

Minutes are the records of meetings and include the following:

◆ an account of those present at the meeting

◆ decisions made

◆ discussions which have taken place

◆ tasks allocated to individuals

◆ reports received from individuals

◆ actions to be taken in the future

◆ details of individuals to whom decisions made refer.

It is the responsibility of an appointed individual (usually a secretary capable of taking shorthand) to record and prepare formal minutes. These are then typed and distributed to those present at the meeting, together with the agenda of the

CHEDISTON SOUTH SAFETY REPRESENTATIVES MEETING

A meeting of Safety Representatives was held in the Conference Centre on Friday 23 June, 19XX at 09.30.

Present Mr B Mills (in the Chair)
           Ms P Taylor
           Mr S Parsons
           Mr H Arfield
           Ms P Olivier
           Mr S Brenner

           Miss S Brown (Secretary)

1   APOLOGIES

Apologies were received from Mr P Kane who was attending the Safety Seminar at Head Office

2   MINUTES OF THE LAST MEETING

The Minutes of the previous meeting were read and signed as being a true record.

3   MATTERS ARISING

There were no matters arising from the previous minutes.

4   REPORT FROM THE CHIEF SAFETY OFFICER

Mr Mills reported that the recent Government legislation concerning Health and Safety at Work procedures would require some careful consideration.

The new procedures would be copied and distributed to all concerned. Mr Mills stated that he would like a sub-committee to be formed to study the legislation and report back at the next meeting.

Ms Taylor, Mr Brenner and Ms Olivier volunteered to form the sub-committee, and agreed to meet on Tuesday 27 June 19XX.

5   IMPLICATIONS OF POSSIBLE NEW EXTENSION TO THE OFFICE BLOCK

Ms Olivier reported that she had seen the plans for the new office block and was concerned that not enough space had been allocated to each member of staff using that block.

After some discussion it was decided that Mr Mills would speak to the architects and report his findings to the next meeting.

6   REPORT ON RECENT TRAINING SESSIONS

It was generally felt that the training sessions were of value, and that they should continue. Mr Kane was attending his session at the present time, and once Ms Olivier had attended, then all staff would have been involved. It was anticipated that these sessions would take place annually, and that all representatives should ensure they attend future sessions.

7   ANY OTHER BUSINESS

Mr Parsons reported that there had been some problems with the installation of the new PCs. The location of some of the machines had meant that wires were trailing in a dangerous way. Mr Parsons had dealt with this problem and all now seemed to be working well and safely.

8   DATE OF NEXT MEETING

The date of the next meeting was set for Friday 27 July 19XX at 09.30. The venue to be arranged

....
Signed

Fig. 3.4 Sample minutes from meeting of Chediston South Safety Representatives

next meeting. This is to ensure that a correct and true account has been made of the previous meeting and that it may be agreed in the next meeting that the minutes present an accurate account of what happened.

Although minutes should be concise and precise, they should not lose any accuracy in this process. The writing style required may seem short and abrupt and often a form of numerical recording is used against each minuted item (*see* the example presented in Fig. 3.4). The subsequent distribution of the minutes further assists those present by reminding them of decisions made and any actions which they personally have to take.

Certain organisations, local authorities in particular, must have their minutes available for public inspection. The details of any motions voted upon or amendments made to these motions must be clearly detailed in the minutes for public perusal.

External communication channels

Most business organisations spend a considerable amount of their time communicating with their customers. Some of this communication, as we have already seen, will take the form of face-to-face or verbal communication. However, it is essential that some of these communications are supported by written evidence of agreements made.

In our day-to-day life we use written communications, and it is just as important when writing a personal letter to a friend or a note to one of the family, as in business correspondence, that we ensure our spelling and grammar are correct. In all organisations, neat, accurate and reliable written communication is vitally important.

Organisations are often very concerned about how they are seen by people external to the organisation. The view that people have is often affected by the way in which information is presented to them by an organisation. The organisation must take care to ensure that its reputation is maintained at a high level in all the communication methods it uses.

Invitations

Informal and formal invitations may be sent or received by organisations. When these are being issued in bulk, they are normally printed by a specialist company and simply prepared for postage within the organisation. An invitation will usually contain the following information:

◆ the address of the person sending out the invitation

◆ the date of the invitation

◆ the names of the people acting as host/hostess at the event

◆ the date of the event

◆ the venue of the event

◆ the time of the event

◆ the reason for the event

◆ RSVP – this is a request for a reply and is taken from the French phrase *'répondez, s'il vous plaît'*. Sometimes a deadline for replies is also given.

Business letters

A business letter, unlike a memorandum, is one that would be sent outside the organisation. It is important that such letters are neat, accurate and well presented.

The headed paper used by the organisation for its business letters would form part of its *corporate image* and would give the information an organisation would wish each of its customers or clients to see regularly:

◆ the name and address of the organisation

◆ the telephone number, fax number and/or telex number of the organisation

◆ the registered address of the organisation, as this may be different from the postal address

◆ the company registration number

◆ the names of the directors of the organisation

◆ any other companies the organisation may represent or be affiliated to.

The layout or format of the business letter will usually also be part of the organisation's corporate image, and different organisations have their own rules about the way in which a letter should be displayed. It is common to use the fully blocked method of display which means that each part of the letter commences at the left-hand margin.

Letters of complaint

Organisations will, in their business activities, receive a number of complaints from their customers, or indeed suppliers. Many will express strong emotions, particularly if money is involved. It is important for the organisation to respond in a helpful and constructive manner. A good letter of complaint from the complainant's point of view should follow these guidelines:

◆ set out the facts clearly

◆ be relevant

◆ be polite

◆ state that the complainant requires a favourable response.

The organisation, in response to the letter of complaint, may have to write a letter of apology. This may involve the following, in addition to the apology:

◆ financial compensation

◆ an offer to replace the goods

◆ an undertaking that the situation will not arise again

◆ an undertaking that an individual within the organisation has been disciplined.

If the organisation discovers that the complaint is without justification then, in order to maintain goodwill, a token offer may be made nonetheless. Whatever the circumstances, justified or unjustified, letters relating to customer complaints should be carefully put together. They should always use restrained language, because even with the best will in the world an organisation is prone to errors and cannot really guarantee that something similar will not happen at some point in the future. All letters of complaint should be dealt with promptly but some may need enquiries to be undertaken before the complaint can be addressed.

Circulars, standard letters and direct mail

Circulars, standard letters and direct mail are often used for advertising purposes. Standard letters can also be used, for example, for inviting individuals to attend job interviews. These sorts of letters take the form of a basic word-processed letter which is merged, using computer software, with a datafile containing names and addresses. In other situations standard letters are not always personally addressed and they may simply refer to the 'occupier'. This is particularly true of circulars as many thousands of these may be distributed in a mailshot.

Circulars have three main goals:

1 To create an impact by using a striking headline or picture.

2 To encourage the reading of the letter by using the appropriate language or stating boldly that the individual will receive a free gift, for example.

3 To be memorable by using appropriate slogans in large type.

Direct mail serves similar purposes to standard letters, but the mailings are addressed specifically to the recipient.

References and testimonials

Many organisations are required at various times to provide references or testimonials for individuals. References are much more common and testimonials need not necessarily relate to an employee of an organisation.

References are often written on a standard form provided by a potential employer. In other cases, a letter can be written in relation to a number of guidelines laid down by the potential employer. These references are always written by an individual who has some knowledge of the applicant and will contain statements regarding that individual's abilities, character, quality and performance.

A testimonial is essentially a letter of commendation. It has not been written with a particular job in mind, but contains general information regarding the individual. Organisations may be asked to write testimonials for individuals who are not necessarily employees.

The writing of references and testimonials provides the organisation with some moral problems. A reference should be truthful as far as the organisation is aware. The organisation must be careful not to make defamatory statements which could harm the reputation of an individual. The writer needs to strike a balance between the truth and tact. In other words, when reading a reference, one should often look for what is not said. There is no legal obligation to provide a reference or a testimonial and much can be inferred from an employer choosing not to give a reference to an individual. It should be noted that employers must grant permission before their name and address be given to a potential employer. In some cases, a potential employer will contact a previous employer by telephone if a quick decision is needed.

Restricted and open communication channels

Whatever the type or size of an organisation, some information that is communicated within it will not be for general use or inspection. It is usual to restrict some channels of communication. Let us look at restricted and open channels separately.

Restricted channels of communication

Restricted channels of communication allow the organisation to keep the information in question available to only a selected few individuals. This information may include:

◆ *confidential material* – only those involved in the development will be entitled to view, for example, the list of materials involved in the production process.

◆ *employee files* – only the personnel department and possibly the line manager of the employee concerned will be allowed access to this information.

◆ *application forms* – only the personnel department and possibly the line manager of the post involved will be allowed access to this information.

◆ *management information systems* – can ensure that information goes to specified individuals only. This can contribute to the control, confidentiality and security of the information.

Open channels of communication

Open communication channels are those types of communication where everyone within the organisation is at liberty to see and be aware of the information involved. Examples of open communication channels are:

◆ noticeboards and newsletters.

◆ minutes of meetings which are circulated to all staff.

◆ non-confidential internal mail which is distributed openly.

◆ multi-user computer systems which offer significant advantages to an organisation in the case of non-restricted information. Access is via numerous terminals throughout the organisation.

In order to ensure that all employees are aware of the limitations of access to restricted information, confidential labels or sealed internal post envelopes will be used. If the organisation uses electronic systems for the communication of internal and external correspondence, then systems will be in place to ensure that monitors are not left switched on or displaying information while the employee is out of the office. Similarly, passwords and user codes will be used to restrict the access to information contained on disk within the computer system.

Administration systems

The operation of administration systems is vital since the activities of the organisation must be co-ordinated and planned. If inadequate administration systems are in operation then the organisation may suffer from a lack of efficiency and effectiveness since it does not have access to all relevant information. We must look at the various areas of business activity, and identify the main types of system and the reasoning behind their adoption.

Business systems

The systems which an organisation has in place should aim to establish a means by which the efficiency and effectiveness of all operations are assessed. All systems rely on the way in which the organisation is structured and the comparative importance with which individuals within the organisation view the system. Any system is only a series of sub-systems which themselves may be split into further sub-systems. It is, therefore, important that the organisation monitors all parts of the system. The systems should be designed in such a way that they can be amended or can evolve to meet the requirements of the organisation. In order to understand the ways in which organisations work, we need to understand how they can assess the efficiency and effectiveness of all their operations.

Controlling business functions

Effective control of business functions is concerned with how the organisation achieves its objectives and goals. At its simplest, if an organisation meets its declared objectives and goals, then it is being effective. However, the amount of resources deployed to achieve these objectives or goals should also be measured in order to assess effectiveness.

In other words, we cannot assess how successful an organisation is simply by considering efficiency or effectiveness separately. We need to consider both, since an organisation needs to operate efficiently and effectively and its operations need to be co-ordinated. Even if only one part of the organisation fails in its task then we cannot state that the organisation is truly efficient or effective. One or more features in the organisation's systems must be deficient if one part of the organisation is under-achieving.

Systems obviously play a vital role here. They are the means by which the organisation is able to operate as a whole entity. Any organisation can have good ideas and well-motivated personnel, but without systems to ensure that vital functions are carried out, these may be doomed to failure. Organisations need not necessarily rely on their own personnel to design and run systems. They may employ outside specialists or consultants who are conversant with organisation and methods (O & M) analysis. In recent years many organisations have employed this vital tool to improve efficiency and effectiveness. They have often done this by engaging outside agencies to study and analyse their existing systems.

Whether the systems of an organisation evolve from existing systems, or are radically redesigned, O & M specialists base their assessment on scientific analysis. Systems are vital to measure the performance of an organisation and to assess whether it is reaching its declared objectives. However the systems have originated, they will always be open to criticism and to the charge that it is the systems themselves that are responsible for inefficiencies or their lack of effectiveness.

We can identify a common thread within administrative systems. Each of the procedures we will look at later consists of a relatively simple process:

Inputs	**Process**	**Output**
Information, via faxes, telephone, quotation, monies, etc.	The system by which this information is handled, e.g. input into computer, analysis costings, etc.	A response, e.g. letter, memo, report, telephone call, fax, etc.

In effect we can split the 'process' into two parts to make it clearer:

◆ storage of information (either manually or by computer).

◆ analysis of information.

This may appear to be too simple a definition. The complexities of the operation very much depend upon the context in which the process takes place.

Defining administration systems

The term administration systems needs to be defined before we can accurately determine the purpose of these systems or the procedures carried out. These are the generally accepted descriptions of administration systems:

◆ activities carried out by managers to determine the aims and policies of the organisation.

◆ control of the day-to-day running of the business.

The running of an organisation requires an organised approach if it is to be efficient and effective. Administrative tasks will be carried out at all levels of the organisation. In a larger organisation, administration will be carried out by the Administration Department, but in smaller businesses the administration may be carried out by a single individual who will be responsible for all forms of administration. Whoever is responsible for carrying out these administrative tasks, the basic purposes remain the same. These are:

◆ providing support systems for all resources used by the organisation.

◆ keeping records relating to the activities of the organisation.

◆ monitoring the performance of the business's activities.

Routine and non-routine administrative activities

The activities of an organisation may be classified as routine or non-routine. We need, at this stage, to look at these in a little more detail.

Routine activities are carried out on a regular basis. Some individuals will be responsible for administration functions which will not differ regardless of any other activities carried out by the organisation. Examples of such functions may include:

◆ the processing of invoices.

◆ the filing of business documents and information.

Other individuals will carry out a series of *non-routine* activities. They will have to be more adaptable as the demands of each day will differ greatly. These individuals will not be able to predict the demands upon them with any great accuracy. On a single day they may have a series of meetings or tasks to perform without prior notice or instruction.

Routine functions of an office can be easily organised through the establishment of systems to handle them. An office organised in this way will base its procedures upon previous experience and will know with great accuracy the demands that will be placed upon it. In situations when an individual or department must carry out a non-routine function, they must be able to rely upon a separate series of procedures to support them. A support system may have to be created for that specific purpose.

Resources supported by administrative systems

Many organisations have found the need to provide administrative systems or procedures in order to support the resources used by the organisation. These resources can fall into three main categories:

1 *Human resources* – many organisations have recognised that human resources are the most important resource they have. The deployment of these human

resources, as much as any other factor, will determine the success or otherwise of the organisation.

2 *Financial resources* – this is the capital (or money) that the organisation has received from its trading activities.

3 *Physical resources* – these are slightly more complicated, and administrative systems need to be in place to fully support the following:
   - land
   - premises
   - equipment
   - plant and machinery
   - copyrights
   - patents
   - trade marks.

In the managing of any of these resources, it is a priority that the organisation establishes a series of systems (which often take the form of a departmentalised structure) to assist in the efficient running of the administration function.

Record-keeping

Maintaining an efficient and accurate recording system of business activity is essential to all forms of businesses. Records are mainly kept for the following four reasons:

1 *To fulfil statutory obligations* – various legislation requires organisations to keep detailed records of business activity. In the main, these tend to focus on financial and staff considerations. A record of business activity should be kept for VAT and tax inspections and with regard to staff, both tax and national insurance deductions and contributions should be recorded. Company legislation requires organisations to provide information for investors, customers and company employees.

2 *To assist future planning* – comprehensive data on the following may be vital to assist managers in future decision making:
   - costs
   - product details
   - market research
   - customer complaints
   - profit margins
   - supplier details.

   These records are maintained in order to allow managers to make decisions on the basis of past experience.

3 *To provide evidence of transactions* – the following records will provide a system for tracking all income and expenditure relating to the organisation's business activity:

- purchases made
- sales made
- dates of transactions
- organisations and individuals with whom transactions have been made
- payments received and pending
- personnel records
- stock levels
- staff training and development
- accurate minutes of meetings.

4 *To monitor performance* – an organisation must attempt to identify any problems arising from its business activities and have in place a system which can quickly highlight these. Finance is the key area to monitor, as financial information may be sourced from various parts of the organisation. Each individual manager is responsible for controlling and monitoring the expenditure of their department and will need to analyse this expenditure to assist in future planning. Expenditure may be compared from two different viewpoints:
- intra-firm comparisons – where expenditure is compared with that of last year
- inter-firm comparisons – where comparisons are made in relation to the expenditure of competitors.

Many organisations have adopted management information systems provided by computer software packages to organise, store and monitor their financial data. The information stored is available to all interested parties within the organisation and can be accessed on an immediate basis. Management information systems are discussed in more detail in the section headed 'The communication process and information and communication technology' (*see* p. 203).

Review questions

1 Describe the process by which a message is transferred from the sender to the receiver.

2 Distinguish between formal and informal models of communication.

3 When communicating, what important considerations should be taken into account?

4 How can quality communications be ensured?

5 Outline the main stages of negotiation procedures.

6 What are the main negotiation skills required of a manager?

7 What are the key characteristics of a good communicator?

8 Explain NVC and give at least four examples of it in practice.

9 How can formal communications reflect the corporate image of an organisation?

10 Explain the nature of, and reasons for, both restricted and open channels of communication.

11 What is 'O & M' analysis?

12 Distinguish between routine and non-routine functions of an administrative department.

3.2

The media of communications

The communication process and information and communication technology

In terms of administrative and communication purposes, the computer has made radical changes to the day-to-day running of a business. It has also changed the daily duties or tasks of the personnel working on the administration side of an organisation. Information technology, essentially, does very much what the manual systems do, but as we can easily imagine, it does this work far faster and (hopefully) more efficiently and accurately. Whenever a business considers a new computer system, two basic points must be established:

1   What is the computer itself capable of?

2   What can the software do and what are its limitations?

Computer operation

Hardware refers to the physical components of the system – the computer itself and its peripheral parts. *Software* refers to the programs which can be used with a particular computer system. The computer is only as good as the software it is capable of running. The actual versatility of the computer is related to the flexibility of the software and its ability to process data (or manipulate it). As you might remember, we defined administration systems as being the process through which information is handled in some way. In many respects, this is exactly how a computer works. Essentially, we can define the operations of a computer as follows:

Input devices	Central Processing Unit (CPU) Memory/disk	Output devices

Regardless of how sophisticated the computer may be, the heart of the machine is the Central Processing Unit (CPU). The CPU is a complex construction of micro-electronic circuitry and components mounted on 'boards'. These boards simply act as a means of connecting all the parts of the CPU. The input devices, as featured above, include the keyboard or a bar-code scanner. These are the means by which information is put into the computer (hence input). Output devices, or how the information is displayed or 'got out of' the computer, include the monitor (screen) or printer. Alternatively, the memory or disk may be the place that you choose to keep the information for further use. Most information that is input is normally in a manner in which humans can read it. Computers need to be able to 'read' this information and to transform it into their own binary language. The principal devices that have been designed to capture information, in other words, to allow the computer access to this information, include the following:

◆ *optical character readers* – which are able to read characters which are also readable by humans.

◆ *optical mark readers* – which enable the computer to read marks in pre-set positions, such as multiple choice papers or market research questionnaires.

◆ *bar code readers* – commonly found in many shops, which enable the computer to read via a light pen or laser scanner.

◆ *magnetic ink character readers* – commonly used for sorting and processing cheques, these are very stylised characters, printed in ink containing iron.

◆ *digitisers* – which automatically transform graphics in particular into a binary format on the screen.

◆ *voice recognition devices* – this relatively new system allows the computer to understand simple words and phrases and interpret them as commands.

Word processors

A word processor is a computer with a keyboard used for entering text. Word processors may thus be used for all forms of business documentation. They have a number of advantages over the manual system (typewriters):

◆ it is comparatively easy to identify and correct typing errors (there is usually a spell-checking facility available).

◆ page numbering may be available automatically.

◆ an instant word count may be available.

◆ the document may be edited and re-edited – particularly useful when sending a similar letter to various addresses.

◆ multiple copies may be made.

◆ all printed copies are of the same quality.

- ◆ documents may be saved for future reference or use.

- ◆ a line-draw facility may be available to aid the ruling of tabulated work.

- ◆ a wide variety of print styles and character fonts is available.

Spreadsheets

Spreadsheets are designed to manipulate data. Spreadsheet programs consist of a number of cells, each of which may be labelled to perform a particular function; the cell may contain a number or text or a formula. Calculations may be made, provided the spreadsheet has been designed to perform a particular function.

Spreadsheets are particularly useful in the displaying of *numerical* data. Spreadsheets offer a number of advantages over their manual counterparts:

- ◆ they are designed to be easy to learn and use.

- ◆ they have a wide variety of uses.

- ◆ they are comparatively cheap.

- ◆ they can be personalised for each organisation.

Further advantages of the use of spreadsheets are shown in Fig. 3.5.

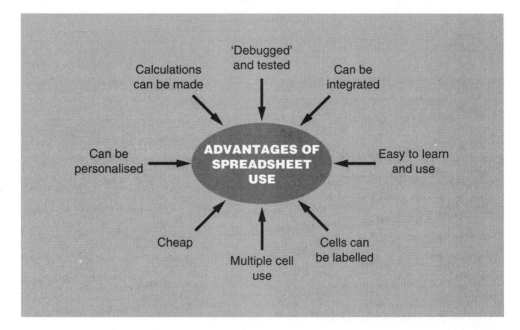

Fig. 3.5 Advantages of spreadsheet use

However, spreadsheets need to be carefully designed prior to use and may suffer from inadequate features by failing to show the correct information in an appropriate format.

Databases

Databases can be used for a variety of purposes. A typical database will offer at least the following facilities:

◆ a personally definable recording format.

◆ a personally definable input format.

◆ file searching facilities.

◆ file sorting facilities.

◆ spreadsheet style calculations.

◆ integration with word-processing packages to enable a variety of report formats to be output.

Graphics packages

Graphics packages are an alternative to the traditional pens or brushes that a graphic artist may use. A graphics package can provide a number of technical and practical advantages and will contain at least the following features:

◆ a comprehensive range of colours, shapes and patterns.

◆ the capacity to move designs around the screen.

◆ options to delete or save designs.

◆ a wide variety of character fonts.

◆ access to a 'library' of pre-drawn graphics known as clip-art.

◆ the option to print the finished graphic design.

Graphics packages are commonly used in business not only for their artistic capabilities, but also to produce charts, graphs and diagrams.

Desktop publishing

Desktop publishing packages combine many of the capabilities of graphics and word-processing packages. They enable the user to produce professional documents, books, posters and articles. Desktop publishing packages will have a number of facilities available, including the ability to:

◆ import text from a word processor.

◆ produce text in a choice of fonts and sizes.

◆ organise text in column form.

◆ import graphics from other packages.

◆ 'scan in' (digitally read) pictures and illustrations and convert them to an appropriate size and shape.

◆ produce various geometric patterns.

◆ merge text, graphics and illustrations.

Accounts packages

Accounts packages offer the user a variety of different facilities, including:

◆ payroll systems which produce payslips and maintain employee records.

◆ sales accounts which maintain records of debits and credits, details of orders made and received, and credit control information.

◆ purchase ledger accounts, which may also provide information in relation to the organisation's buying needs.

◆ general ledgers which maintain and update financial summaries and will automatically produce the following:
  – trial balances
  – trade and profit and loss accounts
  – balance sheets.

Stock control systems

A stock control system is imperative to most organisations and should alert the organisation to the following:

◆ quantities of products stored.

◆ prices of products.

◆ minimum stock levels.

◆ reorder levels.

A good stock control system will also provide a warning to management as to when there are excessively high stock levels of a particular product in the warehouse.

Sales order processing

A sales order processing system should provide the following facilities to the organisation:

◆ order validation.

◆ order checking.

◆ cross-checking with customer's credit status.

◆ production of a 'picking list' for the warehouse.

◆ back-order monitoring so that orders which were not fulfilled in the past may be fulfilled when the item comes into stock.

Computer-aided design and manufacture

Computer-aided design (CAD) is a very flexible system which enables the user to design complex items relatively quickly. CAD is essentially based on a highly sophisticated graphics package which understands the requirements and specifications relating to the item being designed. CAD requires complex calculations to be made and may only be satisfactorily used on powerful computers.

Computer-aided manufacture (CAM), as the name suggests, is involved in the actual manufacturing process. It can control the following:

◆ automated production lines.

◆ robots.

◆ manufacturing systems.

◆ production processes.

Organisations often use an integrated CAD/CAM system which allows the CAD-produced design to be relayed straight to the production line where the process is monitored by the CAM system.

Management information systems

A management information system (MIS) offers a number of features to the organisation. It can:

◆ produce information of a sophisticated nature.

◆ provide information at a crucial period of decision-making.

◆ aid the decision-making process.

◆ process information stored in databases.

Essentially, a MIS should assist managers in making decisions by allowing them access to hitherto unobtainable forms of data.

Information technology as a communication tool

The installation of information technology was initially met with a great deal of scepticism. Many organisations adopted information technology without any serious regard to the uses to which it would be put. However, more recently, organisations have recognised the need to use information technology and to develop employee skills to handle its functions.

The skills required fall into two main categories: *general* and *specialist*. We shall look at these in detail first before considering the nature of the electronic technology itself.

General skills

Nearly all jobs have been affected in some way by the adoption of electronic technology. As a result, most employees must know in general terms how this technology works. Increasingly, technological systems have been integrated via networking systems and are no longer the relatively simple stand-alone desktop computer.

Specialist skills

Nearly one per cent of the working population can now be considered to have specialist skills in relation to the use of computers. Specialists will have particular skills in one or more of the following computer functions:

◆ word processing.

◆ desktop publishing.

◆ databases.

◆ spreadsheets.

◆ graphics.

Features and benefits of new technology

Technology has transformed businesses and as a result many benefits have been enjoyed. These benefits include the following:

◆ cost reductions.

◆ simplified and efficient workflows.

◆ increased responsiveness to customer needs.

◆ additional job satisfaction.

◆ opportunities for employees to learn new skills.

While the adoption of technology can be seen as a positive step, it is essential for all computers to be user-friendly. The recent introduction of the graphical user interface has allowed technology to be more easily understood by its use of icons. All an operator need to do is to use a mouse to click onto an icon which, in turn, redraws the screen and offers a new set of options.

The 'windows' systems allows the operator to undertake a series of simultaneous tasks by overwriting a new screen onto the existing screen. In this way, other files may be perused and referred to and the user may then return to the original document. This system is fast becoming the industry standard.

Computer systems enable an individual to carry out the following main tasks, which include:

◆ recording information.

◆ checking information.

- sorting and classifying information.

- summarising data.

- calculating financial data.

- storing and retrieving information.

- reproducing information.

- communicating information to remote terminals.

Specifically, these processes are covered by the following:

Word processing: the main function of a word-processing package is the manipulation, storage and retrieval of text. In addition, a modern word-processing system will allow graphics to be inserted into the text and, via a database, will provide names and addresses for mailshots.

Desktop publishing (DTP): DTP systems have been developed by merging the functions of word processing and graphics packages. On a DTP system the operator has the facility to use a variety of different typefaces, fonts and styles in conjunction with various illustrations. It is possible to produce a very professional document using a DTP package.

Databases: the storage of information is important to most business organisations. The construction of a database that will provide the information you require needs careful consideration. When constructing a database the designer must know what information will be required from the database and what information needs to be input into the database in order to fulfil these demands. The database is capable of producing information in various forms such as bar charts or line graphs. To get the full benefit from a database it is essential to ensure that the information recorded is constantly updated.

Spreadsheets: the task of a spreadsheet package is to manipulate and organise numbers. Spreadsheets are used when making calculations and forecasts. Provided the correct information has been entered into the spreadsheet package, then the computer can calculate a number of useful totals.

Through networking and the creation of integrated software packages, an operator is able to access all of these key technological functions simultaneously and gain access to information from the individual terminal and the mainframe computer system.

Health and stress issues relating to computer systems

Sources of stress

Working with a computer can be a very demanding job. Someone who is skilled in the techniques of word processing can spend a lot of time looking at the screen. This may not just be for the purpose of entering information, but also for proofreading the text which has been entered. This requires a great deal of concentration if it is to be carried out efficiently and accurately. Similarly, the entering of accounting or other numerical data requires a level of concentration which can be very demanding. Most people using computers find they get very tired very quickly, particularly if they have been looking at a computer screen for more than an hour.

Making the necessary checks

Obviously, being over-tired will affect the effectiveness, efficiency and accuracy of the computer user. In order to ensure that it adheres to government legislation, an organisation must make sure that someone in authority has responsibility for checking that regular breaks are taken and that the correct lighting and screen arrangements are made.

Naturally, if an organisation wants an efficient and happy work-force, then it will do all it can to ensure that they are working under good conditions. This is particularly important when considering the health and possible stress experienced by users of computerised systems. The following should be addressed and constantly monitored:

◆ the temperature in the room – this can affect the performance of the computer as well as the user.

◆ no food and drink should be allowed in the computing room.

◆ regular breaks from the machine should be allowed.

◆ if possible, a variety of tasks should be undertaken during the course of the working day.

◆ the posture of the user should be monitored – a user who is in an uncomfortable position for any length of time will inevitably suffer long-term health problems. Adjustable chairs should be provided with incorporated footrests and correct back support.

◆ the angle and the height of the screen should be monitored. If these are not positioned correctly, then the user becomes tired quicker and errors can result.

◆ avoid the likelihood of having operators suffer from RSI (repetitive strain injury). This is an increasingly common problem for individuals who regularly carry out repetitive jobs such as typing or word processing. If the individual does not vary the tasks, then RSI can occur in the wrists or lower arms.

Additionally, if a user is not sure precisely what is required of them with regard to the work they are carrying out, then this can lead to lack of motivation and frustration which in itself can be a source of stress.

Telecommunications

Three forms of telecommunication

Telecommunications have had a dramatic impact on the communications systems of organisations. At a stroke, many of them have replaced traditional forms of communication. We shall begin by looking at the three forms of telecommunication:

1 Enhanced telephone systems

In recent years modern telephone systems have been developed to provide many new features, including:

◆ visual display of number dialled.

◆ a redial button.

◆ a secrecy button.

◆ a timer so that the call cost may be estimated.

◆ a memory facility for all regularly dialled numbers.

◆ the day, date and time.

◆ conferencing facilities.

◆ a 'voicemail' system where messages can be recorded.

2 Switchboards

These are now much more sophisticated and allow the telephone operator to assess the status of each individual line on the system. It is also possible to identify which extension should be dialled in response to a particular call. Switchboards have the facility to log calls and record them. This assists in the monitoring of unauthorised personal calls made by employees. The logging itself enables the cost of the call to be attributed to a particular department and its budget.

3 Cellular phones

The cellular phone enables individuals to be contacted in remote locations and important information to be transmitted wherever that individual may be. With regard to car phones in particular, a hand-free system has been developed in order to avoid the perils of telephone use while driving.

An alternative to the cellular phone, and in many respects cheaper, is the radio-pager. This enables the individual carrying the radio-pager to be contacted and given a short message or telephone number. Additional facilities available on a radio-pager are:

◆ using the PABX system (private automatic branch exchange) an individual may be 'bleeped' to inform them about a message.

◆ multiple radio-pagers may be 'bleeped' simultaneously.

◆ there is a short visual display consisting of either the telephone number to be contacted or brief details of the message.

Other forms of telecommunication

Answering machines

Answering machines have become a vital part of business communications, despite the fact that people are not keen on talking into machines. When the individual called is not available, or when there is no one to take the message on an extension, then the answering machine can receive the message.

Facsimile machines

Another way an organisation may choose to communicate with its customers or clients is by the use of a facsimile machine, colloquially known as a 'fax'. The word 'facsimile' means *an exact and faithful reproduction of* and applies to text, photographs and graphic images. This means that an added benefit of a fax is that an organisation is not limited to what it can send. It is also useful for organisations which may need to contact companies overseas. A fax machine is generally left on for 24 hours a day, and it does not have to be continually monitored. This means that time differences between countries are not a problem.

Electronic mail

Electronic mail (e-mail) offers all of the facilities provided by fax and telex, but is paperless. Electronic mail offers the additional advantage of being able to store messages when the destination terminal is busy. Electronic mail systems offer a variety of common features (*see* Fig. 3.6). These include:

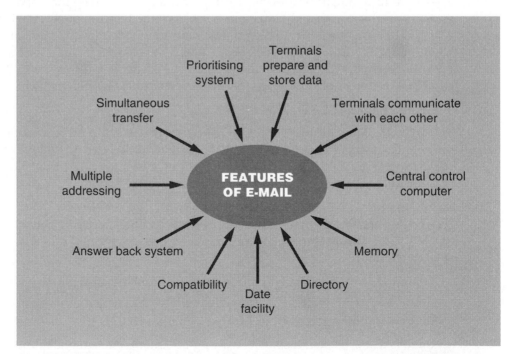

Fig. 3.6 Features of electronic mail systems

◆ terminals to prepare and store messages.

◆ a communication link with other work stations within the network.

◆ a central controlling computer.

◆ a directory of addresses.

◆ a central mailbox.

◆ a system which dates the message.

◆ a function that notes that the message has been received by the addressee.

◆ a facility to multiple-address so that all members of a particular working group are sent the message simultaneously.

◆ a prioritising system so that messages can be identified as important or routine.

◆ a storage facility in order to keep in the memory those messages that have not yet been received.

◆ compatibility with existing equipment and computer systems.

Electronic mail offers a number of advantages in relation to other forms of communication, these are shown in Fig. 3.7.

Another version of the electronic mail system may be found in the electronic data interchange which enables individuals to exchange business documents using the same communication system.

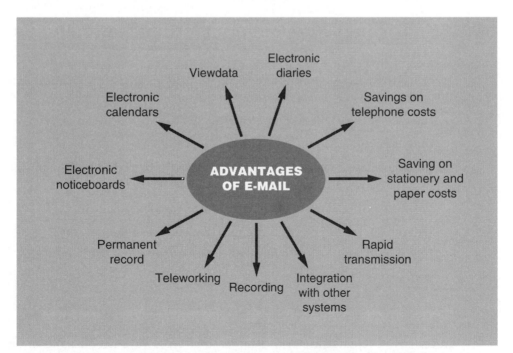

Fig. 3.7 Main advantages of electronic mail systems

Electronic diaries

Electronic diaries and calendars are becoming increasingly common and allow individuals to make diary entries and searches on particular days or events, thus avoiding the need to manually enter information in a personal handwritten business diary.

Electronic noticeboards

Electronic noticeboards and viewdata now allow a mass of information to be accessed via workstation screens. This is provided in the UK by Prestel and is essentially an interactive system which allows not only the viewing of information but the transmission as well.

Videotext

Videotext is the general name for all computer-based systems which make information available to a wide variety of users. Videotext is divided into two main areas: *viewdata* and *teletext*. Viewdata uses the telephone system to make contact, whereas teletext is broadcast via a television signal.

The Internet

Companies are increasingly making use of the Internet to establish web sites which give out information about their business to existing and potential clients. Web sites can be accessed from all over the world by anyone connected to the Information Superhighway via a computer terminal and modem.

◆ Effectiveness of communication – efficiencies and deficiencies

In order to analyse the effectiveness of any form of communication used by a business organisation, it is important to consider the following factors:

◆ the ease of use of the communication.

◆ the ease of access to the information.

◆ the efficiency of use in terms of the user, with regard to health and the stress experienced by that individual.

◆ its effect with regard to the interaction between people.

◆ will the interaction between organisations be affected?

◆ how confidential will the information be?

◆ will security become an issue?

Ease of use and access to communication systems

In order to evaluate ease of use and ease of access, we need also to think about the person who is using the system. Obviously, the system itself is only as effective as the person using it. It is imperative that all business documentation is produced in an error-free way.

Communication systems specialists take the view that the reduction in human involvement with the processing of information and communication takes many of the errors out of the processes. If a business can rely on a foolproof communications system, then the accuracy factor is taken for granted. Others may take a more sceptical view and state that reliance on electronic technology means that humans are less aware of the process, therefore they find it more difficult to identify errors and inaccuracies. The sophistication of systems should mean that they are largely reliable.

A sophisticated communications system should offer flexibility and the ability to respond to change and market requirements. With improved communications between remote parts of an organisation there should be a greater interchange of information. The sharing of ideas can be problematic at a more traditional level based on paper. Paper-based filing systems, for example, lack the immediacy of access that can be enjoyed from on-screen systems. A good communication system should also help efficiency in terms of work flow and operations by ensuring that congestion and delays in the interchange of information can be identified and information re-routed by an alternative channel.

With increased efficiency the organisation will receive a useful additional benefit in that it will appear to external organisations to be more responsive and professional. If the communications system is sufficiently user-friendly then employees will enjoy a more stimulating and satisfying work experience. If employees can be freed from boring and routine tasks, then there is more opportunity for them to stretch their talents to the benefit of the organisation. This will, in itself, increase efficiency since fewer employees are involved in mundane duties.

Interaction between people and organisations through communication systems

When you are analysing a communication system in terms of its efficiency, you will also need to address the question of whether it is adequate in terms of its capacity to allow members of the organisation to interact. In addition, you will also need to look at the system with regard to its potential for interaction with other organisations.

Interaction between people within the organisation could include different communication systems which may take the following forms:

◆ internal telephone systems

◆ documentation used within the organisation only

◆ electronic mail

◆ a mail distribution system

◆ a filing system

◆ a computerised system which is used for internal use only.

Confidentiality and security in communication

Whatever the nature of the organisation's business activities, there is always a need for certain security measures to be in place. This may simply mean that the organisation does not wish its competitors to know:

◆ any information regarding it's customers.

◆ any information regarding the rates of discount offered.

◆ any information regarding the credit limits offered to the organisation.

◆ any information relating to the production costs and targets of the organisation.

◆ any information relating to the distribution arrangements of the organisation.

◆ the current financial status of the organisation.

Organisations which are involved, for example, in the production of military equipment may be even more sensitive than most on matters of security and confidentiality.

Security codes and limited access

The communication systems of an organisation are particularly vulnerable in terms of security to unauthorised users. Communication systems rely on shared channels to transfer the information from machine to machine. Confidentiality and security devices in common use are those which allow limited levels of access into the system. By means of a security code numbering system, individuals can only gain access to certain levels of the system. In this way more junior members of staff are restricted in relation to the type of information they can access, while, at the same time, the procedure serves as a back-up security system. Because access is limited, a 'hacker' would need to know the correct procedure before being able to break in to the system. In addition, where information is not necessarily security sensitive, but nonetheless confidential, a security code system makes it less likely for it to be accessed by unauthorised individuals within the organisation.

Review questions

1 Name four data input devices, and explain their use and benefits.

2 How have computers improved the methods by which organisations communicate?

3   What are CAD and CAM and how would an organisation use them?

4   What is MIS, and what features does it offer an organisation?

5   Distinguish between general and specialist skills in the use of computers.

6   Identify the most common forms of telecommunications used by businesses.

7   'E-mail has all but made the fax obsolete.' Discuss.

8   Explain the main advantages of e-mail systems.

9   How would an organisation judge the effectiveness of its communication systems?

10 Identify the main advantages of computer-based filing systems over paper-based ones.

11 What health and safety considerations need to be taken into account when installing computer systems in an organisation?

12 List the ways in which an organisation might communicate with another business.

Section 4

IDENTIFYING AND CHANGING ORGANISATIONAL CULTURE

After reading this section you should be able to:

◆ identify organisational cultures, rules and norms.

◆ identify and analyse the factors which influence changing organisational cultures, rules and norms.

◆ identify and evaluate the relationship between organisational cultures, structures and performance.

◆ influence and adapt to organisational change.

4.1

Culture

Essentially, business or corporate culture is the organisation's personality. It is the way in which the organisation thinks and how it does things. The culture is something that most members of that organisation share. By being an employee, the culture is gradually learnt.

The management will try to create a particular organisational culture. Some organisations do have very strong cultures. Perhaps the best way of looking at a culture is to examine some of the work-related values which are shared by all. There are four basic core values. These are:

1 *Power distance* – this addresses the fact that individuals accept the way in which the organisation is structured. It also includes the realisation that not all members of the organisation have equal power. The subordinates trust the management and receive trust in return.

2 *Uncertainty avoidance* – this is a measure of how individuals within the organisation feel in situations when they are unsure of themselves. An integral part of this is to encourage employees to take part in decision-making through empowerment. This will greatly reduce the uncertainty and allow for greater expression and participation.

3 *Individualism* – certain organisations stress the importance of personal initiative and achievement. Indeed, they reward employees for personal performance. On the other hand, other organisations will stress the importance of co-operation, but will positively encourage competition between departments or sub-divisions of the organisation.

4 *Masculinity or femininity* – the former puts forward the notion that individuals should be assertive and fosters a competitive working environment. This form is particularly common in organisations in the USA. On the other hand, some organisations favour a caring approach, sometimes described as a feminine approach, as they feel that this is more employee orientated. Further, it also suggests that the organisation positively nurtures their employees.

Some examples of organisational culture

Having looked at the core values, we can now turn our attention to some particular examples of organisational culture.

Clan culture is based upon teaching employees to share values. The organisations which favour this form of culture will develop their ability to pass it on from one employee generation to the next. These organisations are inclined to be traditional, and all members of the organisation will have characteristics of a particular style and manner of conduct.

Alternatively, there may be a *market culture*. This is rather less formal. The individuals within the organisation conform to the culture which offers rewards for performance. There is little pressure from the organisation to conform; in fact, the culture almost demands that individuals remain different: they thrive upon differences. The market culture does not generate loyalty or co-operation, but it does generate initiative, responsibility and entrepreneurial approaches.

Two key theorists, Harrison and Handy, developed and proposed four different types of organisational culture. These are known as:

1 *Power cultures* – which have a central source and depend upon trust and personal communication. Within these organisations there are few rules, although the central power of the organisation controls the individuals and the decisions. Typically they are controlled by a charismatic leader. These organisations are strong and effective in most cases.

2 *Role cultures* – which are based on logic and rationality. All individuals are controlled within their roles and by the rules of the organisation. The only way to achieve in an organisation such as this is to attain a certain level of performance. The organisation is stable and predictable. Individuals who thrive in this kind of environment will be efficient. It is not, however, an organisation that adapts well to change.

3 *Task cultures* – where power is based on ability and expertise. Project teams are the most important aspect of this form of culture. Typically the organisation will be structured as a matrix. These organisations are strong and flexible. The teams which have been established to handle certain situations can be changed or redeployed.

4 *Person cultures* – which emphasise the importance of the individual. In these organisations there is a tendency for like-minded people to co-operate. Power is shared and based on ability. Organisations such as these find it difficult to control the various individuals. In many cases, a person culture is found within larger organisations which are predominantly role or power culture orientated.

If employees share the cultural values of the organisation then they will be more likely to be committed to it. Organisations, however, need to be able to adapt and change their culture if they intend to remain competitive and adaptable. There may be a degree of resistance to proposed changes if employees feel that their status within the organisation may be affected by the change. Equally, employees may have become used to certain forms of behaviour and approach. They will feel less secure with, and may consequently fear, the unknown.

We will now take a more systematic look at the various aspects of organisational culture and the norms and rules that pertain to each of the different cultures.

Culture and theory

Theories and theorists

The concepts of organisational culture have been developed in recent years. For many theorists organisational culture is something of a departure from the mainstream or more contemporary approaches to organisational theory. There is, however, a growing number of theorists who have added to the debate regarding theories on organisational cultures. Essentially, organisational culture states that each organisation has its own particular miniature society or a particular form of configuration which is unique to itself. This means that, rather like modern society, it will have its own beliefs and values, myths and heroes and will, to all intents and purposes, behave very much like a larger form of society. Naturally the differences in perspectives from which organisational culture is approached are enormous. We will begin by having a brief look at some of these. Arguably the work of Argyris and Bennis provided much of the foundation upon which the majority of organisational culture theories have been developed. They were part of the *human relations school* and concentrated primarily on beliefs, values and attitudes, all of which are useful in shaping an individual's cultural perspective.

Modern structural theory does not really add a great deal to the organisational cultural debate. Since it is largely interested in goal orientation and mechanistic ways of explaining an organisation's activities. This is of course typified by their interest in organisation charts. *Systems theory*, which has been in existence since the 1940s, offers us some help in understanding organisational culture. Many of the modern day theorists use some of the terms which were made popular by systems theorists of the 1960s. To some extent *cultural theory* has been influenced by systems theory because it has a similar outlook on the organisation's life. They both emphasise the importance of analysing the information within its own environment and the importance of uncertainty. Not only this, they also identify the fact that there is often limited scope for employees to show their true individuality within an organisation.

During the late 1970s theorists such as Kanter and Mintzberg, representative members of the *power and politics* approach to theory, developed a number of ideas which help us further the cultural perspective. Principally these include the notion that most organisations act irrationally; that their goals and objectives tend to have been developed over a period of time through negotiation; and that they comprise a number of different groups, often referred to as coalitions or subcultures.

Organisational artefacts

When we investigate organisational culture there are a number of terms which we need to understand because they are commonly used by many theorists. The first of these is the term *artefacts*. This refers to any physical aspect of the company which has been created by the company itself (see Fig 4.1). It would include annual reports, dress codes, fixtures and fittings; the location of car parking space (and its allocation); the general appearance of the buildings; the use of information technology. It also relates to the use of language within the organisation, ceremonies or celebrations which reinforce behaviour and the creation of the various rules, systems, procedures and programmes, such as appraisal, meeting structures and quality assurance. With all these observable artefacts we can begin to see that any organisational culture can be quite complex. No single classification system is sophisticated enough to cover all of them.

Fig. 4.1 Examples of organisational artefacts

Language, stories and myths

At the very least these artefacts give us some form of indication as to the nature of the culture in operation within the organisation. If we refer to language for example, the use of jokes, metaphors or jargon can give us some strong clues as to the acceptability of certain types of behaviour. In this respect organisational culture does not just view language as a means of communication. Within a particular organisation, language will be used on the assumption that a basic level of understanding has already been established between the individuals, and in this respect the language will be modified. This will be further reinforced by other artefacts such as the use of metaphors. Typically, for example, military metaphors may be used, suggesting aggressive behaviour. More typically the constant use of words and phrases such as 'high quality', 'excellence' or 'optimum' all assist in reinforcing a particular approach and have become part of the organisational culture.

Another type of artefact is the organisational story. Organisational stories, which may have developed over a period of time, tend to focus on a single sequence of events which were part of the organisation's history. The value of these stories is, of course, to help employees remember information and to generate a particular type of belief; to legitimise a particular point of view which is in accord with that of the organisation. As we know, stories and other such methods of conveying information are popular across all areas of society. They help people understand situations and events and in effect 'paint a picture', albeit an imaginary one, to reinforce their knowledge and insight into how something works.

Many similar comments can also be attributed to myths, which are often developed by organisations. The one major difference between myths and stories is that the myths have considerably less foundation in reality. Back in the 1980s, several theorists tried to identify the different types of myths. These are:

◆ Myths that try to create, maintain or legitimise certain forms of action or consequences; in other words, which legitimise a particular approach.

◆ Myths that attempt to maintain or hide the interests and value systems which are linked to the power structure of the organisation – this will often help to legitimise enormous differences in pay and serve as a means by which unfair or unethical situations can be explained away.

◆ Myths that help explain cause and effect – most individuals operate from a basis of not having a full quota of information available to them. One example is the myth, held more commonly in the past than in the present day, that women may be unreliable workers since they will marry and then leave to have children. If this myth is accepted then women can be passed over in promotion. In some respects, situations like this become self-fulfilling; women faced with the prospect of these 'unseen' barriers based on unreliable myths may turn to alternative forms of self-expression, or they will seek out employers who actively operate an equal opportunities policy, thus taking their skills and experience elsewhere.

◆ Myths that attempt to justify chaotic action – with most individuals in an organisation faced with a prospect of having to cope with very complex and turbulent activities, myths can assist in trying to reduce their anxiety and uncertainty. The myths attempt to establish the workplace as being solid and reliable with a series of ethical codes that it will not break under any circumstances.

Ceremonies, rites and rituals

Ceremonies, rites and rituals are commonplace in most organisations. They serve to reinforce the cultural values of the organisation. We can identify three main areas of activity here, the first being the *rites of passage* which include training programmes, induction programmes and retirement dinners or events for leavers. These enable the organisation to show changes in the status and role of individuals. The second area is that often referred to as the *rites of questioning*. This involves the use of external consultants or adherence to critical reports in order to challenge the established order of the organisation. Finally there are the *rites of renewal*, including office parties, employee participation in change and job redesign, which help refurbish the status quo within an organisation. Many of the rites or rituals are dramatic planned set pieces such as prizegivings and sales conferences, that are in some way extravagant. They are extremely important because they can consolidate the organisational culture through social interaction.

Cultural norms and symbols

You may have already come across the concept of 'norms'. These are rules for behaviour which indicate to an individual what is appropriate and inappropriate in certain circumstances. In relation to organisational culture, these norms help an individual to understand how they should react and deal with particular sets of circumstances. Symbols such as words or objects are another important aspect of organisational culture. Use of logos, for example, can help reinforce the corporate culture and identity. They essentially perform three main functions: the first is purely descriptive; the second is to control, so they would be used on posters and reports as well; and the third is to assist the maintenance of the various systems, so they would be used on the covers of handbooks, code books and rule books. Symbols provide clearly identifiable ways of saying things or presenting things which are acceptable to the organisation. In other words, they are company standard approaches.

Heroes

One of the stranger aspects of organisational culture is the identification of corporate heroes who are seen or meant to be seen by members of the organisation as exemplars in success. Why is it important for an organisation to identify particular individuals as being heroes? There are a number of good reasons for this:

◆ ordinary individuals who have obtained this status can be copied by others.

◆ they provide excellent role models and set the standards for performance required.

◆ they can be used to identify a particular aspect of the organisation to external organisations.

◆ they can help to reinforce the prevailing organisational culture and show what is unique about it.

◆ they can illustrate to employees that their own personal success is very much linked with the success of the organisation.

Having extolled the values of heroes, many theorists in recent years have alerted organisations to the dangers of over-emphasising their importance. Remember that heroes tend to be individualists and, in a prevailing environment which extolls the virtues of teamwork, there is perhaps no room for the hero. Co-operation is considered to be far more important than individual excellence. There is also a great danger in perhaps choosing the wrong person. The organisation's knowledge of this individual may be limited to their activities at work and they may become something of a liability. Setting someone up as a hero also tends to demotivate individuals who are performing reasonably well but not spectacularly so. There has certainly been a decline in the number of individuals being set up as heroes.

Values and beliefs

As we have mentioned already, *values* are the codes which indicate to an individual how things should be done. *Beliefs* help us recognise what is and is not true. Attitudes connect these beliefs and values with feelings. This allows us to behave in a particular way towards a specific idea. We will return to this concept later. As we said, beliefs and values have a common link and allow us to react in particular sets of circumstances. Many beliefs and values which have become attitudes are tainted by prejudice and actually represent more of a stereotype, but they do have an enduring impact on the way in which individuals will react.

Assumptions by and about people and relationships

There are a number of basic assumptions which are shared by most individuals within an organisation. These tend to revolve around feelings and emotions. As we said, beliefs are relatively easy to detect but assumptions are rather more unconscious feelings. Beliefs can be debated and modified whereas assumptions are somewhat more nebulous. Beliefs are based upon knowledge but assumptions are an individual's interpretation of that knowledge and that belief overlaid with a veneer of values and emotions. Back in 1985, Schein suggested that there were five different types of basic emotion.

1 *Humanity's relationship to nature* – some organisations assume that they can completely dominate the environment in which they operate; others feel that they are completely dominated by the environment and have to try to find some kind of way in which they can operate within it.

2 *Reality and truth* – many organisations have based much of their tradition and consequent rules and procedures upon accepted ways of doing things. This rational legal process has established particular ways of approaching a problem or a situation. The organisation has in effect its own 'truth' and is therefore less pragmatic since it is assumed this truth is correct.

3 *The nature of human nature* – some organisations, adopting McGregor's Theory X approach, assume that the majority of their employees are very lazy individuals.

On the other hand, some organisations may adopt the opposite theory and view their employees as being considerably more self-motivated. In the vast number of organisations the assumption is, of course, that employees are motivated purely by money, or perhaps by some form of organisational approval. It is the nature of human nature or rather the view of human nature which will colour the organisational culture.

4 *The nature of human activity* – the predominant approach in this respect is that individuals should be proactive and *do* rather than *react*. In this respect, great emphasis is placed upon self-development since it is through self-development that success can be achieved.

5 *The nature of human relations* – organisations do differ enormously but they all assume that there should be some form of relationship between the individuals within that organisation.

Some organisations will tend to encourage collective approaches to their operations and favour co-operation whereas other organisations will encourage individualism. In addition to this, organisations which tend to be somewhat autocratic in nature may favour individualism, whereas more democratic organisations will have a tendency towards the collective approach. Again we can see that the nature of human relationships within an organisation will have a marked effect upon the cultural development of that organisation.

Sources of organisational culture

We have looked at many of the different aspects of organisational culture; however, we have not described exactly how organisational culture comes into existence. Where exactly does it originate? There are the more obvious sources of culture: the organisation's mission statement; perhaps the use of technology within the organisation; the adoption or amplification of the national culture of the country; an adoption of the characteristics of charismatic leaders within the organisation; or indeed the type of business activity involved. All of these are equally relevant and likely sources of organisational culture. However, we need to look rather more deeply than this. David Drennan, for example, identified some 12 different factors or sources of organisational culture:

1 The influence of a dominant leader.

2 The company history and its tradition.

3 The technology, products and services used and supplied.

4 The industry itself and the competition.

5 The customers.

6 The organisation's expectations of itself and of its products and services.

7 The information and control systems used by the organisation.

8 The legislation and external business environment.

9   The policies rules and procedures adopted by the organisation.

10 The reward systems and measurement of those reward systems to the employees.

11 The organisation itself; its structure and resources.

12 The goals, values and beliefs of the organisation.

The primary sources of organisational culture are shown in Fig. 4.2.

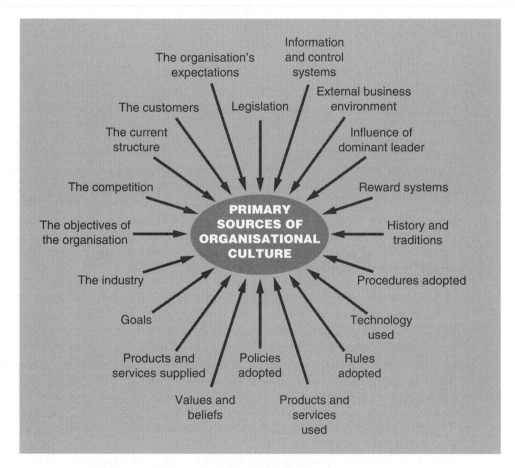

Fig. 4.2 Primary sources of organisational culture

Broadly, we can split the probable sources of organisational culture into three main areas since these are, by and large, the more dominant areas of influence.

The role of the predominant national or social culture

The first refers to the society's or the nationality's predominant culture. It is certainly true that, given a strong national identity in particular countries, there could be a tendency for organisations within that country to adopt many of its cultural norms. It is interesting to note, however, that this is not necessarily the case.

Hofstede, a theorist and researcher working in the 1990s, put forward the proposition that national cultures and, by implication, organisational cultures have five very different dimensions:

1 Power distance

2 Individualism or collectivism

3 Masculinity or femininity

4 Uncertainty avoidance

5 Confucian dynamism.

By doing this he managed to identify a number of different nationalities in his view which held particular types of attitudes and values relating to their national culture.

Power distance, he suggested, was the extent to which the less powerful members of a particular organisation expect and accept that power is distributed unequally throughout the organisation. In instances of low power distance the inequalities within the organisation will be minimised as the subordinates will tend to be consulted more frequently by their managers. However, in high power distance organisations there are enormous inequalities which are less desirable. Power is centralised and subordinates tend to be very widely separated from their managers, both in terms of consultation and salary.

Individualism or collectivism refers to the extent to which an individual is tied by the society itself. In highly individualistic organisations employees are free to make mutually advantageous relationships with the organisation, and promotion would be purely based upon skills. In very collective organisations there is a greater degree of integration and the requirement to be involved in teamwork. There is also a greater level of security which is related to the loyalty which both sides give to one another.

The question of *masculinity or femininity* refers to the distinction between the social gender roles. Men on the one hand are required to be assertive and tough and show outward signs of success. Women on the other hand would be expected to be more concerned with the quality of life, rather more modest and somewhat less abrasive. In work, this distinction would be encouraged with men being the high performers and women providing a more controlling and levelling background.

Uncertainty avoidance, as we have mentioned in a previous section, is the extent to which individuals within an organisation feel threatened by unknown sets of circumstances. Some organisations may find themselves in a position where their management and their employees are ill-prepared for uncertainty. They will find it difficult to deviate from generally accepted and expected patterns of behaviour or rules and regulations. However, the likelihood is that the more able the organisation is to cope with uncertainty the more possibility there is for it to succeed.

Finally, *confucian dynamism* refers to the long-term or short-term attitudes of the employees and the management. Organisations which have only short-term goals and objectives will be somewhat less stable in their nature since these will be prone to radical changes in direction over a period of years. Organisations which have a more long-term approach with clearly specified goals and objectives stretching out over a number of years will have rather more stability. The organisation's culture will be very much determined by the relative prevalence of short termism or long termism. It is interesting to consider which approach would have a more dominant effect upon the individuals working for that organisation. It very much depends upon the nature of the individuals employed and their ability to assimilate the organisation's culture.

The role of leadership in shaping organisational culture

Leadership plays a very important part in shaping organisational culture. It is said that a single charismatic leader can create an organisational culture of their own. Given the fact that most organisations are created as a result of the fusion of several individuals' views on reaching a number of different objectives then, at least in the initial stages of the organisation's life, the organisational culture will reflect their views. During this early period the founders of a particular organisation can have an enormous influence on the nature of the organisation and the way in which it will operate. These founders will tend to set the rules, procedures and systems which will become commonplace within the organisation throughout its life. They will also be able to set the limits of acceptable behaviour and patterns of activity and involvement for all levels of management. Obviously as organisations will often outlive their founders, the influence that the founders have upon the organisation will wane as time passes. However, good practice will always remain in place.

The business environment as a cultural influence

Just as leadership can affect the organisational culture we should not forget that one of the primary influences will be the nature of the business environment in which the organisation operates. Deal and Kennedy, for example, state that the business environment is probably the single greatest influence in shaping corporate culture. This is perhaps very true. A service orientated, manufacturing orientated and public sector orientated organisation will each have radically different ways of doing things and of communicating with the public and their customers.

However, it is the nature of the market itself, principally the activities and the nature of the competitors, which may have a drastic effect on organisational culture. Markets which have a degree of stability will tend to create organisations which are equally stable, integrated and slow changing. In markets where a more dynamic approach is necessary, the organisational culture will encourage individual managers and their subordinates to be somewhat more competitive and ambitious.

Stakeholders in the business

Within the more general view of the influence of the business environment we should not forget that a number of different stakeholders may have a radical impact and influence on the nature of the organisational culture. Stakeholders are of course groups of individuals who have a stake or an interest in a particular organisation. Among these, at least in the private sector, are included customers. Naturally customers seek to acquire the ability to influence the organisation itself by expecting improved quality and reliability of products and services. This is often referred to as a *quality culture*. Some organisations have readily embraced this approach as they wish to satisfy the requirements of their customers as a paramount and overriding issue.

For privatised or private organisations we would assume that the largest single influence upon the organisational culture would be the owners of the organisation. Certainly we would expect shareholders to have an effect on the organisational culture. However research has shown that this is not the case. Writing in 1984, Davis suggested that there are relatively few occasions when the management of the organisation will take any notice of the wishes of the shareholders. Principally, these occasions revolve around the concentration of ownership of the organisation and the potential external threats. Management would certainly take notice if the organisation was owned by a single individual or several members of a particular family, as their influence on the organisational culture as major shareholders would be enormous. On the other hand, in situations where the organisation faces the possibility of takeover or merger then the wishes of the shareholders and the reflection of their particular points of view would be taken on board by the organisation.

Other influences on organisational culture

The government has a considerable influence on the organisational culture. Perhaps the most radical influence that the government can exert is in relation to the process of privatisation. Certainly the organisational cultures which were prevalent in the nationalised industries in the UK prior to privatisation are radically different from what we now see in the deregulated and privatised utilities. Not only has the legal framework surrounding the organisation radically changed but so too has the management. The organisations have had to cope with dramatic and radical cultural changes in a highly competitive market-place.

Although the general public can be considered to a large extent as being the customers or potential customers of the organisation we can broaden our interpretation of the term 'public' to reflect the national culture or trends in the national culture within a particular country. Primarily we can consider the impact of equal opportunities, for example upon the organisational culture.

In addition to this we can see that gradual changes in the public's attitude towards the environment have also had a dramatic effect on organisational culture. It is now very difficult for an organisation to operate in a non-environmentally friendly way without drawing the attention of the general public. This in turn means that the organisation has to internalise many of the concerns of the general public and modify its own culture accordingly.

Cross-cultural similarities – and differences

For organisations which are professionally based such as hospitals, accountancy practices and educational institutions, we could assume that there would be a degree of similarity between the organisational cultures. The management or the bulk of the workforce, having been trained in a similar way, particularly having had to cope with the rigours of a professional course or qualification, should perhaps reflect a similar form of organisational culture. The presumption is that there is a form of professional culture. Whether this is true or not there are certainly a number of values and beliefs which are put forward by professional associations or at least members of professions. Similarly trained professionals in a large organisation may have broadly similar approaches to organisational culture.

If we broaden this debate and consider managers, for example, to be a profession in their own right, then we could try and identify some values and beliefs that are common to them. Certainly there is evidence of 'jargon' or language common to the majority of managers. There may even be a degree of loyalty that we can associate with managers. In addition to this we can identify the fact that most managers are highly competitive, either within the organisation itself or certainly externally. It is also true that the managerial culture which is predominant in some organisations is directly related to the nationality of the different managers. There is likely to be an enormous gulf between managerial culture in the USA and managerial culture in any number of African states.

◆ The development of organisational culture

How cultures develop

Once an organisational culture has been established we should not assume that it remains static. It will inevitably develop over a period of time. There are two basic ways in which this can happen. The first is known as *trauma*. It is assumed that when the original culture was established at the beginning of the organisation's existence there was a degree of uncertainty as to whether the organisation would survive or be successful in the long run. This degree of uncertainty is said to be traumatic for the employees and the management concerned. There will be a period when the individuals working for the organisation are uncertain as to whether they should push for particular work patterns or codes of behaviour, since their overriding concern is the long-term success of the organisation. Over a period of time the influence of the founders of the organisation will reduce allowing the management and their subordinates to gradually amend the organisational culture. Eventually the organisational culture should be established as a result of negotiation and consensus.

From time to time, organisations will face traumas or crises. At various times individuals in the organisation will have to develop ways in which they can overcome their problems. The trauma theory rests upon the fact that all development of organisational culture is carried out on a gradual learning basis. It also assumes that the development of organisational culture is continuous and that the individuals within the organisation will seek to develop an ever more acceptable version. Organisational culture which derives from trauma-based learning is considerably more reinforced than other forms of organisational culture. It is certainly true that, if the organisation attempts to modify organisational culture which has been developed on the basis of trauma, they will find it extremely difficult. The very nature of trauma-based learning means that it is more fundamental to the culture itself than any other form.

An alternative to trauma-based learning is that of *positive reinforcement and feedback*. Individuals operating within an organisation will have a tendency to repeat particular forms of behaviour providing they discover that this way of operating is successful. Equally, where a type of behaviour is not successful, the organisation will move away from this particular type of culture. This is a natural process since positive feedback leads to reinforcement of a particular way of doing things and negative feedback means that the organisation will not adopt this method of operation in the future. Positive reinforcement requires the organisation to continually test the way in which it has coped with certain situations. This also means that, as the external environment changes the organisation may discover that previously successful ways of doing things are no longer valid. Steps must then be taken to modify the culture in order to take account of the changing external environment. Most organisational culture is shared, where the majority of people in the organisation have learnt that particular codes of behaviour and practices are acceptable and successful. In this way a more integrated culture can emerge.

How cultures continue

It is important for the organisation to ensure that any organisational culture which is prevalent within the business continues over a period of time providing, of course, that that culture is successful. This is usually facilitated by the way in which the organisation chooses new entrants into the organisation, an integral part of the recruitment and selection procedures. For senior positions in particular, individuals who are considering joining the organisation will have a considerable amount of knowledge regarding its working practices and objectives. Indeed, in the initial stages of employment new recruits will take steps to try to learn about the organisational culture and history. This will enable them to operate far more effectively in their jobs. In some respects, the acceptance of the prevalent organisational culture will determine whether a new recruit is suitable or not for a post. If their attitudes accord broadly with the organisational culture, then they will probably fit in rather more successfully than someone who is unaware of the organisational culture or who finds their own views at variance with it.

Once an individual has joined the organisation they will find themselves part of a socialisation process. Socialisation within an organisational environment can be both formal and informal. This is often referred to as *enculturation*, which refers to the process by which individuals are gradually exposed to the various types of behaviour; the values and beliefs of the organisation. By embracing these different views which form part of the organisational culture the new recruit will become an integrated member of the organisation itself. Not only does this process affect new recruits to the organisation but it also has an impact on those who are moving within the organisation itself. It is a learning process which is important for all individuals, whether they are climbing up the hierarchical levels or moving laterally or horizontally into other areas of the organisation. Indeed, we will discover that in the majority of organisations there are subtly different approaches from department to department or within the different subdivisions within the organisation. In addition to the more formal socialisation process which will of course include such systems as induction, there is an informal system in operation. This system itself is probably the more primary means of transmitting the organisational culture from one individual to another. Colleagues will be able to guide the new recruit or the transferee and convey to them the importance of particular codes of behaviour and the adoption of specific beliefs and values.

Socialisation, however is a fairly effective way of incorporating new recruits into the business itself. Some organisations favour a high level of socialisation which demands that the new recruit conforms fully to the way in which the organisation operates. There is a danger of course that over-socialisation will lead to a stifling of creative ability and objective overviews. The ultimate outcome of over-socialisation is to become a 'company person'. This may not be what the organisation really needs. We should also bear in mind that socialisation is a continual process, not only for the new recruits but also for the existing employees. This is an integral part of the gradual development of an organisation which cannot rely upon accepted organisational cultural practice in a changing business environment.

When new recruits join an organisation they will be faced with an organisational culture which is relatively complex and at times rather ambiguous. They will of course be unaware of many of the situations in the past which have determined the culture, and they may find that some of the generally shared views of the organisation are difficult to grapple with. Codes of behaviour which have become generally accepted by existing employees can prove to be difficult to understand for the new recruit, since they have not shared the same learning experience. The reactions of new recruits differ widely. Obviously, some will openly embrace the shared organisational culture while others will find that they need to question it. Gradually, however, the shared experiences and values which operate within the organisation will be relayed to the new recruit. It is only after this process has been completed that the individual may find themselves in a position that they are fully integrated and fully appreciative of the various nuances of the organisational culture.

Some organisational cultures will be considerably more difficult to accept and become part of than others. In certain cases it can be simple and relatively straightforward but in others there is a high degree of complexity. There may also be some differentiation between the organisational culture which operates at subordinate level to that which is expected and accepted by senior management.

As we referred to earlier in this chapter, there are a number of basic assumptions, beliefs and artefacts that determine the nature of the organisational culture. We can also see that there is a diversity of different cultural items which affect the overall culture. Not only this, but there are a number of subcultures which will be more or less dominant within the structure itself. These subcultures can be rather complex and may operate as counter cultures to the main organisational culture of the business.

The ongoing scenario

In the final analysis the individual who has joined the organisation will either be fully integrated within the organisational culture or may find that they need to reject or have been rejected by the organisational culture itself. In the initial stages of the new employee's relationship with the organisation there may be a period of probation in which the organisation and the new employee size one another up and decide whether they are truly compatible. Obviously the onus is on the new recruit to adopt the organisational culture rather than the organisational culture amending itself to suit the needs of the new recruit. If, after a period of time which may last anything up to two years, the new recruit cannot fully accept the nature of the organisational culture then the two parties may choose to disperse.

 # The uses of organisational culture

Reducing conflict

As we have seen organisational culture includes the sharing of assumptions, beliefs and values. Individuals within the organisation will learn how to act in certain sets of circumstances. One of the principal reasons for the development of organisational culture is that it helps to reduce the amount of conflict within the organisation. In other words, there is a degree of *social cohesion* within the business. Providing individuals can accept a particular type of organisational culture, we can see that it will assist them in being able to cope with external pressures in the business environment. Not only this, it will allow them to survive and adapt to changes by developing a series of integrated internal processes.

There needs to be a generally accepted way in which the mission statement and objectives of the organisation are interpreted. Since the principal goal is to achieve the various objectives of the organisation the business needs to develop a generally accepted strategy in order to achieve this. This form of consensus allows the organisation to develop its personnel in such a way that they will act together, understanding how and why things need to be done. It will also reduce the degree of ambiguity in certain situations.

Co-ordinating and controlling

Organisational culture is not only important to reduce the level of conflict within the organisation, it will also help the management to co-ordinate and control the organisation itself. Certain courses of action will become an integral part of the organisation's operations. This will enable the management to make a series of decisions without any reference to the employees themselves since they will be expecting this particular type of response. There will be a series of pre-conceived ideas and expectations in certain situations. Individuals will readily accept the fact that they need to respond in a particular way. This will facilitate the co-ordination of various activities. The adoption of various rules and procedures will also reinforce the control that management have and there will be a generally accepted recognition of power and authority within the organisation.

Reducing uncertainty

Just as we mentioned earlier, there is a degree of uncertainty at the beginning of an organisation's existence, and indeed a level of uncertainty from new recruits entering a business. However, the adoption of a standardised form of organisational structure will generally reduce the level of uncertainty present. If there is a coherent culture within the organisation the individuals can attempt to predict various courses of action which may be put forward by the management. This means that when there are conflicts of interest for example, there will be generally accepted ways of coping with these conflicts. This is not to say that the resolution of these problems will necessarily be rational, even though they may be predictable.

Improving motivation and effectiveness

If the organisation has developed a culture then the individuals within the organisation are generally considerably more motivated, making them more efficient and effective. This is, of course, assuming that the organisational culture is one which is fully embraced by most members of the organisation. The individuals working within the organisation will understand the ways in which demotions, punishments, bonuses and wage differentials are calculated. If the employees can readily identify with an organisation and its culture, then they have a tendency to be far more loyal. This means they have fully embraced the beliefs and values of the organisation itself. It is then assumed that the performance of these employees will be greatly enhanced.

Types of organisational culture

As mentioned in the introduction to this chapter, there are a number of ways in which we can classify the different types of organisational culture. Essentially we should consider the main classification systems as suggested by Harrison, Handy, Deal and Kennedy, Quinn and McGrath and Scholz. Over a period of 20 years the classifications of organisational culture have become considerably more developed. This allows us to attempt to make some broad generalisations regarding the organisational cultures which we will find in the majority of businesses.

Harrison and Handy's classification

It was Harrison in 1972 who suggested that there were four different types of organisational culture. These were *power*, *role*, *task* and *person*. By the end of that decade Handy had reworked a number of Harrison's theories and had more clearly identified the nature of each of these cultures.

Power cultures

For Handy the power culture was one which was based on trust and on good personal communications. He suggested that there was little need for rigid bureaucratic procedures since most power and authority was based on a small number of individuals. This meant that the power culture was quite dynamic in the sense that it could react to various changes very quickly, but was highly dependent upon a small number of fairly powerful individuals within the organisation. He also suggested that these types of culture were fairly tough on their employees, that the primary goal of these organisations was largely related to the success of the organisation and not the feelings of their employees. There was also a tendency in this form of culture to have a relatively high turnover of staff since the individuals would need to very clearly identify with this form of culture in order to accept it.

Role cultures

Role culture rests very heavily on bureaucracy. In other words, the processes in the organisation need to be extremely logical and rational. Role cultures are very good at performing particular functions, especially those which need a degree of co-ordination. Again the control within the organisation is held by a handful of managers. Great emphasis is placed on rules and procedures. These are ways in which the organisation can determine the level of performance of individuals within the business. Certain individuals will have power based upon their specific abilities to carry out particular functions and this means that they will be able to exercise a high degree of authority in certain areas. The vast majority of role culture organisations are extremely stable. This means that they operate in a rather predictable environment where their products and services have a long lifespan. These organisations tend to be very good at adapting to slight changes in the external environment but they are not very good at innovation. They prefer gradual change rather than radical revolution.

Task cultures

Task culture rests upon the expertise of individuals rather than the position of individuals within the business. In this respect task culture organisations tend to have matrix structures. In other words, project teams and teams of specialists predominate within the organisation. The overriding concern for this form of organisation is to complete the tasks in hand in the most appropriate manner by making efficient use of all available resources. This means that these types of organisation need to be adaptable and flexible with a number of individuals who have a high degree of autonomy. They also need to have a degree of respect for the status and approach of other individuals within the organisation. Typically, advertising agencies would be an example of a task culture where the onus is upon innovation, ideas and creativity. This type of organisation also needs to be able to react quickly to changes in the external environment and to have procedures and regulations which are adaptable and flexible.

Person cultures

The person culture refers to situations where decisions tend to be made on a more collective basis. This would perhaps be the ideal culture for a partnership. Compromise is the important feature here: individuals working within their own allocated areas of expertise will co-ordinate their activities in order to satisfy the objectives of the organisation. The majority of individuals at a certain level within an organisation will be relatively autonomous. They will have a high level of expertise and be able to perform a number of tasks without having to report to other members of the organisation.

Deal and Kennedy's theories

Deal and Kennedy in the early 1980s developed theories about the way in which organisational culture can be related to the market-place and the way in which the management of the organisation makes decisions and frames its strategies. They were pragmatic in the sense that they were proposing theoretical cultures. They did not necessarily mean that any organisation actually adhered fully to these typologies. However they did manage to identify four main types of organisational culture.

Macho cultures

In their first form of organisational culture, which they called the *macho culture*, they recognised that these types of business have to make fast decisions as an integral part of their operations. They had to adopt a very tough attitude toward their employees and their fellow managers. There is a high degree of internal competition within these organisations. This is largely related to the fact that the operations were extremely high risk. As a result the majority do not enjoy any form of long-term planning or strategy. Indeed most actions are based on short termism. One of the principal features of this form of culture is that the level of co-operation within the business is extremely low. As a result there is a very high turnover of staff and the net result is that the organisational culture is not very strong. Typical examples are organisations operating in the entertainment field and in management consultancy.

Work hard/play hard cultures

The *work hard/play hard culture* is one that is generally associated with sales. The majority of individuals are sales orientated; however the level of risk is comparatively low. The individuals operating within this organisation are required to make a number of repetitive sales to different customers but are not reliant necessarily on one sale itself: it is the cumulative number of sales which determine success or failure. These are team-based organisations which also encourage a high degree of external social activities. The onus is almost certainly on competition, albeit competition based on mutual success. In this respect these organisations would encourage competition and reward individuals for comparative or relative success against other members of the organisation. There is often a tendency in organisations like this for volume of sales or volume of success to be more important than quality of success.

Company cultures

The third form of organisational culture is known as the *company culture*. This refers to organisations who are in high risk areas and operate on the basis that decisions take a long time to come to fruition. Most decision making exists at the top end of the organisation itself. The organisation is extremely hierarchical and the employees are expected to accept and respect the authority and technical competence of more senior managers. The nature of these organisations means that the level of investment in a particular project is extremely high. Although returns are expected in the long term, there is a considerable level of risk attached to each invention or technical breakthrough. In this respect the organisation continually lives on the edge and may fail as a result of decisions made many years ago.

Process cultures

The final form of culture which Deal and Kennedy identify related to process. Their *process culture* organisation operates in a low-risk, slow feedback environment where employees are more encouraged to consider the way in which they do things rather than what they actually do. These cultures tend to be rather protective and are very heavily based on systems and procedures. The onus on employees is to be orderly and to give enormous attention to detail. There is also a predominance of meetings and work groups in order to legitimise decision making and the position of individuals within the hierarchy. In fact, in terms of the hierarchy we will find that process cultures have very rigid levels of management. Great emphasis is placed upon the position which the individual has within the organisation. Having said this, these organisations operate in a rather predictable environment and as a result they are often slow to react.

Quinn and McGrath's cultural types

Quinn and McGrath identified four different organisational cultures. These were known as the *rational or market culture*, the *ideological or adhocracy culture*, the *consensual or clan culture* and the *hierarchical culture*. Much of their theory is based on the fact that when individuals interact within an organisation there is an exchange of ideas or facts. The way in which these exchanges are undertaken is determined by the status of the individuals involved. In order to understand this we need to have a look at the theories in a little more detail.

Rational cultures

The rational culture is very firmly based on the needs of a market. The organisation places a great deal of emphasis on productivity and efficiency. Not only this, the organisation encourages its management to be much more goal-orientated and decisive. In other words, all activities are focused upon tangible performance and as a result individuals are rewarded on an achievement basis.

Adhocracy cultures

The adhocracy culture is an adaptive, creative and autonomous culture. The authority within the organisation is largely based upon the abilities and the charismatic nature of the leaders. These organisations tend to be rather risk-orientated and there is a great emphasis placed upon employees' adherence to the values of the organisation itself.

Consensual cultures

The consensual or clan culture is concerned with equality, integrity and fairness. In this respect, much of the authority within these organisations is based on some form of informal acceptance of power. Decisions tend to be made on the basis of collective agreements or consensus. Dominant leaders are not common within these forms of culture. The overriding concern is that the majority of employees or members of the organisation have maintained a high level of morale. In this way, they are able to co-operate and support one another in order to fulfil the organisational objectives. Loyalty in these organisations is extremely high.

Hierarchical cultures

The hierarchical culture, which we have referred to a number of times already throughout this book, relies upon stability and control. This is achieved through a rigid set of regulations and procedures. Decisions are nearly always made on the basis of facts and the management has a tendency to be rather more cautious and conservative than in any other form of culture. The employees are very strictly controlled through a series of systems aimed at ensuring predictable responses in similar circumstances. It is important for the organisation that they combine the total obedience of their employees with a decision-making process based upon logic.

Scholz's dimensions of culture

Finally we refer to Scholz who developed three different dimensions of culture which he referred to as *evolution*, *internal* and *external*. Evolution refers to how the culture can change over a period of time. The internal consideration is how the circumstances within an organisation affect its culture, and the external is how the outside business environment will affect the culture of the organisation. Out of these three considerations, Scholz developed five particular cultural types which he called *stable*, *reactive*, *anticipating*, *exploring* and *creative*. If you refer to Fig. 4.3 you will see how all of these considerations fit together. It is

The evolution-induced dimension				
Culture	**Personality**	**Time Orientation**	**Risk Orientation**	**Change Orientation**
Stable	Introvert	Backward looking	Risk averse	No change
Reactive	Introvert	Present	Minimum	Minimum
Anticipating	Introvert and Extrovert	Present	Familiar only	Incremental
Exploring	Extrovert	Present and Future	Risk/gain trade-offs	Radical
Creative	Extrovert	Future	Unfamiliar	Novel

Fig. 4.3 The evolution-induced dimension

also interesting to note that he developed three further cultural types based on the nature of the business itself. These he called *production*, *bureaucratic* and *professional*. If you refer to Fig. 4.4 you will see how this fits into his overall theory.

Scholz's internal-induced dimension				
Culture Type	Predominace of Routine Operations	Level of Standardisation	Skill Requirements	Input and Relevance of Culture to Most Employees
Production	High	High	High	Negligible
Bureaucratic	Medium	Medium	Medium	According to hierarchical position
Professional	Low	Low	Low	Only those with significant skills and knowledge

Fig. 4.4 The internal-induced dimension

One of the major problems with identifying different types of culture is that it is all too easy to try to pigeonhole particular organisations. No organisation necessarily fits into any of these particular categories. The majority of organisations are far too complex for this rather generalised approach. The best that any of these classifications or typologies can offer is the fact that they give us some point of reference between extremes.

So far we have investigated the different types of theories which can be applied to the study of organisational culture. It is now appropriate to turn our attention to some of the specific forms of culture and try to identify some of their key characteristics.

Formal and informal cultures

The establishment of a formal culture, which is clearly identifiable to all members of the organisation and has been developed as a result of the management deciding to impose a particular way of approaching all operations, is likely to have been clearly thought through and may cover all aspects of activity and behaviour. Obviously, formal cultures can develop over a period of time, but the formalisation process may be inconsistent, leading to differences in culture in different parts of the organisation. In other words, to create a formal culture may mean beginning from the basics and slowly building the culture into a fully integrated and encompassing system of behaviour. On the other hand, an informal culture may have developed as a result of a more loose-knit organisation, needing to be able to adapt in a changing environment, where it would be inappropriate to try to impose anything like a formal culture. The very nature of the informal culture allows each individual within the organisation to develop along different lines and hopefully be far more responsive as a result.

Typically we would find a formal culture in a bureaucratic organisation which relies on formalised behaviour and standardisation as its key controlling mechanisms. For organisations which have a more flexible production requirement, an informal culture may be more appropriate, as this will allow decisions to be made without reference to stultifying decision making, which needs to pass through various stages of the hierarchy before its implementation.

Positive and negative cultures

It is probably best to think about these two aspects of culture in terms of their overall impact on the organisation's ability to develop its employees, as well as having adaptable structures and procedures which are capable of coping with a number of different circumstances. A positive culture would rest firmly upon the ability of the employees to feel free enough and confident enough to make valuable recommendations and contributions to the organisation as they feel appropriate. On the other hand, a negative culture would place the vast majority of employees in either a position where they feel that their contribution is undervalued, or their views are under-represented. As a result, employees will have a tendency to be led from the top of the organisation, rather than feeling that they can make any kind of impact on the structure or the procedures of the organisation.

Backward-facing and forward-looking cultures

Typically, a bureaucracy or an organisation which rests upon traditional ways of doing things will have a tendency to be rather backward-facing in terms of culture. They will find it extremely difficult to embrace cultural development within the organisation, since they cannot appreciate the fact that any of their systems or operations need to be adapted or changed to cater for new challenges and opportunities. This will be typified by strict rules and regulations governing the majority of policies, procedures and operations throughout the length and breadth of the organisation. There will be considerable resistance, both at managerial level and in other parts of the organisation, to any hint of change or development. This will be particularly true of organisations which appear to be relatively successful, while still resting upon traditional ways of doing things.

A forward-looking organisation will either tend to have a culture that is in a continual state of flux, or will have developed a culture which positively encourages employee-involvement, continual change and investigation into new ways of carrying out various procedures and operations. It is probable that these forward-looking organisations are somewhat smaller and younger than those which have adopted a backward-looking stance. For an organisation which has a relatively short history, there will not have been many opportunities to develop a systematic culture which can determine the behaviour and approach of the organisation and its employees.

Autocratic and democratic cultures

We have mentioned both of these terms in previous sections of the book and in many respects we can see how these two different approaches to culture and hierarchy can influence the way in which the organisation will develop or retain its cultural identity.

In an autocratic organisation all decision making and operations will be controlled by the upper tiers of the management; those who have direct responsibility for supervising employees will have little opportunity to amend policy and procedures as they are required to follow the instructions of their line managers. Decisions will be made within these cultures purely on the basis of authority; there will be little opportunity for discussion or input at lower levels in the hierarchy.

A democratic organisation, on the other hand, may not only embrace many of the forward-looking attributes, but may also positively encourage considerable involvement at all levels of the organisation. While some organisations may strive for consensus in decision making and work patterns, others may have stylised or formalised ways in which they encourage employees to make a contribution to the decision-making process and the development of the organisation in general.

Profit-driven cultures, social responsibility and public image

It is probably fair to say that the vast majority of organisations in the private sector have a profit-driven motive behind most of their decision making and operations. The profit-driven motive is a matter of degree. At one end of the spectrum, some organisations will be completely focused upon the acquisition of profit before any other consideration. To this end, employees will be encouraged to cut corners, drive hard bargains with suppliers and try to obtain the best possible prices for all of their products and services. This will be at the expense of any other external stakeholder, although they may have to consider the probability of having to adhere to legislation and other controls within the markets in which they are operating. The vast majority of organisations would, however, state that they do have a degree of social responsibility, although for the most part this refers strictly to changes in their operations related to legislation and environ-mental controls. There are only a few organisations who have taken their social responsibilities further than they legally need to and, to this end, have attempted to make as much capital out of this approach as possible.

Realistically, organisations which have an awareness of their social responsibility will have a view to developing the way in which they operate beyond what is legally required at present. In strategic planning terms, it would be foolish for an organ-isation to move slowly and consistently with the developments of legislative control over their operations. This may mean that the organisation will have to develop its social responsibility in a slow and meticulous manner. If it does this it may have to constantly change the way in which it operates to compensate for changes in the law. It may be more cost-effective to consider moving ahead of the legislation, taking short-term advantage of this fact, while making the investments proactively.

The ways in which customers and other external stakeholders view an organisa-tion can be extremely important in terms of the business's ability to perform well and retain market share. The ways in which these external groups perceive the organisation is integral to the organisation's structural development in terms of making it both attractive and understandable.

Tribal or clan features

Many organisations positively encourage involvement and co-operation at all levels beyond what would normally be expected. Taking the basic premise that all em-ployees exchange labour for wages or salaries, the tribal or clan culture encourages involvement beyond contractual obligations. From the organisation's point of view, they are offering considerable security and loyalty to their existing employees. From the employee's standpoint, they are offering, in return, loyalty to the organi-sation and a commitment based on mutual interest. The success of the organisation will determine the prosperity of the employees and the organisation itself.

Tribal or clan features are developed through a thorough socialisation process, which seeks to develop unity within the organisation. There will be a clear career path available to all employees and those who have been in the organisation for a considerable number of years will be accepted as role models and mentors to the newcomers. The values and norms of the organisation will remain in tact through-out several generations of employees. Each organisation will have a unique history, which is not only kept alive in the hearts of the employees, but also by celebrating the way in which certain key historical developments have influenced the organi-sation. All members of the organisation will have a shared image of the business's style and conduct and will also share a pride in their membership of the organisa-tion. In these organisations all roles will be interdependent and there will be an extensive network of informal relationships between different individuals in sepa-rate areas of the organisation. By having shared goals, perceptions and behaviour, communication, co-ordination and integration will be greatly enhanced. The clan culture, above all, promotes feelings of personal ownership for all employees.

There will be no need for the organisation to establish autocratic or authoritarian decision making or rules upon the employees.

Rules and codes of behaviour

We have already looked at the various types of organisation. You will now be aware that each organisational type will have its own peculiarities or personal identity. Establishing clear rules and codes of behaviour enables the organisation to ensure that all employees share a similar and familiar approach to duties and tasks. While, on the one hand, a formal organisation may establish a comprehensive handbook that clearly indicates the way in which employees are expected to behave, others may take a less formal view and seek to gradually socialise carefully selected employees, who they feel are capable of embracing the organisation's viewpoint and behavioural patterns. The vast majority of organisational cultures are unstated, with the employees not really appreciating the fact that they are reflecting this culture in everything they say and do. Just because an organisational culture is not verbalised does not mean that it does not have a considerable influence on its employees. Some organisations will have a strong culture, but the majority, as we will see, have strong sub-cultures, which have developed in various parts of the organisation and, if not adequately controlled, will lead to considerable conflict and power struggles.

Sub-cultures

As the organisation establishes autonomous or semi-autonomous groups, variations or radically different cultures will develop in these parts of the organisation. Providing these sub-cultures do not actively work against the core values and norms of the organisation, they may prove a positive benefit, particularly if the nature of the work carried out by those in the sub-cultures requires a radically different approach. Physical separation, in terms of remote geographical location, may be one reason why sub-cultures will develop. However, in other organisations it may be simply as a result of those members of the sub-culture undergoing training and development which differentiates them from the rest of the organisation. Individuals in different departments or divisions of the organisation will naturally have a number of shared values which will lead to the development of a sub-culture which does differ from the norm. The larger the organisation, the more likely there is to be a profusion of small sub-cultures in various parts of the business.

Review questions

1   What are the four basic core values when considering organisational culture?

2   Describe Harrison and Handy's typologies.

3   To what does the term 'artefacts' refer in an organisational context?

4   What are organisational 'myths'?

5   In terms of organisational culture, what are the 'rites of passage', 'questioning' and 'renewal'?

6   What purposes do symbols have in organisational culture?

7   Why would an organisation identify a corporate hero?

8   What are the five different types of basic emotion identified by Schein?

9   Identify at least ten sources of organisational culture.

10   Why is leadership so important in the shaping of organisational culture?

11   What are the nature and purpose of sub-cultures?

12   What theories did Handy rework and how did he more clearly identify the nature of different cultures?

13   What kind of culture would be used for a partnership and why?

14   What were Quinn and McGrath's four organisational cultures?

15   Describe the five culture types described by Scholz.

16   What are the main differences between formal and informal organisational culture?

17   Distinguish between positive and negative cultures.

18   Distinguish between back-facing and forward-looking organisational cultures, and explain the advantages and disadvantages of each.

19   Describe the differences between autocratic and democratic organisational culture.

20   To what extent has social responsibility influenced organisational culture?

Influencing factors

There are a number of different influencing factors that can determine the nature of the organisational culture and any probable changes which are either underway or need to be implemented. Broadly, these influences can be broken down into two major areas: one which can be considered as internal influencing factors, and the other as external cultural changes in the environment or the market-place. As a result of this, the organisation may choose to adopt either organisational or product ethics in order to fully broadcast its intentions and stance to stakeholders. This approach will involve considerable changes in the business practice and trading policies of that organisation.

Internal influencing factors

History, ownership, size and technology

Just as all of these factors will affect the way in which an organisation chooses to configure itself, we will also discover that they will have a marked impact upon the nature and development of organisational culture. As we have seen in the previous chapter, organisations which have a formal, backward-facing and auto-cratic nature, coupled with the tendency to be somewhat bureaucratic, will have established a very rigid organisational culture, which is resistant to change. Alternatively, those organisations which have a less formal, more positive, for-ward-looking and democratic approach will be more able to cope with cultural changes when faced with different sets of circumstances.

The ownership of the organisation will naturally have a bearing on the predomi-nant culture. Those organisations which have had a stable ownership over a peri-od of years will have had the time to develop and establish a recognisable organ-isational culture. Others, which have been subject to mergers or takeovers, may find that radically different organisational cultures are imposed upon them by the new owners. While, in the short term, this may be somewhat disquieting to the employees and managers, it is an inevitable result of an ownership change.

Naturally, the new owners will seek to impose their own culture, possibly based upon their experience in other organisations, or the predominant culture in the new parent company. This is not to say that ownership changes are necessarily negative. In fact, many ownership changes will allow an organisation to seriously reconsider the nature of its culture. It is also important to realise that an ownership change may be precisely *because* the prevailing culture in the organisation that has been acquired is exactly in accordance with the wishes of the new owners. In this respect, they will seek to replicate the culture of the newly acquired organisation into their existing areas of business, having had the opportunity to closely examine all of the mechanisms.

Naturally, as an organisation grows, it may need to radically reconsider its culture. For cultures which have operated successfully in smaller units, there may be a need to update or amend in order to compensate for the increased size or any radical changes in structure. Typically, as an organisation grows and diversifies, it will find that certain aspects of its organisational culture are no longer appropriate or desirable. The organisation will simply have to change its culture in order to survive.

As we have mentioned previously, the implementation and use of technology will have serious repercussions on all aspects of the organisation's structure and culture. Enhanced communications, for example, may break down many of the sub-cultures which were predominant in the pre-technology stage of the organisation. Equally, the widespread introduction of technology relating to production will mean that smaller working groups are required, to operate in a far more interdependent way than in the past. This will all lead to cultural changes, and while different parts of the organisation may resist this change, the management will seek to move towards a position where all areas of the organisation embrace technology and accept the resulting changes in their culture.

Goals and objectives

The development of organisational culture, as we have seen, is related to creating an environment where the organisation's goals and objectives are dominant throughout all parts of the business. It is obvious that if goals and objectives change then so too will the culture. The business will not be able to allow a mismatch between the new goals and objectives and a culture which is related to a previous set of strategic aims. In reflecting the new goals and objectives, the organisational culture may need to embrace many of the factors which we have already considered, such as a change in ownership, size, or the widespread implementation of technology. Whatever the case, the management needs to carefully consider the impact of a change in goals and objectives and how this will affect current working practices and relationships. It would be difficult for most organisations to cope with sudden changes in their strategic ambitions, perhaps in relation to challenges or opportunities in the external environment, as well as handling considerable cultural changes internally.

External cultural environment

Perhaps the most dominant influence on changes in organisational culture is the external business environment. The corporate culture of the organisation needs to be able to incorporate any factor in the external environment that will help it succeed or meet its goals and objectives. Given the fact that the majority of organisations in a particular market or sector differ widely, they will all be aware, nevertheless, of changes or influences in their external environment. An organisation that cannot cope with a dynamic and competitive environment will be at a grave disadvantage compared to those who are able to adapt more freely. As we will see when we consider changes in ethics, practice and trading policies, competition is only one of the many influences which an organisation has to deal with.

This situation is further complicated as an organisation moves from being a national to a multinational operation. They will have been able to, in the past, embrace many of the national cultural characteristics of their own country, but as they expand into new markets they will have to become far more multicultural in their outlook. Given the fact that the majority of countries are now multicultural themselves, organisations will have become aware of the need to consider different values, religions, attitudes and regional differences. An organisation may find itself in a very difficult position if it cannot strike the correct balance in terms of the different multicultural pressures demanded of it.

Organisational responsibility

Regardless of the type of business or organisation, there are always groups or individuals who are affected by or affect the organisation itself. In many respects these can be seen as imposing some kind of responsibility upon the organisation. For most businesses the groups or individuals are commonly known as stakeholders and they include the following:

◆ *employees* – whose major areas of interest and concern are working conditions, job security, wages and development.

◆ *the management* of the business – whose main interests are their own job security, their status in the organisation, their power (compared to others) and the growth and profitability of the organisation.

◆ *shareholders* – whose main aim is to receive dividends on their investment, ensure that the market value of their investment is secure and to make sure that the liquidity of their investment remains high.

◆ *creditors* – whose principal area of interest lies in the security of the loans they have made to the business, the interest received on those loans and again the liquidity of their investment.

◆ *suppliers* – whose interests include the security of contracts made with the organisation, maintaining regular payments from the organisation, the growth of both their own and their debtors' organisations and the general development of the market.

◆ *society* – who, through various government departments, voluntary organisations and codes of practice are concerned with safe products, protection of the environment, equal opportunities and ensuring that there is no discrimination.

We can now identify the stakeholders as being groups which are affected by the business's policies, operations and other decisions. It is obviously important for the business to take these stakeholders' views and needs in mind when formulating their aims and objectives. However, this does make decision making a much more complex process. Clearly, certain stakeholders will have more influence than others and the business needs to be aware of how much power each of these stakeholder groups may have, not only now but in the future.

So if businesses are answerable to various stakeholders, then we can identify those which are directly involved in the organisation and those which may become involved in the organisation at a later date. The traditional stakeholders would obviously include shareholders, customers and employees. Indeed, very many of the basic definitions of stakeholders only consider these three main groups.

Changing attitudes to growth and development

It has often been argued that economic development and growth in business activity is beneficial to society as a whole. It is also an important influence on the quality of life of that society. In this respect businesses have developed processes and practices which are designed not only to increase their production as well as the consumption of those products and services, but also to reduce the detrimental effects on the environment. While economic growth is still a primary concern of both businesses and the government, the protection of the environment, and more broadly the protection of consumers, has been seen as an extremely important consideration. Given that many natural resources are reaching stages of depletion and there have been marked increases in the number of accidents which could be attributed to business activity, it has been argued that many countries have overridden environmental concerns in the pursuit of economic growth. Factors which point towards this view are the high levels of pollution and reduced quality of life in major cities and other areas with high industrial concentration.

What many governments and businesses are looking to find is a balance between environmental protection and economic development. It seems that the only way to overcome the dangers which face this continued degradation of the environment is for businesses to accept responsibility for their own behaviour and the consequences of that behaviour. However, if we consider the fact that many businesses simply serve as a means by which products and services are provided to society, then we are narrowing the number of groups they may become involved with. Given that businesses do affect many of our lives, either directly or indirectly, the development of environmental perspectives has become an integral part of many corporate plans. This means that businesses need to apply concerns about their sphere of activity to their working practice when it comes down to day-to-day operations. As we will see shortly, this leads to a business culture, which is responsible on a corporate basis.

Business ethics

Broadly speaking, we can define ethics as a particular code of behaviour, which to most people is considered to be a morally correct approach. Obviously if we refer back to stakeholders, their interpretation of morally correct behaviour will differ. For most businesses, ethics concern the activities they should and should not become involved with. Ethical issues will invariably concern certain businesses more than others.

The tobacco manufacturers and distributors have found themselves at the centre of a moral and ethical dilemma. The basis of their business depends upon individuals choosing to smoke. However, since research carried out on behalf of various government institutions and cancer-related pressure groups has led to a causal link between smoking and diseases, they find themselves at times spurned by government, but at the same time needed by government. It is true to say that tobacco provides a considerable source of income for most governments, and, as such, there is a split in loyalty when one considers this income and the relative costs to society. In the face of widespread opposition in developed nations, tobacco manufacturers have switched their marketing towards the less developed countries. These countries with a slightly less aware consumer base are now the major growth areas in tobacco distribution. Equally, there has been considerable debate regarding advertising of products aimed at children during commercial breaks between children's television programmes. While this is prime advertising space for these toy and game manufacturers, it places parents or guardians in a position where their children are exposed to persuasive advertising, thus creating a demand that cannot always be fulfilled.

If you refer to the section which considers European Union and UK law and policies you will see that there are a number of codes of practice and pieces of legislation which cover many aspects of advertising and marketing. It is certainly much harder, given this comprehensive range of laws and policies, for an organisation to make incorrect claims about its products or, more broadly, be misleading.

One of the key debates which surrounds business ethics concerns the notion that business ethics are merely a public relations exercise. Many organisations in any case find themselves in a position where they could not make false claims about their product. Equally, their advertising which aims to be informative, as well as persuasive, purely seeks to gain a temporary advantage over their competitors. Most organisations operate within an ethical code whether they recognise this or not. Normally this will be part of the organisation's culture and the decisions made by senior management will reflect this. Given that individuals within an organisation, particularly the senior managers, are members of the society in which the business operates, they will be influenced by the society's general attitudes and ethical codes. In a competitive environment, however, many businesses face the dilemma of having to incorporate ethical standards and concern for the environment with a need to maximise profits. Any system or code which aims to put these ethics to the forefront may, inevitably, have an effect on profits. Ultimately business activities are only justifiable in as much as they reflect the requirements of the stakeholders. It is often a question of identifying the requirements of the stakeholders and reconciling them against any ethical code.

In today's business world organisations face far more scrutiny from the various stakeholders and coupled with this they operate within an environment which is far more controlled by regulations and legislation. The question of business ethics and public relations tends to rest upon a notion of public trust. Any organisation which appears to violate this trust faces the danger of being beaten in the market-place by others that are more eager to please the customers and reflect their beliefs more accurately. Having said this, the majority of business activity does not involve any question of business ethics, indeed not many of the activities involved are controversial at all. In cases when they do, which may relate to abuses of power or breaches in legislation or regulation, the organisation will face public exposure which would harm not only the image of the organisation, but its long-term economic viability.

Business ethics, however, have grown in stature and importance. The consumer does demand that businesses act in a more ethical manner. The government ensures this through regulation and legislation. The true measure is when the organisation incorporates these business ethics within the framework of their normal business activities and does this in a sustainable manner.

Enironmental management

Any business response or action which involves expenditure has a trade-off cost. Any resources which are ploughed into ethical or environmental concerns mean that money, time and effort are not being directed towards making profits. This is an opportunity cost. Businesses do not have infinite resources so any investment decision in relation to environmental concerns must be taken very carefully. Taking environmental responsibility is, of course, a long-term policy and, as we have said earlier, a business which is endeavouring to survive in an ever more competitive market may need to concentrate on short-term returns. Many businesses would actually like to be environmentally responsible, but their stakeholders may wish them to concentrate on matters which are in the best interests of the business in order to optimise their own rewards. If we take the statement that many businesses are principally concerned with short-term profits, then it is the shareholders or those who have provided finance who have the most influence. The organisation would have to prioritise its objectives and make sure that there is a development plan as part of the major corporate plan. The key question

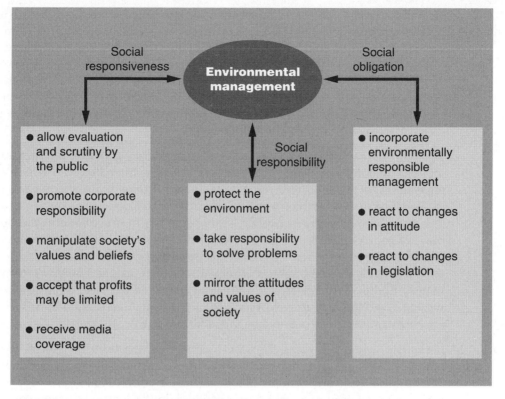

Fig. 4.5 Different approaches to environmental management

is whether we can rely on businesses to have sufficient responsibility towards society and the environment or whether they actually need to be forced to take these matters on board through legislation and regulation. We can best address the various ways in which an organisation can implement some form of environmental management by looking at the three different ways of approaching this problem (*see also* Fig. 4.5):

1 *Social obligation* – in this approach the organisation tends to react either to legislation or to changes in the attitudes of society or, more particularly, the market. They will only incorporate environmentally responsible management when they have to. In this particular approach the most important stakeholder is the shareholder and consequently profit is the most important goal

2 *Social responsibility* – in this example the business tends to go beyond the basic requirements as laid down by law and will try to mirror the current attitudes and values held by society in general. The business will attempt to take responsibility by attempting to solve environmental problems and will also take steps to protect the environment. While this form of business is also bound by the wishes of their shareholders, profit is important but it is not the dominant influencing factor.

3 *Social responsiveness* – this particular approach is far more proactive, in fact organisations which fall into this category are actively attempting to manipulate society's values and beliefs. Typically these businesses will be at the forefront of promoting corporate responsibility, will open themselves out to evaluation and scrutiny by the public and also be ready to accept that profits may be damaged or limited by their policies and procedures. In return, of course, the business receives considerable media coverage and a high profile as an exemplar of corporate responsibility.

The last approach takes the view that a better society provides a better environment in which to operate. There are, of course, other benefits which can be enjoyed by the business as a result of taking environmental policies to their logical conclusion. As a direct result of environmental policy the business may be able to reduce its energy costs or wastage. As an indirect benefit, the business may, of course, increase its market share due to its higher profile in the media. Cynics might suggest that by taking this proactive view an organisation will find itself less likely to be the subject of regulations or threatened by any external regulatory bodies. Whichever environmental management system an organisation wishes to put in place, they will have to face the fact that there will be short-term expenses and the pay-back will be much longer term.

Perhaps a way of assessing the costs against the long-term benefits is to undertake a cost–benefit analysis which would allow the business to set out and evaluate the social costs and benefits of any particular policy. It is, of course, extremely difficult to put any price on environmental gains or losses, but monetary values do offer some way of being able to make meaningful comparisons. On a global level, of course, you could compare the desire or demand for certain products and services against the need to try to protect the environment and reduce the use of scarce resources. It is extremely difficult to measure physical items such as products or services against improvements or reductions in the quality of life. Whether the business intends to incorporate some form of environmental management may be taken out of its hands. It will always need to have some form of contingency plan in mind which addresses the possibility of new regulations or legislation coming into force which may force the business to do something in respect of their operations that they do not at present undertake. This contingency planning obviously involves second guessing society's opinion as it develops, reflected by government policy, and the incorporation of this into forward planning which lays the foundation for the organisation to adapt as required.

Social costs

Pollution and other environmental concerns

An obvious example of a social cost is air and water pollution. These result from production methods but no account is then taken of the ill effects such pollution may have on others. Social costs are considered to be those costs borne by society as a whole or incurred by individuals who did not consume the good or service which generated the cost. However, it is often very difficult to measure social costs and put a value upon them. Indeed it is often very difficult to notice them in the first place, let alone find the cause.

Social costs can occur due to:

◆ *production on consumption* – the adverse effects of pollution on recreational areas, e.g. chemical pollution in rivers and lakes causing a danger to water sports.

◆ *production on producers* – the adverse effect of one production pollution on another production, e.g. chemical pollution in rivers and lakes causing diseases in livestock.

◆ *consumption on production* – examples are traffic congestion caused by private motorists, increased transport and delivery costs for businesses.

◆ *consumption on consumption* – litter caused by some consumers, preventing others from using recreational facilities.

Governments, consumers and businesses are becoming more and more aware of what effects their actions have on the environment. As mentioned, an obvious social cost of production is pollution to air and water. Factories churn out by-products into the air, such as sulphur dioxide and smoke, and dump chemical waste into rivers. However, it is not only private businesses which are to blame; consumers are also at fault. Each time consumers purchase and use products containing CFCs (chlorofluorocarbon), for example, they contribute towards pollution. Consumers may only consider the private costs involved but not the social costs of their activities on the environment. In recent years several important environmental considerations have been highlighted by the media. Some specific social costs include:

◆ *global warming or the greenhouse effect* – the more pollutants released into the atmosphere the thicker the atmosphere becomes, preventing heat generated by the sun's rays from escaping.

◆ *holes in the ozone layers* – increasing concern is being generated by the decrease in the ozone layer surrounding the earth. It is feared that as the ozone layer is eroded, more and more of the harmful UVA and UVB rays from the sun will penetrate earth's atmosphere causing universal incidence of skin cancer and, probably worse for the planet, restricting plant growth. This could turn large areas into virtual deserts; consider the recent droughts in central and northern Africa.

◆ *acid rain* – the expulsion of acidic gases, such as sulphur dioxide, into the atmosphere and the mixing of them with moisture in clouds, causes the rain drops to have a slightly acidic content. The result of this is 'acid rain' which has destroyed large areas of Scandinavian woodland and damaged flora and fauna throughout the world.

Other environmental considerations

Other environmental considerations that should be considered are, for example, the destruction of the South American rainforests. In many cases this takes place not for the wood the trees provide, but to make way for mines to extract metals and minerals or to be used as farmland. Lastly we must consider the effect of rubbish generated by humans. Every single business activity and household in the UK generates waste, over 20 per cent of which is dumped into the sea. We are not even going to attempt to discuss the effects of nuclear by-products and nuclear accidents such as the meltdown at Chernobyl.

Drawing on finite resources

Alongside these considerations of pollution we should also look at the effect we are having on the level of natural resources around the world. Take British Gas, for example – every time somebody lights up their gas oven they are burning a scarce and finite resource (i.e. once burnt the gas cannot be reclaimed and re-used; it is gone). Also, by not taking into account the full cost of businesses activities such as pollution, the price system will not bring about efficient allocation of resources, (allocative efficiency), which means not putting resources to their best use.

Social costs and effects on health

The social costs and effects on the health of the nation of such activities is obviously quite extreme. In some cases air pollution can cause respiratory infections, cancer, burning eyes and skin infections, not to mention the effects caused by water pollution to humans, fish and wildlife in general. Such an effect on health carries a cost in itself: the more people who suffer from such conditions, the more strain is put upon healthcare systems and the more costs incurred in treating them. Another effect is that as resources become more and more scarce they become more and more expensive. Thus those families and individuals on low incomes can no longer afford them, which again if we take our example of gas, would cause adverse health conditions as people can no longer afford to heat their homes.

Employment considerations

The effects generated by social costs on employment are twofold in nature. First, if all companies were to take into account the organisational costs of production – plus the wider social costs – this would necessitate a rise in prices causing the level of demand within the economy to fall. However, consumers already pay for these social costs in terms of rates and taxes. Thus the offsetting of social costs on employment can be seen as being adverse.

If we assume that this adverse effect means that people are either being underemployed or are unemployed then they will suffer from a lower income than if they were in full-time employment. The more disposable income a person has the more goods and services they can afford to buy. Lower income brackets conversely can afford less, and not being able to afford goods and services can lead to poor or ill health, for example if you cannot afford a balanced diet, suitable clothing and shelter. Along these lines, concerns about future employment can cause ill health as well, ranging from tension and stress to depression and nervous breakdowns. Coupled with ill health from pollution this could be a serious problem. The effect upon employment can spiral as employers may be reluctant to employ, somebody who suffers from poor or ill health and is liable to take time off; they will opt for someone who is fit and healthy. Another aspect to be considered is that, as businesses become more aware of their social responsibilities, and as consumers demand 'greener' and cleaner goods, they may well invent more modern machinery and production techniques, which could, as is often the case, lead to job losses as increasingly new innovations and modern production practices become less and less labour intensive.

However, there is another side of this. The pressure on business and the demands of consumers have created new industries and markets for 'green' environmentally friendly products and have created some employment opportunities along with them.

Social or environmental audits

In the USA, corporations began to consider environmental audits some 30 years ago. These audits are now fairly common practice there and they are becoming increasingly important in Europe also. Typically, an environmental or social audit would involve the following professionals:

◆ lawyers

◆ scientists

◆ economists

◆ engineers

◆ environmental specialists.

A business will access these individuals through consultancies, the government and from its own workforce. In the USA there is an Environmental Protection Agency which publishes guidelines and recommends that businesses go beyond the legal requirements.

So what exactly is social and environmental auditing? It is a check on the environmental performance of the business as well as an investigation of the management systems which have been created to bring about improvements. The audits usually begin with the business establishing a baseline to make an assessment of current practice. From this baseline the business is able to compare its performance in succeeding years. Subsequent audits will show whether the business has reached its target objectives. Audits are regular, systematic, objective and well documented. Since the audit aims to measure the business's performance it should help the management to control environmental practices and ensure that statutory requirements are met.

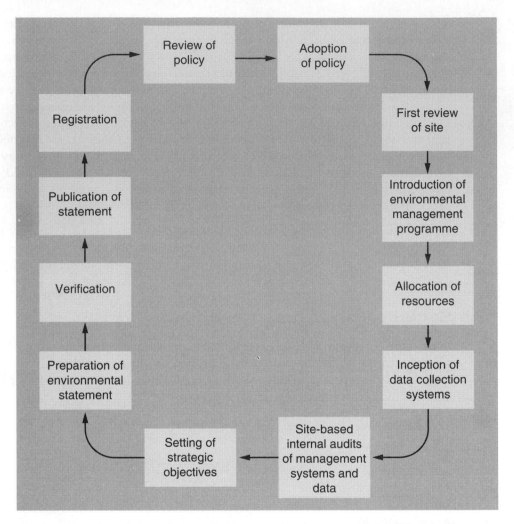

Fig. 4.6 The framework for environmental management, auditing and disclosure
Based on the requirements of the European Union Eco-Management and Auditing Scheme. Prepared with the assistance of Steve McIvor of The Body Shop.

The framework for environmental management, auditing and disclosure and for social auditing and disclosure as practised at The Body Shop are shown in Figs 4.6 and 4.7. The key objectives of an environmental audit are to:

◆ consider whether the environmental management systems are operating well.

◆ compare the business's practice with any legislation.

◆ ensure that the business is complying with its own corporate policy.

◆ develop procedures which will allow the organisation to achieve and develop its environmental objectives.

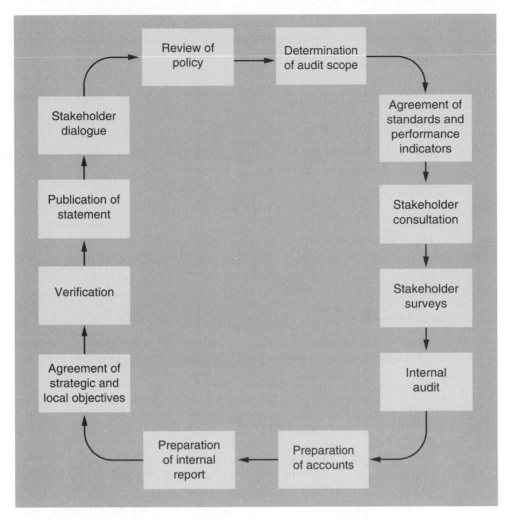

Fig. 4.7 The framework for social auditing and disclosure at The Body Shop
Prepared with the assistance of Steve McIvor of The Body Shop.

◆ ensure that employees and the public in general have adequate protection in terms of health and safety.

◆ carry out risk assessment on environmental failure.

◆ sample air, water and soil around factories.

◆ suggest ways in which the organisation can make improvements to its environmental practices.

Advantages and disadvantages of environmental audits

The key benefits which a business can enjoy by carrying out an environmental audit include the avoidance of legal action being taken against it, and consequent fines, reduction in the cost of energy, waste minimisation and improvements in quality (in conjunction with other measures such as quality circles).

There are, however, a number of disadvantages or costs which may be incurred. These include:

◆ the cost of the audit.

◆ the cost of complying with the audit.

◆ the disruption in production while the organisation accommodates the suggestions arising out of the audit.

Three basic stages in an audit

There are three basic stages to an audit. These are the *pre-audit stage*, *the audit stage* and the *post-audit stage*. We will now have a look at these in a little more detail beginning with the pre-audit stage.

The pre-audit stage

◆ In order to ascertain the scope and framework of the audit, the business needs to set goals and objectives which aim to develop strategies.

◆ The selection of the members of the audit team is crucial. The business will need to identify individuals who have both expertise in environmental matters and a knowledge of the operations of the business.

◆ The members of the audit team also need to have an awareness of the industry at large and a detailed knowledge of the internal workings of the organisation itself. They will need to familiarise themselves with the premises, the production processes and the location of each of these sites. Often the audit team will produce questionnaires for the management to fill in, in order to gain further insights into the workings of the business.

◆ The audit team may also make use of questionnaires which they will send to the workforce. These will aim to cover such areas as health and safety and working conditions.

The audit stage

Turning to the audit stage itself, which of course is carried out on site, the following aspects will need to be addressed:

◆ The audit team will inspect records and other documents held by the organisation which would include waste licences and discharge consents.

◆ The audit team will also investigate and inspect the maintenance programmes and ascertain what the business intends to do in the case of accidents or spillage. The organisation will have to have developed a control programme and the audit team will look at the management procedures, equipment available and any engineering considerations.

◆ The management will be investigated in terms of its competence and its ability to authorise activities.

◆ The audit team will confidentially interview various members of staff in order to collect information concerning the effectiveness of systems and waste management.

◆ Finally, the plant itself will be inspected together with the working practices, the safety equipment and any sampling or monitoring procedures carried out by the business. At this stage the audit team will also take soil, air and liquid samples, and if appropriate noise samples.

The post-audit stage

The final stage of the audit concerns the post-audit. The key features here are:

◆ An evaluation to ascertain whether sufficient information has been collected to make a meaningful audit.

◆ The next part of this stage is to put the findings into written form so that discussions can begin with the management of the business. It will be important for the audit team and the management to look at the audit findings to see if there are any misinterpretations or misunderstandings. At this stage the management will be able to take note of what steps they need to take. As a consequence of the audit the business will be able to develop an action plan to deal with any deficiencies within their operations. They will be able to establish a schedule and work out some practical solutions to deal with any problems which may have been highlighted.

Product ethics; eco-management and eco-labelling

Eco-management

In 1991 the European Commission established a European Union Eco-Management and Auditing scheme. The regulation came into force in March 1992. It provides a framework for organisations to plan and assess the impact they have on the environment. It encourages them to commit to a policy of reducing the environmental impact. It further encourages them to make statements and record their progress to the public. While this is a voluntary scheme it is expected that the system will come into full force and become compulsory, particularly for larger businesses. The key objectives of the scheme are:

◆ to set up and implement an environmental protection scheme.

◆ to carry out regular and systematic evaluations of the environmental systems to ensure that the public is informed about the environmental performance.

If a business wishes to join the eco-audit scheme, it has to make a commitment to adopt the eco-audit cycle shown in Fig. 4.8. Essentially this involves the following:

◆ define environmental policy

◆ set targets within specific time frames

◆ establish plans and systems to aid the reaching of these targets

◆ constantly monitor these systems

◆ regularly audit the progress

◆ report the findings to the public and have a third party independently audit them

◆ establish new targets built upon the initial successes and continue the procedure.

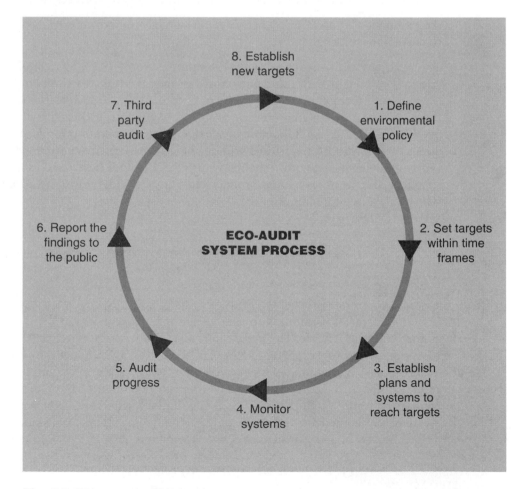

Fig. 4.8 The eco-audit process

The key aspects of the eco-auditing scheme include the following:

◆ an assessment of the environmental impact of the business's activities

◆ the careful management of energy, raw materials and water, etc.

◆ a reduction in the amount of waste produced by the business

◆ a careful consideration of the design of products and the processes used to make them

◆ the prevention of accidents

◆ to encourage employees to become involved in the system

◆ to involve the public as much as practicable.

By taking the eco-audit scheme on board a business will need to amend its policies, targets, objectives, action plans and systems. While many of these changes can be made internally, there may be a need for the business to use the expertise of external consultants. Once the business has carried out a full auditing operation it can then call in an accredited environmental verifier who will be able to state whether the environmental report is true and fair. Once this has been carried out then the business will be included on the Eco-management and Audit Register.

Eco-labelling

The fact that only around 2 per cent of plastic used in consumer products is recycled indicates that, there is a poor infrastructure to recycle these products. There has been a gradual development in the way in which the lifecycle of a product can be managed to attempt to ensure that there is a minimum amount of impact to the environment. This is known as *product stewardship* and is very much incorporated in the eco-labelling system. Basically product stewardship involves the following:

◆ considering the design of a product and looking at its efficiency

◆ examining the energy, raw materials and components used and attempting to discover whether there are any more environmentally friendly substitutes available

◆ looking at the production process itself to see if there is a better way to produce the product which would involve less energy and result in less pollution

◆ examining the waste and recycling during the production process

◆ looking at the packaging and the after-sales service to identify a safe and energy-efficient way to dispose of that product after use.

When we consider the eco-labelling scheme we can see that it addresses the whole of the lifecycle of the product. Stages under consideration are:

◆ pre-production

◆ production

◆ distribution

◆ utilisation

◆ disposal.

The environmental considerations included at each of these stages are:

◆ waste

◆ soil pollution

◆ water contamination

◆ air contamination

◆ noise

◆ consumption of energy

◆ consumption of natural resources

◆ effects on the eco-system.

The EU's eco-labelling regulation which was produced in 1991 aims to promote products which have a less harmful effect on the environment. However, one of the major riders is that the production of the product should not affect employee safety or the performance of that product. The eco-label itself should obviously affect all organisations that handle the product along the distribution chain. In many respects the label is very much seen as a minimum standard. The labelling system excludes drink, food and pharmaceuticals. It is important to also note that any products which include substances that are considered dangerous are excluded from the eco-labelling system. Eco-labelling is voluntary and self-financing and gradually the criteria which have been established to obtain an eco-label are being tightened up.

Once the European Commission receives an application from a manufacturer or importer, it contacts all member states who have 30 days to raise any objections to the recommendations made by the Commission concerning the awarding of an eco-label. Providing there are no objections then the manufacturer or importer is awarded an eco-label for a specified period. If there are any objections then the Commission will use national experts in order to assess the importance of the disagreements. Businesses applying for an eco-label will have to pay a fee to cover administration costs and a further fee for the use of the label. The businesses awarded with eco-labels can, of course, use this to their advantage by promoting eco-labels in their advertising.

Further environmental considerations

There are a number of reasons why a business may be encouraged to consider the environment. Principally these include government intervention, the market mechanisms, external pressure and self-regulation.

Reactive responses to environmental concerns

Certainly the experience in the UK has shown that only regulation and legislation is really effective. Given the fact that most law tends to be reactive, the government is merely taking action as a result of visible environmental degradation such as global warming or acid rain. Many businesses, particularly multinationals have to cope with a number of different legislative controls in the different countries in which they operate. It is certainly true to say that some businesses have moved their more dangerous and environmentally worrying production processes to less developed countries. One only has to consider the Bhopal disaster to see that more lax legislation and control of business operations in the less developed countries allow processes to be used which would not be allowed in Europe or the USA.

At the other end of the scale, Germany, for example, has legislation which requires retailers and manufacturers to recycle 80 per cent of all packaging. So conforming with the different requirements in different markets can, at some points, improve the competitive position of businesses and at other times seriously reduce them. For the most part government legislation establishes a minimum standard. Businesses which look at these minimum standards and decide to exceed them may have a long-term advantage since they are considerably ahead of the majority of other businesses. There are still a great many businesses who are very slow to react to new legislation and find themselves in a situation of crisis management when new legislation is brought into force. Legislation does have an important role to play. Many businesses do have a distinct advantage over governments since they are intimately involved in various production processes. They can think ahead and put action plans into force well before the government has collected the necessary information needed to bring legislation into being.

Let us turn our attention now to the market and the awareness of the consumer. It is certainly true that all major stakeholders are much more aware of their responsibilities towards the environment. In this respect they can take a considered approach when looking at the objectives of the business and incorporate some form of responsibility. Businesses have certainly noticed a high degree of product switching. This is despite the fact that consumers do not have access to the full picture. As we discussed earlier when we looked at eco-labelling, consumers will then have the opportunity to identify products which have matched the stringent criteria and make informed purchasing decisions on that basis. It should be relatively easy to identify these eco-labels. The Blue Angel eco-labelling scheme is available in many of our high street stores.

Proactive responses to environmental concerns

The establishment of the British Standard in environmental management systems (BS7750) follows the same basic approach as the British Standard quality system (BS5750) and it emphasises the business's responsibilities to the environment. Perhaps another consideration is that premiums paid to insurance companies by businesses which have been responsible for environmental damage have greatly increased. Just like a household insurance, those which have established security systems are rewarded with lower premiums. Likewise, if a business is able to install environmental safeguards they, too, will enjoy lower premiums. This has also been evident in the fact that providers of finance have been more inclined to lend money to organisations which have environmental safeguards. After all, payment to clear up environmental disasters is extremely high. Polluting industries such as scrap merchants, businesses which deal with hazardous waste, pulp and paper mills and petrol stations have slowed up significantly.

Self-regulation

One of the key responses to the various forms of external pressure has been to implement effective regulations. Clearly many business activities are covered by government legislation and regulations. However, certain industries have recognised the fact that they need to self-regulate and adopt various environmental controls *before* legislation comes into force. This can be seen as a way in which a business can offset the impact of legislation.

Self-regulation does have very positive impacts. First, it allows the business to appear credible as it seems to have environmental considerations uppermost in its mind when conducting business. Second, it provides a convenient way of deflecting public awareness of certain business objectives and activities onto more mundane yet popular concerns. Given that the public has a greater level of awareness regarding the environment, and that through government legislation businesses are no longer allowed to take decisions without reference to the environmental impact, there is an assumption that self-regulation is a means by which businesses will adhere to certain rules and norms. This involves placing some trust on those businesses that have adopted an approach to their activity which is based on self-regulation. However, while some businesses are capable of being left to their own devices, ultimately, the government does need to step in from time-to-time to enforce environmental policy.

Business benefits of foresight

As we mentioned earlier, businesses do need to operate within a framework of strict legislation. However, many organisations have begun to realise that it is within their own best interests to take a proactive stance which enables them to be considerably ahead of potential legislative change. This sense of social responsiveness, while it may stand in the way of profit maximisation in the short term, can be seen to be profitable and responsible in the long term. Organisations need to try and anticipate the mood of the public and to put in place strategic management processes which can develop a sense of responsibility and may help to avoid the need for governments to regulate or legislate.

Pressure groups and their impact on organisational and product ethics

Business responses to external pressure

We now turn our attention to pressure from external groups. Principally we can identify the main pressure groups as being either those based in the local community and national organisations or indeed international organisations such as Greenpeace. The scale or size of these pressure groups differ; however, their objectives are fairly similar. They will attempt to influence decision making and have indeed made strenuous efforts to broaden the decision-making process. This is known as 'democratisation' and calls for greater access to decision making on the basis that the decisions made by businesses may adversely affect both the environment and society in general.

Unlike political parties, pressure groups do not seek political power in the sense that they do not have parliamentary candidates. They are groups of like-minded people who try to influence the government. There are two main types of pressure group:

1 *Interest groups* – also known as protective groups. These groups protect the interests of a particular section of society (examples would include professional associations and trade unions).

2 *Cause groups* – also known as issue groups. These groups promote or support a particular cause (examples include animal rights and environmental issues).

Pressure groups do provide the government with useful information that would not normally be available to them. They are extremely important for the following reasons:

– to help defend and support various minority interests
– to provide communication between the government and other decision-makers between elections
– to help in the framing and implementation of government policy and legislation.

During the health service reforms the British Medical Association (BMA), who represent doctors and the various trade unions representing other workers in the health service, were closely involved in consultations aimed at improving the service to patients.

At times the government and pressure groups work quite closely together. In certain areas this consultation can be quite formal, which would include:

– serving on advisory bodies
– membership of consultation groups
– membership of committees of enquiry
– membership of royal commissions.

Much of the consultation is also undertaken informally. These include:

- 'off the record' meetings between government ministers and pressure groups
- the use of professional lobbyists
- 'insider status' which means that the pressure group is regularly, though informally, included in the decision making.

The methods used by the various pressure groups to influence government decision making may differ, but typical actions could include some of the following:

- direct consultation
- negotiations or bargaining
- marches, strikes and demonstrations.

Some of the larger and more established groups have a number of employees or experts who are able to advise and give an extra air of responsibility to these activities. Typical groups in this category would include:

- the Confederation of British Industry who represent and support the employer's side of the argument
- the Trades Union Congress who represent and support the employee's side of the argument.

Environmental pressure groups are by no means the badly organised fringe which many critics have described them as in the past. They have excellent information-gathering processes and access to experts in order to target their power. What is certainly the case is that those organisations who merely thought that environmental concerns were a passing fad have realised to their cost that, by refusing to respond to external pressure, they not only face significant reverses in public relations but also, as government legislation has caught up with current public opinion, they now face legal action too.

Benefits from positive responses to pressure

We have looked at many of the pressures upon businesses and the potential costs which they must accept in implementing credible environmental policies. We now turn our attention to the benefits.

Many of the major organisations which operate in the UK have significantly increased their spending on environmental policy. ICI, for example, has increased their spending fourfold. This now accounts for some 20 per cent of ICI's total expenditure. McDonalds, often cited as one of the major corporations responsible for deforestation and intensive farming, has rapidly become one of the leading exponents of recycling. British Telecom has stated in many publications that they wish to reduce the impact of their goods and services on the environment. Even oil companies such as Mobil have stated that the environment is one of their most important considerations. This does show a level of commitment but if we analyse the organisations which are at the forefront of implementing environmental policy, we can see that they are largely multinational or based in the USA. It is certainly the case that UK-based businesses are falling behind.

Certainly the implementation of environmental policies has brought about a whole new range of business jargon. Principally, these include the following:

PPP (Pollution Prevention Pays)

WOW (Wipe Out Waste)

WRAP (Waste Reduction Always Pays)

Setting a good example

Although we have said that UK businesses tend to lag behind in the implementation of environmental policies, there are organisations which have become dominant, perhaps not in terms of their market share and influence but certainly in terms of being at the forefront of the public's mind. The Body Shop, for example, during a recent energy audit, have managed to save themselves considerable amounts of money. Indeed, The Body Shop can be used as an example of a UK-based business which operates throughout the world as a key influence on ways in which to identify environmental concerns and attempt to address them. The implementation of environmental policy brings with it the opportunity to improve market image. Organisations which appear to be more responsible on a corporate level, coupled with their ability to inform the customer about this, should be in a position to improve their market share. The various new initiatives which we have already outlined, including BS7750 and eco-labelling, provide businesses with a clear opportunity to show that they have taken environmental considerations on board and that the consumer can make a more informed decision about their purchasing habits.

Niche marketing

An additional feature of the implementation of environmental practices is that this accords very closely with the changing nature of customers' lifestyles. Niche markets are growing and there are considerable numbers of consumers who take far more care in choosing the types of products and services that they use. They aim to have some kind of effect on the market-place by their informed purchases. These market niches have developed considerably and businesses have been fast to recognise this. Some consumers are willing to pay at least marginally more for these products providing they are assured that they are less harmful to the environment. This has proved to be very valuable to many businesses, particularly in competitive markets where margins have been squeezed. The margins for these environmentally friendly products, based on the fact that consumers are prepared to pay more, is of course greater. Such opportunities only arise when a business is prepared to accept its corporate responsibility, rather than simply trying to prove to the public that it has done so.

In conclusion, a business which makes an initial investment in ensuring that environmental practices are an integral part of its activities can reap the benefits of greater revenue if it provides the right product or service. Not only this, particular niche markets have developed which address energy saving, waste control and pollution reduction issues. These are targeted not only at other businesses but also at households. It is presumed that this series of niche markets is sustainable and will present additional opportunities as environmental procedures develop.

Ethical investment

Finally we turn our attention to ethical investment, particularly relating to financial institutions that invest and manage money. The Co-operative Bank, for example, has long taken the position that they will not invest in countries which have questionable regimes. Equally, they do not invest in organisations that have been involved in business activities which are environmentally unfriendly. This has broadened out in recent years to include businesses that can prove certain acceptable levels of care for their employees and concern for their local environment. A further example is that of Marks and Spencer who were accused of having a long-term business relationship with a North African supplier. Allegedly, this North African manufacturer of woollen garments routinely employed under-aged workers and paid them very low wages.

The concept of ethical investment extends also to businesses who are considering the establishment or acquisition of new plant and machinery both in the UK and beyond. It is no longer possible for a multinational to consider undertaking dubious production processes in less developed countries as this will almost certainly come to light and prove to be detrimental in their consumer markets in the West. Perhaps the main reason for businesses to consider the importance of ethical investment is that they find themselves under constant pressure from their home markets and regular consumers. Certainly the awareness of the consumer is an overwhelming consideration which far outweighs the potential benefits that may be accrued by the business in involving itself in questionable activities elsewhere.

Consumerism and its impact on trading policies

Consumerism is a term used to describe the general movement which aims to influence the decisions of organisations in terms of their business activities. The pressure is on suppliers, manufacturers and distributors to make sure that their products are not dangerous or unreliable. The pressure even goes as far as to attempt to make sure that advertising and marketing activities stay within the limits of truth and reliability.

It is worth noting that consumerism is far more common in countries with developed economies such as most of Europe, and the USA. With added choice and organisations competing for our custom, businesses are keen to respond to our needs and demands.

Many experts believe that the main reason for the growth in consumerism was the emergence of various media communications. The producers and manufacturers of consumer products need to be able to consistently sell very large volumes. To do this they must use the best persuasive skills available, via television, the press, radio and other advertising media. Gradually this influence has reduced, although we all are open to persuasion in what we buy.

After the Second World War, after several years of doing without, the consumer was hungry for products and was also already tuned into persuasive advertising because of the successful propaganda used during the war.

By the 1950s, the UK had begun to mirror the mass broadcasting that had already been so successful in the USA. By the late 1960s commercial radio was broadcast throughout Europe. As the new decade dawned, the UK entered a period of almost full employment and relative prosperity. Commercial television was here and with the rise in home ownership the UK consumer wanted every available domestic product.

From the 1970s, consumer legislation tackled all aspects of selling, from guarantees and advertising to credit. As the decade ended, the consumer was demanding more and more from even the most basic products. The 1980s saw uncertainty about the future and the economy and with it even greater demands for high quality and better specifications.

Today we see the chain stores dominating the market, with massive influence and power in the media; but a new force is in the arena. Consumer-led groups, set up to defend the rights of the public, flourish. There is a marked dislike of credit cards, poor quality mass-produced goods and the dominance of large multinationals.

'Green' (i.e. environmental) issues are very important. Not only do they address the excesses of industry and demand greater responsibility by manufacturers, but they also urge the consumer to think more carefully about aspects such as recycling.

The consumer has, at times, been led by the manufacturer, but perhaps the balance has tilted in favour of the consumer. Consumerism demands change, not only for better service and quality but in relation to all aspects of product cycle, including distribution and selling.

Review questions

1   List the factors which influence organisational culture.

2   Identify the major stakeholders in a business.

3   How do business ethics influence the organisational culture?

4   'Many business are principally concerned with short-term profits rather than business ethics'. Discuss the implications of this statement.

5   What are the three main aspects of environmental management?

6   List the reasons why social costs can occur in a business context.

7   What are social and environmental audits?

8   How does eco-management encourage an organisation to behave?

9   What are the key aspects of an eco-auditing system?

10 What does eco-labelling exclude?

11 What is the purpose of BS5750?

12 What is 'democratisation'?

13 What benefits can an organisation expect to receive from implementing environmental policies?

14 List the methods used by various pressure groups to influence government decisions.

15 What has been the effect of consumerism on the trading policies of organisations?

4.3

Influencing and adapting

It is particularly important for businesses to understand why their employees behave the way they do. In fact this consideration is crucial in the management of human resources. Most management theory rests upon certain assumptions which are:

◆ all people behave in a particular way for a reason.

◆ much human behaviour is based on their wants, their needs or their motives.

◆ people naturally try to attain certain goals or objectives in order to satisfy their needs.

There is definitely a link between motivation, job satisfaction and job performance. This link will almost certainly determine an individual's behaviour. The more motivated an individual is the more keen they will be to realise their potential and develop themselves. A key to this study of motivation is an analysis of the job, recognition and responsibility.

Why employees behave as they do

The work of F.W. Taylor

As an engineer, F. W. Taylor began with the assumption that people only work for money. Writing in the latter half of the last century he developed a series of work study techniques which he thought would enable jobs to be made simple so that they could be undertaken quickly and efficiently. Indeed, he left any planning or organisation to managers and supervisors. He believed that by encouraging individuals to work harder with the promise of additional payments as a reward, they would be sufficiently motivated. But unfortunately Taylor was wrong. It seemed that employees would only work hard when they were under close supervision and while not under supervision they worked their normal pace. If you follow Taylor's theory which is now also known as 'scientific management' then it is true to say that a major motivator is money. However, money does not motivate in all cases. We can see examples of Taylor's scientific management in practice to this very day. Some workers are, in fact, paid by results or by attaining pre-set quotas.

Elton Mayo and the Hawthorn Effect

During the 1920s and 1930s Elton Mayo was employed to attempt to improve productivity in an electrical company. This was called the Hawthorn Works and it is the factory's name which is perhaps even better known these days than Elton Mayo himself. He began by adopting Taylor's scientific management principles. He wished to find out exactly what environmental features of the workplace could affect productivity. He made a number of changes in the lighting, the heating, the availability of refreshments, the length of the working day, the length of the working week – and in every case productivity went up. Rather puzzled, he set about gradually eliminating or reversing many of the things that he had done in the first stage of his research. He withdrew teabreaks; he reduced the level of lighting. Amazingly, productivity continued to improve. Now extremely confused, the researchers finally hit upon the explanation. In consultation with the work-force Mayo had discussed the various changes that he was about to make. He had noted that the work-force had a good relationship with their supervisors, with one another and that in general the working environment was pleasant. Mayo gradually came round to the opinion that productivity had increased in each instance on account of the fact that they had been consulted, they had been involved and, of course, that the improvements and changes that were made were desirable. This has become known as the *Hawthorn Effect*.

Mayo did not stop his studies and research there. He investigated another department in the same organisation. In this particular department there were two different groups working on fairly complex equipment. One group considered themselves to be high in status as they were doing the most complex jobs. The other recognised themselves as being somewhat lower in status. This created a sense of competition between the two groups. Each group had their own set of rules and codes of behaviour. Both groups had also established that each individual within the group should work at a particular pace and produce a certain level of output every day. They simply had set themselves to produce a fair day's work for a fair day's pay. Individuals who did not comply with this rule found themselves under considerable pressure from other members of the group. The company established a number of output targets per day. On some occasions the groups exceeded these targets, but most of the time the targets were reached or they were slightly under. What Mayo discovered was that on some days they had actually produced more than they were reporting and they simply saved up the excess output to be included in the next day's totals. The conclusion of his research and analysis was that two important factors were in play: first that they had a benchmark to compare their own output (this was the employer's output targets); and second they had established for themselves a concept of a fair day's output. As a result of this the groups did not feel obliged to exceed these predetermined targets.

Perhaps the lesson that can be learnt from this, and it is certainly one that Volvo have taken a lot of time and effort to develop, is that the group's rules need to accord with the organisation's rules. The targets need to be the same or very similar and the only way that this can be achieved is through consultation, with the day-to-day responsibility for monitoring these levels of output falling upon the supervisor or foreman.

Maslow's theory of human needs

Abraham Maslow was an American psychologist. He was principally interested in human needs and this formed the basis of his theory which was published in 1943. He established five classes of human needs:

1 *Physiological or basic needs* – which means the basic minimum requirement of a job is that the wage or salary satisfies the person's needs in terms of food, drink and accommodation.

2 *Security or safety needs* – which refers to an individual's need to be protected and safe; to have shelter and warmth. In addition, there is a need for job security. (In some respects the development of trade union activity since the Second World War is related to this consideration.)

3 *Belonging or affection needs* – most individuals within the working environment value companionship and friendship. They see this as being an integral part of belonging.

4 *Esteem or ego needs* – perhaps the easiest way of describing this is in terms of status. Most individuals value being recognised as good at their job. In work terms this would include being in a position of authority, being on circulation lists for information or more ego-based considerations, such as having a carpet in your office.

5 *Self-actualisation needs* – basically most individuals feel that they need to be fulfilled. In the working environment the vast majority of employees may find themselves without a great deal of opportunity to satisfy their needs in this particular respect. Only those who have a recognised skill or who are managers may find self-actualisation a reality.

Maslow's pyramid – a hierarchy of needs

In many instances you will see Maslow's hierarchy of needs portrayed as either a pyramid or a series of steps (*see* Fig. 4.9). This is meant to put across the point that without the lower level needs such as security then an individual cannot possibly hope to attain the higher level needs such as esteem or self-actualisation. In other words, the hierarchy of needs does have a definite order. An individual, for example, who receives a high salary may be satisfying their physiological needs alone. The mere fact that their office environment is poor and they have little room in which to operate may preclude them from attaining any of the higher level needs. Alternatively, someone who has been unemployed for a considerable length of time may be prepared to take any job, even if it is a lower status than their previous occupation, purely to satisfy their physiological or security needs. Maslow sees this as being an integral part of human nature and human behaviour.

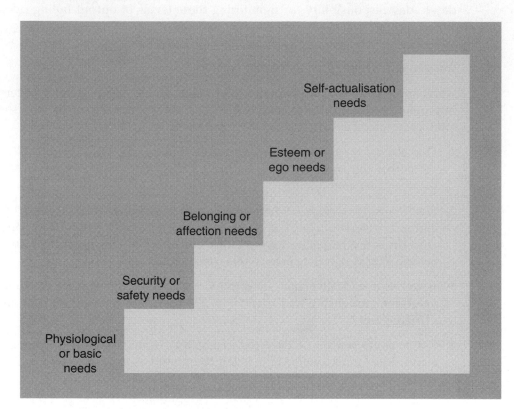

Fig. 4.9 Maslow's hierarchy of needs

Existence, relatedness, growth

There have been many attempts to modify Maslow's theory. One version by Alderfer is of particular note. In this theory Maslow's hierarchy of needs is reduced to just three levels of need:

1 *Existence needs* – which are broadly similar to Maslow's physiological and security needs.

2 *Related needs* – which include belonging and affection and a certain degree of the esteem associated with personal relationships.

3 *Growth needs* – which incorporate self-actualisation and the esteem related to individual performance.

This theory is known generally by its shorthand ERG (existence, relatedness, growth).

Some criticisms of Maslow's theory

Maslow's theory has been criticised on a number of different levels. Since Maslow believes that individuals only seek to achieve the higher level needs after the lower level needs have been fulfilled, he ignores the fact that some individuals may wish to attain the higher level needs before the lower level needs are met. There are certainly many instances of individuals craving for status rather than income or security. Maslow's theory has been criticised on the basis that it does not account for individual ranking of needs. Some of the needs which he identified would not be considered to be important by certain individuals. Equally, his theory does not take into account culture, lifestyle or the traditions of the society in which the individual lives.

Herzburg and the motivational hygiene theory

Herzburg's motivational hygiene theory divides the factors related to the working environment into two separate categories. One he calls *motivators* or *satisfiers* and the other he calls *hygiene* or *maintenance factors*. Herzburg developed his theory after interviewing engineers and accountants. He asked them two very basic questions. The first question was 'What has happened at work that has resulted in a marked increase in your job satisfaction?' Then he asked 'What events at work have happened which have shown a marked reduction in your job satisfaction?' The replies that he received were not all that surprising. The experiences of the individuals that he interviewed showed that the events which had brought about an increase in their job satisfaction were not exactly the opposite of those which they had found to be very dissatisfying. From this analysis Herzburg developed a list of elements of a job which could produce satisfaction. These were:

◆ achievement

◆ recognition

◆ responsibility

◆ promotion prospects

◆ the work itself.

These he called motivators or satisfiers.

The second list of elements were those which could bring about dissatisfaction. These included:

◆ pay

◆ relationships at work

◆ how the individual was supervised

◆ the company's policies

◆ the physical working conditions or environment

◆ the availability or otherwise of fringe benefits.

He called the second group hygiene factors.

The reason he called them this was because he felt that these factors made the job bearable and that they needed to be maintained in order to ensure that the individual remained in the job. It is important to understand the principal differences between these two lists. If you refer to the first list – the motivators – it was unlikely in Herzburg's findings for an individual to wish to leave the company if they had achieved a high status position. Certainly an individual would work harder and be more motivated had they achieved a high status, but it was not a reason for them to leave. However, the hygiene factors were of principal concern in many situations. Poor pay or inadequate working conditions would cause individuals to consider leaving the company.

Herzburg's theories have been the subject of considerable discussion ever since they were written. What he is virtually saying is that by improving pay or fringe benefits, for example, employees will not be sufficiently motivated for any great period of time. They may have a short-term impact but will gradually be forgotten in terms of motivation and performance. Basically, if we ignore the second set of factors, and focus in on the motivators or satisfiers we can see that they are very similar to Maslow's hierarchy of needs.

Fayol's 'top-down' theories

Writing in 1916, Henri Fayol was a French industrialist. His views and theories are generally accepted, almost without criticism, by many management consultants and exponents.

He realised that the problems commonly experienced by organisations in respect of their management and personnel was the root cause of industrial failure. Fayol is a 'top-down' theorist (believing that changes must begin with the managing director) as opposed to a 'bottom-up' theorist (starting with the worker) like Taylor.

He began by identifying and defining the three main aspects of management:

1   The activities of the organisation.

2   The elements of management.

3   The principles of management.

We need to examine these in rather more detail.

Activities of the organisation

As Fayol said, 'All activities to which industrial groups give rise can be divided into the following six categories':

1   *Technical activities* (including production, manufacture and adaptation).

2   *Commercial activities* (including buying, selling, and exchanging).

3 *Financial activities* (including the seeking of finance and its best use).

4 *Security services* (which include the protection of the organisation, property and employees).

5 *Accounting services* (including balance sheets, costing, statistics and stock checking).

6 *Managerial activities* (including forecasting and planning, organising, commanding, co-ordinating and controlling).

Fayol identified these key activities through extensive research, finding them to be the most common activities from the respondents and through personal experience.

Elements and principles of management

The elements of management are simply what management actually does. Fayol set out 14 basic principles (*see* p. 285). He also identified 'rules' or 'laws'. These were:

◆ The division of work meaning that if an individual specialises then they will become more skilled, efficient and effective. Unfortunately, this does lead to boredom and repetition.

◆ The accountability of the manager or leader (which means the power and authority that this person has).

Vroom's expectancy theory

Vroom put forward a theory known as *expectancy theory*. He believed that the way in which an individual seeks to satisfy their needs is based on the individual's belief or feeling of how their efforts may be translated into an outcome that will bring them their desired reward. He believed that an individual's behaviour is governed by the following:

◆ what the individual wants to happen

◆ the individual's estimation of the probability of that happening

◆ how much that individual believes that a particular event or action will satisfy a need.

Most individuals, according to Vroom will base their behaviour on what has happened in the past. In situations where the individual does not have any previous experience then there will always be a level of uncertainty. It is this uncertainty that relates to motivation. If an individual does not have prior knowledge, then they may find themselves in a situation of not knowing what to do. This confusion may affect their motivation. A detailed analysis of Vroom's theory indicates that:

◆ the managers of a business always need to tell their employees exactly what to expect, particularly in the case of the introduction of new working practices.

◆ employees must be able to see why and how their efforts are translated into rewards.

◆ rewards should always satisfy workers' needs.

◆ bonus schemes, for example, are unlikely to mean that employees will work harder because they may not realise the link between their efforts and the reward.

Using the motivation theory, the business should be able to identify the characteristics of the job that would allow some of the following:

◆ self-development

◆ opportunities for satisfaction

◆ recognition

◆ independence.

The major characteristics that would encourage motivation are:

◆ a variety of tasks

◆ different surroundings

◆ interaction with others

◆ independence in deciding how tasks should be handled

◆ having clearly stated goals which are sufficiently challenging and with some kind of indication as to the performance expected by the organisation.

Motivation and job design

As we develop the argument throughout our investigation of motivation in practice, we can see that if the business takes care in its job design, then there is every chance of increasing motivation. A business which decides to undertake job design will aim to improve satisfaction and performance. It should be pointed out that, of course, job design does not simply revolve around motivational theory. There are a number of other factors which may determine or limit the job. Technology, the cost of providing necessary equipment, resistance from employees or unions and the way in which the organisation is managed can all have an impact and a reducing effect on the job design. As we will see when we consider job enrichment, job enlargement, job design, job rotation and job evaluation, all of these play an integral part in formulating and creating a job which aims to motivate and satisfy, as well as addressing the basic need of the job to perform a series of tasks.

Job design forms an integral part of ensuring that motivational theory and practical experience are incorporated into the nature of work. Perhaps one of the starting points in job design is to analyse the job itself. This can be undertaken in a number of different ways, which include:

◆ *direct observation of the job in progress* – this, of course, has its drawbacks including the fact that an experienced worker will make the job look easy. There is no indication as to the mental processes going through the job holder's mind and some jobs are carried out so rapidly that it is almost impossible to analyse them.

◆ *interview* – there are two basic versions of interviewing that we can consider. The first is with the job holder. Naturally the interviewer has to get over the fact that the job holder may be suspicious about the questions being asked and may naturally try to exaggerate the importance of the job. So, in other words, the interviewer has to take into account the fact that the worker's attitude may influence the responses and in some cases the employee may be unco-operative and, perhaps, have a poor memory. The second interview variation is that of an interview with a supervisor. Unfortunately many supervisors, despite the fact that they may have done the job previously, may be out of touch with it. Some supervisors may have never done the job at all.

◆ *a study of the materials used* – this will include an investigation of the materials, machinery, communications and documents used as an integral part of the job.

◆ *self-analysis* – in this version the job holder actually analyses the job themselves. While there is a danger that the analysis may be subjective, this offers the best opportunity to discover all of the intricacies of the job.

◆ *questionnaires* – although these are used on a widespread basis they are somewhat unreliable. The current job holder is asked to fill in a questionnaire, but again they may be suspicious of the reasons behind the questionnaire itself.

◆ *work diaries* – this method encourages job holders to detail all of their activities over a period of time. A well-maintained work diary can prove to be very useful.

This job analysis process presupposes that the job already exists and that the organisation intends to redesign it. Many of the problems arise when the job does not necessarily exist at present or the organisation wishes to merge or radically change existing job roles. Having adequately considered the job design and analysed any existing job roles, the business may now consider a variety of different measures in order to facilitate motivation.

Measures to facilitate motivation

Job extension and rotation

Job rotation falls under the category of *job extension*. It involves the training of employees in several basic skills so that they can exchange jobs with one another at predetermined intervals. There is evidence that employees undertaking job rotation experience more job satisfaction as they have a greater understanding of the work process. They manage to achieve this by experiencing different jobs at different stages of the work process. In addition to this the employees are far more versatile and multiskilled. This is particularly useful if the business encounters a period of sickness in their workforce.

Job rotation does provide employees with variety in their work. It also enables them to cope with certain jobs that would place unnecessary strains upon them if they had to undertake them every day of the working week. It is relatively cheap and fairly simple to organise and, as a result, it is one of the most popular forms of job extension. In some organisations the job rotation system is directed by the management and in others it is carried out on a voluntary basis.

One of the major drawbacks with job rotation is the feeling that individual employees are never given sufficient time to develop their skills in a particular job role. They are simply moved on at regular intervals and never attain a high degree of expertise. Equally, problems arise when employees are swapped over from one job to another. This is particularly true if the rotation occurs at busy times. An employee moving into a new job role may find themselves in a situation where the previous post holder has not tied up all the loose ends of work in progress. At the end of the day, job rotation may be counter-productive. Unless the variety of jobs available to the employees on the job rotation scheme is wide enough, then they will become familiar with all of the job roles and at this point the job rotation system is no longer of any great value since they are not motivated by a new change. Job rotation is ideal for unskilled or semi-skilled employees. It is also used extensively in white-collar jobs (some 16 per cent of businesses use this system for white-collar occupations).

Job enlargement

Job enlargement is a particular way of redesigning the parameters of a job which incorporates the expansion of tasks normally carried out in a particular job role, to similar activities which are related in some way. The individual, having expanded into additional tasks, finds themselves less dependent upon other employees. This means that individuals are less task-orientated and also they are less specialised. With the widening of tasks the individual employee is far more able to pace and organise their own work load. There are considerable costs which would be incurred in introducing job enlargement. Unfortunately, the benefits are uncertain. One of the principal problems which arise from job enlargement exercises is that eventually even the enlarged job will become boring. If the business merely enlarges jobs which are repetitive to incorporate similarly repetitive tasks, then the whole exercise is self-defeating. One of the benefits which has been associated with job enlargement is that it does mean that individual work loads need to be heavier and, as each employee is not dependent upon other colleagues, then interaction is less likely. Research into job enlargement has shown that the majority of employees are far more satisfied with their jobs after the enlargement has taken place. In fact, their performance was far better than those who are still in restricted job role situations.

Job enrichment

There are two basic forms of *job enrichment*. The first is known as 'vertical job enrichment'. This means that an individual employee is given the opportunity to see a task through to its final stage of completion. Compared with job enlargement, job enrichment allows the employee to become involved in related but not similar tasks. Job enrichment has been particularly successful in blue-collar work. Employees who are undertaking a relatively limited set of tasks are given the opportunity to carry out inspection checks and machinery checks. Taking responsibility for an entire task or job has been positively identified as a key motivating factor. The introduction of job enrichment schemes has so far penetrated some 10 per cent of organisations (for blue-collar job roles).

The other form of job enrichment which we referred to at the beginning of this section was *horizontal job enrichment*. Effectively this is very much like job enlargement and seems to have had a limited value in most cases. This form of job enrichment is different from vertical job enrichment in as much as it incorporates only tasks of a similar level and complexity.

Research has shown that job enrichment schemes have short-term and long-term effects. In the short-term, which has usually been measured at around three months, the performance of employees who have been job enriched has dropped off. This may be due to the fact that they have had problems in embracing the extent and the complexities of the new job role. After six months, however, performance is considerably up. This again may be a result of the employees gradually coming to grips with the needs of the new job post.

Job evaluation

Job evaluation is an altogether different kind of process. It involves placing all of the jobs within the organisation in some form of ranking order. This is done in order to ensure that employees are paid fairly and in accordance with the demands and conditions of the job. Broadly speaking, job evaluation processes look at the following:

◆ tasks involved in the job

◆ responsibilities and obligations of the post holder

◆ skills used

◆ knowledge required

◆ initiative to be used by the employee

◆ individual ability to cope with stress

◆ requirements for planning

◆ need to control other employees

◆ co-ordination of the working environment.

Ideally, all of these criteria are examined in an objective manner. Once the ranking order has been established, a monetary value needs to be applied to each of the jobs. The main purposes of job evaluation are to:

◆ to make pay administration easier

◆ to harmonise internal rates of pay

◆ to fix a reasonable rate of pay for jobs within the organisation

◆ to facilitate a reasonable promotion system based on job grades.

There are three main types of job evaluation:

1 Ranking – which is a way in which the job is valued as a whole.

2 Grading – which considers the job specification primarily.

3 Points rating – which is extremely analytical and again looks at the job specification.

Let us have a look at these in a little more detail.

If an organisation uses the *ranking* method then a committee is established which is responsible for putting the jobs in a ranking order according to their worth. This is a relatively quick system which requires little administration and it should be fairly well understood by most members of the committee and the employees. It is usually used in organisations which already have a reasonable pay structure. However, it is not a very practical way of carrying out job evaluation in very large companies and experience has shown that ranking has brought on a number of industrial tribunal actions which relate to equal pay.

The second system, *grading*, provides a framework into which most of the jobs can be fitted. Normally the lowest graded job is one which requires very little in the way of skills or is extremely closely supervised. Each grade above this basic job increases in terms of the skills, knowledge and responsibilities required. Once the committee has read the specification it can then match the grade definition against it. This again is a very simple and quick way of job evaluation. However, there are a number of jobs in many organisations which are very difficult to categorise. The system is less objective since some arbitrary decisions have to be made in order to push a particular job into the grade.

The final version, known as *points rating*, is probably the most commonly used. Typically, the organisation will establish a number of factors against which the job can be measured. These may include some of the following:

◆ skill required to do the job

◆ the effort put into the job

◆ the responsibility of the job

◆ the working conditions in which the post holder has to operate.

Although this system may seem to be crude, many organisations have further refined it by establishing sub-divisions under each of these main headings. For skill, for example, there may be sub-divisions which include *experience*, *dexterity* or *education*. Each of the different factors are considered by a committee and they will allocate a number of points which are then added together to place the job in a points rating. A hierarchy of jobs is then established. Other organisations have decided that weighting is a way in which the points system can be more fairly administered. Some jobs may rely far more on experience than on education. Others may be more dexterity orientated rather than experience orientated. In order to reflect the true nature of the job, some of the points which have been allocated against particular skills required are doubled, trebled or quadrupled in order to reflect the importance of one particular skill.

Work groups

A logical extension of many of the techniques and processes revolving around job design are encompassed in the formation of autonomous work groups. These groups incorporate many of the advantages of job enrichment since individuals within these work groups have a greater degree of flexibility. In this respect job rotation is commonplace. These work groups are able to carry out complex tasks and take full responsibility for the full range of tasks and skills required to carry them out. The work groups are self-regulating and self-organising. Each individual has the opportunity to use a wide range of skills, including basic management. Organisations which have encouraged autonomous work groups have noticed that there has been a considerable performance improvement, coupled with a decline in the number of days lost due to stoppages. In addition to this, the quality of products produced has increased tremendously. Typical examples of autonomous work groups can be found in Volvo, where vehicles are produced using this working practice.

Empowerment

If an individual employee is allowed to control their contribution to the organisation, complete tasks and attain targets independently without reference to management, then this is an example of empowerment. It involves the management trusting their employees to make reasonable decisions. It is also an example of delayering, as it reduces the importance of administration and further reduces the number of managers at various levels which control the working practices. In effect it streamlines management and improves communication and control. It is somewhat different from delegation in as much as it devolves many of the duties down to operational level. Empowerment allows individual creativity and initiative, it improves the commitment of the employees and encourages team spirit. It allows decision making to be taken at various levels of the organisation and it is a true reflection of performance. Autonomous work groups provide a prime example of empowerment.

Teamworking

As we have seen, many of the motivational practices which are realised through job design, and job extension, incorporate features of teamworking. Equally, autonomous work groups and empowerment also incorporate the concept of teamworking. Rather than relying on individual employees carrying out a series of tasks in isolation, businesses have begun to realise that the advantages of teamworking far outweigh the benefits of specialisation. Interaction with other individuals as an integral part of working life considerably improves performance and motivation. Providing the teams are established in such a manner as to provide complementary skills, experience and viewpoints, then there is ample opportunity for these teams to pay back for the reorganisation or restructuring in a meaningful and profitable manner.

Management styles

Each management role involves the use of authority and some degree of leadership. Organisations can be described as 'power systems'. Individuals who become employees have to give up some of their independence in order to function within the organisation.

Just how the authority is used in the organisation can determine how the organisation actually functions and also affects all of its internal relationships. In the army, for example, a clear line of responsibility, authority and power has been established and is clearly understood. The new recruit knows they report to the sergeant, and the sergeant knows to salute and take orders from an officer. In a business organisation, these clear distinctions may not be so obvious. What is clear is that any leader or manager does require a degree of obedience from the subordinates. The notion of leadership implies that the individuals in a management position have the 'right' combination of skills and abilities. The manager needs to be able to obtain effective performance from the employees. The manger also needs to be aware of the employees' needs. As we shall see, some leadership styles ignore the needs of the employee entirely.

Theories on leadership and management

The term 'leadership style' refers to the way in which one individual manages others. The leader's style may result in the following:

◆ respect

◆ affection

◆ trust

◆ loyalty.

The two key aspects of leadership hinge upon the managers' *attitudes* and *abilities to delegate and consult*. This is a recurring theme in the leadership style we will now consider.

Max Weber's theory of management style

The German social scientist, Max Weber, was very interested in management style and organisational structure. He identified three different types of organisations and used these to illustrate his theory:

1 *Charismatic leadership* – where the employees were devoted to their leader and worked hard as a result (eg a political party).

2 *Rational-legal leadership* – due to the skills and expertise of the leaders, they are respected and accepted by the employees.

3 *Traditional leadership* – when the authority is derived from custom and practice.

Fayol's principles of management

Henry Fayol, a French social scientist, developed a list of key management qualities and functions:

◆ *division of work* – all employees know what their duties are.

◆ *authority* – clear, unambiguous and complete.

◆ *discipline* – rigid and firm if required, but in any case clearly understood.

◆ *unity of command* – all aspects of the organisation are managed in the same manner.

◆ *unity of direction* – the organisation has a clear corporate strategy.

◆ *sub-ordination* – individuals within the organisation put the business first and their personal interests and needs second.

◆ *remuneration* – a fair wage for a fair day's work.

◆ *centralisation* – essentially a cost-effective measure, but ensures that like tasks are concentrated and not duplicated.

◆ *clear scalar chain* – all individuals within the organisation know their own position within it; achieved by the production of an organisational chart.

◆ *internal order* – the organisation does its best to avoid conflict within the organisation.

◆ *equality* – basically, equal opportunities, regardless of age, sex, sexual orientation, disability or creed.

◆ *stability of tenure* – making sure that the employees are not concerned and worried about their job security.

◆ *initiative* – the organisation encourages the creation of ideas and readily accepts them if they will work; certain decisions can be made without reference to senior managers.

◆ *esprit de corps* – a French saying, derived from the military, which means that there is a 'company spirit'; in other words, individuals are proud to support the aims and objectives of the organisation.

Mayo's solidarity theory

The Australian, Elton Mayo, investigated factories to discover why individuals feel more or less content with their job and role. Mayo made three quite interesting observations, which form the basis of his *solidarity theory*:

1 Output and motivation (interest in the job) improved when employees were being observed by him.

2 Peer pressure (from work mates) contributed to the level of support by the individuals within that group.

3 The group had strong feelings about what was possible and reasonable and that this was as important as their reaction to demands from the management.

Maslow's self-actualisation theory

The American sociologist, Abraham Maslow, produced a theory that motivation and leadership style should be based upon the employees' needs. This is perhaps more commonly known as the *self-actualisation theory*. Although this may sound one-sided, it showed that it was in the organisation's best interests to consider the fact that a well-motivated employee needs to acquire or be given certain support and incentives.

The 'hierarchy of needs' as it became known is a well-researched and applied leadership style of management. What it says is that every individual needs a series of ever-more complex achievements and goals in order to be truly motivated. The first needs are 'physiological'. These are the most basic 'life-supporting' needs, such as food, housing, warmth and clothing, and an individual's first motivation in working is to satisfy these needs.

The second level, known as 'safety', refers to the employees' belief that they are secure in their job and will not face dismissal for a trivial or an unimportant reason.

Building on to this is the third need, 'social belonging'; which means that the individual is socially acceptable. This may be seen in the nature of the job, the job description, job title or the way in which society in general views the job they do. The fourth level of need is known as 'esteem'. This is the way in which the individual is viewed as a person and as an employee. An individual who has achieved respect from their colleagues and has good solid standing in the country in respect of the job they undertake is likely to be more motivated than others who have not.

The final level of the needs of the employee is called 'self-actualisation'. This refers to the individual's belief that they have achieved (career-wise) what they set out to achieve. The individual is content that they can do the job well and have received the recognition for doing so. It should be noted that an individual cannot be expected to achieve the higher states of motivation until the basic ones have been gained first.

Herzberg's theory of motivation

Frederick Herzberg's investigation of accountants and engineers in the USA brought forward another angle to the theory of leadership, motivation and management. He identified five major motivations, and we will look at these first.

1 *Achievement* – the individual feels that something has been accomplished by their labours.

2 *Recognition* – others (and management) realise that the role the individual is playing in the organisation is important and is appreciated.

3 *The work itself* – the job provides variety and interest and is not crushingly boring.

4 *Responsibility* – the employee has enough freedom to make decisions and is given a job role that meets or reaches their potential.

5 *Advancement* – the employee perceives that they can be promoted if their skills and performance warrant it.

The hygiene factors that Herzberg identified are features of the work or organisation that help to maintain an individual's 'good feelings' about the job, but do not necessarily motivate in themselves. Typical hygiene factors include:

◆ wages/salaries

◆ bonuses/commission

◆ working conditions

◆ quality of supervision

◆ working environment

◆ job security.

McGregor's Theory X/Theory Y

McGregor, an American management consultant, identified two radically different leadership and management styles. These were:

1 *Theory X* – where organisations and their management believe that the employees are lazy and do not work hard unless they are very closely supervised. In these organisations tough and unrelenting managers would be common.

2 *Theory Y* – where the organisation and their management believe that their employees do want to work hard. They can be relied upon and will perform well if the organisation provides a reasonable and supportive working climate

Likert's management theory

Likert, another American theorist, put forward the notion that if the management created an environment where individuals were encouraged to 'network' and support one another, then the employees would be able to work well together. Specifically, he cited that a good and effective leadership style would:

◆ be helpful and friendly

◆ be concerned with employees welfare

◆ be supportive

◆ be fair, but firm

◆ encourage employees' development

◆ support staff with problems

◆ protect weaker employees

◆ be expert and well organised

◆ be good at planning

◆ live up to employees' expectations of them.

Other management theories

In *trait theory*, a number of key qualities were identified which helped map out the ideal management and leadership style. These were:

◆ ability to articulate (good speaking skills)

◆ ability to convince

◆ willingness to co-operate

◆ decisiveness

◆ determination

◆ drive

◆ initiative

◆ ability to get things done

◆ insight (forward-looking)

◆ perception (can see future pitfalls)

◆ self-assured attitude

Style theory maintains that the leadership style of the management is first dependent on the following:

◆ the nature of the organisation's business.

◆ the historical management.

◆ the structure of the organisation.

The above mentioned theorists then propose that leaders will be in one of the following categories:

◆ *dictatorial* – where the leadership style is harsh and unremitting and employees are expected to do as they are told at all times.

◆ *benevolent autocratic* – where the leadership is less strict, but adheres to very clear (and historical) sets of rules and procedures.

◆ *consultative* – where the organisation encourages employees to take a role in the decision-making.

◆ *democratic* – where the organisation positively encourages participation from all employees at all stages of the decision-making process.

Several management consultants have supported the *leadership grid theory* of management style. Essentially, it is a follow-up of style theory. This theory contends that leaders believe either that:

◆ employees need support in achieving a goal or completing a task.

◆ that the task and job in hand are more important than the needs of the employee.

The ideal leadership style may lie somewhere between the two.

Fielder, yet another American theorist, put forward the theory that leaders switch from being task orientated to employee orientated, depending upon how the leader is getting on with their employees at the time. Many theorists do not accept this view as research has shown:

◆ the task-centred approach was always successful regardless of the leader's relationship with their employees.

◆ an employee-centred approach was always most successful, regardless of the relationship status.

In *best fit theory*, the balancing of three elements make up the leadership style. The three elements are:

1 *The task* – the job in hand.

2 *The employees or team* – those who will undertake the task.

3 *The leader* – the individual responsible for directing the team and allocating the tasks.

If you imagine a triangle, with a short base and longer verticals, you will begin to understand the nature of this theory. The two most important elements are represented by the long verticals, and the subordinate third element occupies the base. In a situation where a quick decision and action needs to be undertaken, then the leader and the task occupy the verticals with the employee on the base (subordinate).

Pay-back theory is typified by the phrases 'nothing for nothing' or 'what's in it for me?' Career-orientated employees would drive hard bargains and always negotiate with their managers on the questions of role, tasks and duties.

Using *management by objectives* theory, the organisation establishes and supports a range of meetings to discuss the following:

◆ objectives and targets to be achieved by the employees

◆ a timescale for the above

◆ negotiation of the objectives

◆ agreeing the objectives with the employees

◆ setting the deadlines

◆ quantifying the objectives (i.e. how they will be measured).

The outcome of this theory is a more task-based leadership style. It is a feature of the implementation of this theory that employees are often ignored during the process and they then have to suffer the consequences of ill-considered demands and deadlines.

Arising out of the management by objectives theory was the development of staff appraisal, performance measuring and more reasonable pay scales.

Vroom, Lawler and Porter put forward *expectancy theory* to suggest that the relationship between people's behaviour at work and their goals was not as simple as was first imagined. The theory proposed that:

◆ each individual has different goals.

◆ individuals will only try to achieve their goals if they think that they have a reasonable chance of achieving them.

One way of classifying goals is as follows:

◆ a direct goal is achieving better performance.

◆ an indirect goal results from achieving the direct goal.

The value of the goal, in personal terms, affects motivation and behaviour.

Increasing motivation

As we have seen, there are a number of different ways of attempting to increase the motivation of employees.

Using McGregor's Theory X/Theory Y

If we apply McGregor's Theory X and Theory Y we can see that the choices of an organisation may be determined by their view of employees using this theory. Each manager will have their own personal theory about motivation. McGregor's theory accommodates both differing viewpoints. Theory X states that most individuals do not like work and will attempt to avoid it if they possibly can. The only way to motivate these individuals is to closely control their activities and threaten them when needed. Theory Y, on the other hand, states that most individuals are willing to accept responsibility. They find that physical or mental activities at work are natural to them. They respond to reasonable management behaviour and positively encourage employee involvement. It is certainly true that managers who have a Theory X point of view or a Theory Y point of view will develop very different payment arrangements.

Let us have a look at Theory X and Theory Y in a little more detail, bearing in mind that these are two very extreme positions:

Theory X managers believe that their workers are lazy. The only way in which they can make them perform is to reward them with money or make them fear punishment from the management. There is also the feeling that these employees are incapable of thinking for themselves. They have to be given very clear instructions and, above all, cannot be trusted to complete a task without close supervision. The solution in this instance is for the manager to break the individual tasks down, to give clear instructions and to make sure that they are carried out by using their authority to control. Money is considered to be the main motivator.

Theory Y managers have the complete opposite view to Theory X managers. They believe that employees actually enjoy their work and will be responsible and show initiative. Also that employees can be trusted to work without being closely supervised. There is also a sense that the employee will do their very best for the organisation and put the organisation first. In organisations that prefer Theory Y you will find that employees will be involved in the decision-making process of that organisation. They will also have much greater freedom. These employees will be kept informed of their progress and rewarded according to their performance. Most Theory Y managers will be on very good terms with their employees and will be rewarded by being shown respect.

A Theory Y manager may appear to be soft and easy to manipulate whereas a Theory X manager may seem to be autocratic and dictatorial. What McGregor suggested was that a manager needs to try to use their authority to encourage employees to enjoy their job and improve their performance at the same time. Both of these goals will end with the organisation benefiting.

Using Drucker's communication theory

Writing in 1970, Peter Drucker identified four fundamental aspects of communication:

1 Perception.

2 Expectation.

3 Involvement.

4 Not merely information but practical benefits too.

You may think 'how does this fit into motivation?' Well, Drucker was saying that it doesn't actually matter *what* is said to an employee; this is only as he calls it 'uttering'. What is important is that the employee responds. For an employee to perceive or understand a particular system, they need to be able to understand what they can expect from it; they also need to be involved in it. Above all, the communication or system does not just simply have to be information; it needs to have a practical basis. In the development of any performance-related or payments-by-results or incentives scheme, the employee needs to recognise the fact that there is a definite advantage in including themselves and involving themselves in the system. Drucker, therefore, suggests that most effective incentive or performance-based systems need to have included the employee at the earliest possible stage. They also need to be clearly understood by the employee in order to ensure that they operate effectively.

Using a traditional approach

Team-based versus *them-and-us* is a traditional point of view which expresses the divide between managers and employees. Both groups see the other as 'them'. Many organisations reinforce this viewpoint by recruiting managers directly from educational institutions when they have no understanding of working on the shop floor. This is also fostered by something known as *separate status* where there is a clear divide between those who work in the factory and those who work in administration or managerial positions. To begin with, the working hours will be different, with factory workers starting earlier and perhaps finishing earlier too, whereas the administration staff will start later and will also finish an hour or so after the factory work has been completed. In terms of pay, the factory employees will be on either an hourly rate or a piece rate whereas the administrative staff will be on a monthly salary. Pensions also differ with the factory employees generally being on a state-only pension whereas the administrative and clerical staff will have access to the company pension scheme. The employment contract will have significant differences, for example the period of notice for a factory employee will normally only be around one week whereas the managerial and administrative may have to work up to three months' notice. All of these considerations conspire to generate the 'them-and-us' approach. While this is a very old-fashioned viewpoint it is still very dominant in a number of traditional organisations.

Against this theory, as we have seen, is the team-based approach, where all members of the organisation, regardless of their status or their involvement in the activities of the organisation, consider themselves to be a member of a team. Many of the incentives such as profit share and share ownership, make this approach a reality where even the most lowly employee, as a shareholder, or as someone who has access to a profit share, will feel that they are an integral part of a team, working together to try to improve profits and overall business performance. Many newer businesses will try to foster this approach from the first day of operations. It is only the more old-fashioned organisations that will still have aspects of the 'them-and-us' opinions.

Many organisations have decided to develop a single status for all employees. This means, in effect, that regardless of the grade of the employee, they will share the same canteen, car park, access to the company superannuation scheme and other benefits. Fringe benefits such as pensions and sick pay are considerably improved across the board, hours of work generally are shortened and the control of employees becomes slightly less important. This has been exemplified by the fact that clocking in machines in these organisations have been removed. Generally speaking, employees who were on wages have been shifted across to salary payments, even though many employees prefer to be paid on a weekly rather than a monthly basis because they have geared up their payments to deal with this kind of system. There are a number of reasons why organisations have moved to the single-status system. These include:

◆ many have realised that there is no longer a wide divide between manual and non-manual work.

◆ employment law has been brought into force which equalises payment so men and women receive equal pay for work of equal value.

◆ many have realised that production workers are very important and that they need to be motivated at all times, for example through the development of quality circles and teamwork.

◆ health and safety, for example, has been applied to all categories of employee and more broadly EU directives have implemented all aspects of employee protection.

◆ experience has shown that single status results in a much lower labour turn-over among the manual workers.

◆ single status definitely addresses the jealousies which used to be prevalent between manual and non-manual employees.

◆ industrial relations in these organisations has been considerably improved (*see also* Fig. 4.10).

Some of the specific advantages which can be enjoyed by developing a single status situation are:

◆ that all employees are able to identify with the organisation as a whole rather than a particular grade or status.

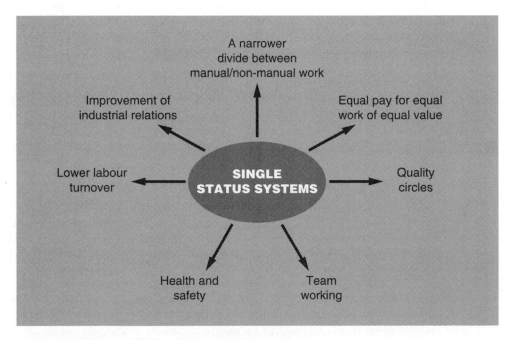

Fig. 4.10 Reasons for a single status system

◆ the work-force is considerably more flexible and this allows the organisation to deploy its employees into areas where additional effort is needed.

◆ most employees will develop a more responsible attitude to their work; they will be willing to involve themselves in problem solving and decision making at all levels.

◆ the climate of the organisation is one of fairness.

There are, however, a number of disadvantages that can be associated with single status organisations. These are:

◆ there is a high cost in developing terms and conditions which are common to all employees throughout the organisation – this harmonisation process is particularly difficult in borderline cases.

◆ while many employees may consider themselves to be in a slightly better position in a single-status organisation, others who have specialised roles may find that their status has been undermined.

◆ there are certain groups, particularly skilled workers, who will aim to maintain their own particular privileges.

Group, task and individual needs

Group development within the organisation is obviously influenced by the individuals involved, their tasks and objectives, the size of the organisation, the nature of leadership and the physical working conditions. Organisations will attempt to balance group, task and individual needs as best as possible within the constraints of having to address the needs of the business itself. It is useful to appreciate the ways in which groups develop and the stages that they pass through in normal sets of circumstances. These are:

◆ *The forming stage* – where the group attempts to become orientated towards its goals and procedures. At this stage the group needs to have as much information as possible and the individuals will begin to appreciate the interdependencies that will be an important aspect of behaviour and relationships within the group. They will begin to understand leadership roles and also the skills and knowledge of other team members.

◆ *The storming stage* – individual group members will have begun to recognise that there are conflicts arising as a result of interpersonal hostility and different task demands. Some group members may openly challenge the leadership and isolate themselves from group interaction. Conflict resolution is imperative at this stage and may well involve the redefinition of the goals and tasks assigned to the group.

◆ *The norming stage* – at this point group members are beginning to fully co-operate with one another. They have adopted and embraced the various tasks which have been assigned to them and are more willing to communicate and express their own opinions. This stage is typified by a synergy developing within the group, which enables a higher level of work output, greater morale and more sense of a team rather than a group of individuals.

◆ *The performing stage* – members are beginning to accept and trust one another. They will still have a diversity of viewpoints, or may have begun to conform to more dominant group behaviour. There will be a strong sense of shared objectives and despite any differences or disagreements, most group members will work in a co-operative manner. The team will now know why it exists, what procedures they must follow, the fact that truthfulness and openness is important and that they can receive help from other members of the group. This all derives from a sense of belonging, where members have appreciated the fact that conflict will exist, but they are able to deal with it. This will go a long way towards encouraging individual members to appreciate and improve their own performance.

◆ *The adjourning stage* – this presupposes that the group only needs to exist for a limited period of time and that after the successful resolution or achievement of objectives, that the group can be disbanded

Reactions to change

Acceptance, resistance and conflict

Given the fact that change aims to move an organisation from its current situation to another, we should appreciate the fact that change will cause uncertainty or unwillingness to give up existing practices. To begin with, many individuals will deny that the change is actually necessary and will resist it utterly, or avoid the changes once they have been introduced. The management structure needs to be able to determine why there is resistance to change and attempt to overcome it. If individuals feel threatened by change, they will not be able to recognise the potential advantages of embracing the change. If management can explain why the changes are necessary and the opportunities that are presented by this action, then there is more possibility of commitment being received from those who are hesitant. There are a number of different reasons why individuals will feel a need to resist change. These include situations where:

◆ their security has been undermined

◆ their competence is being questioned

◆ familiar relationships are under threat

◆ their territory or responsibilities are being impinged upon

◆ they do not understand the direction in which they are supposed to be moving.

For all individuals involved there needs to be a period of transition from resistance or denial to exploration and commitment. This would include the need for the organisation to fully appraise all employees and give them time to understand and internalise information. Those that are resisting will not acknowledge, accept or respond to this approach, but should be encouraged through support to explore the potential advantages of the change. Once this has been achieved, commitment will be gained through team-building activities, rewards, and the gradual move towards the new objectives.

Force field analysis

Kurt Lewin put forward the theory of *force field analysis*, which considers that situations of change can be best visualised by two mutually opposing forces operating against one another. As we have mentioned, when we considered the driving and restraining forces in the second section of this book, one set of forces supports the change and the other resists the change. The main purpose of force field analysis is to enable the management to identify the nature of these forces in advance of any implementation of change. The next step would be to attempt to remove or minimise each of the forces which restrain the organisation from making the change, while, at the same time, bolstering the forces which support or encourage the change.

We can best see the current state in which the organisation finds itself as a solid line with, some distance away, a dotted line showing the desired state. The driving forces can then be seen as arrows pushing the current state line towards the desired state line. There are matching arrows attempting to restrain the current state line from moving towards the desired state line. Some of the forces will be stronger than others. It is the manager's responsibility to try to match and exceed the restraining forces in order to push the organisation towards its desired state. If the two opposing forces are equal, then the organisation will remain where it is. If the driving forces are stronger, or the restraining forces become weaker, then the line will move towards the desired state.

Quality circles

Many organisations have begun to use *quality circles* as a means by which problems can be identified and solutions offered. These groups of volunteers are led by a supervisor or team leader, whose role it is to establish the group and to try to develop it into a cohesive team. Normally, a quality circle would consist of up to 12 members, with a variety of different experiences, viewpoints and ideas. The managers of the organisation do not involve themselves in the decision-making processes within the quality circle, but are supportive and considerate towards the suggestions made by the team. It is of vital importance that any proposals made by a quality circle are, at the very least, considered seriously and not simply ignored.

Quality circles are an integral part of Japanese culture and are seen as a way in which employees can be encouraged to be even more loyal to the business.

Naturally, the majority of quality circles' activities involve performance and quality issues and are used extensively by organisations such as Marks and Spencer, Rolls Royce and Ford. In most UK-based organisations there has been considerable resistance to the introduction of quality circles, or at least acceptance of their suggestions. Quality circles are most typically found in organisations which encourage participation and a practical approach to the resolving of problems.

Monitoring change, review and feedback

While many plans to change the operations of the organisation may appear to be perfectly workable in theoretical form, there may be a tendency for some aspects to be overlooked and for others to be inconsistent. Once any change has been implemented, the organisation would be wise to not only monitor the impact, but also to systematically review the situation after the dust has settled. This would probably involve a relatively formal review and evaluation period, which allows the organisation to step back from the situation and examine precisely what has been the outcome of the changes. In order to make this as comprehensive a review as possible, it would be desirable for the organisation to seek feedback from the employees and to include in their deliberations the experiences that other lower levels of the hierarchy have undergone.

Communication strategies

At all points the organisation needs to ensure that adequate communication channels are open to all parts of the organisation and above all, these need to be two-way. Not only does the organisation have to inform the employees of the nature and implications of change, but they also need to appreciate the fact that certain individuals will have cause to seek assurances and, perhaps, offer suggestions as to how this change could be implemented.

In order to do this, the organisation needs to be specific about what needs to be accomplished. Any opportunity to measure differences between traditional practice and new proposed procedures should be made. It is also important that the targets which are set are attainable and that results or milestones are clearly identified, so that some sense of accomplishment can be achieved. In addition to this, the organisation needs to superimpose a time limit on the changes so that the management and the employees know the extent and timeframes involved.

Development and influence of corporate culture

An organisation's corporate culture will naturally exert a considerable influence over its strategies. There are a number of stages or reasons why a culture will have such a marked effect upon strategies, and a number of aspects to take into consideration:

◆ The organisation needs to continually scan the environment to identify situations with which they are uncertain, but feel that they are capable of controlling. There will be certain cultural assumptions within the organisation that will affect this scanning process.

◆ The organisation needs to be aware that it will have various filters in place that will determine the attitude towards certain information and activities in the external environment. This selective perception of different situations will have been built up as an integral part of the organisation's culture.

◆ The organisation needs to not only collect and interpret information, but also to appreciate the fact that their own culture will have a different set of demands arising out of the information and this will determine their response.

◆ The organisation's culture will have an ethical component to it which will determine the way in which strategies are formulated and implemented. Whatever the dominant sets of values and norms within the organisation, there will be a variety of different ways in which the organisation will either restrict their response or direct their actions.

Any new strategy will put forward at least two questions which can be directly related to the culture. These are:

1 What behavioural changes are required of the culture in order to incorporate the new objectives?

2 Does the behavioural change or degree of change determine whether the objective can be achieved?

The organisation could take a number of different approaches to culture while considering its strategic possibilities. These would include:

◆ actually ignoring the culture itself, but this may be dangerous unless the organisation's culture is not fully developed.

◆ trying to manage the strategy around the culture by making adjustments and modifications to the plans.

◆ trying to modify the culture to fit the strategy.

◆ trying to adapt the strategy to fit the culture.

Miles and Snow put forward the concept that there are three basic types of organisation in terms of culture and strategic approach. These are *defenders*, *prospectors* and *analysers*. As we can see from Fig. 4.11, there are a number of differences between each of these culture and strategy mixes.

Mission statements

The mission statement of an organisation is often referred to as its vision or, more explicitly, what it feels it is about. Some mission statements are very broad or bland, but others may more clearly state the organisation's aims and objec-

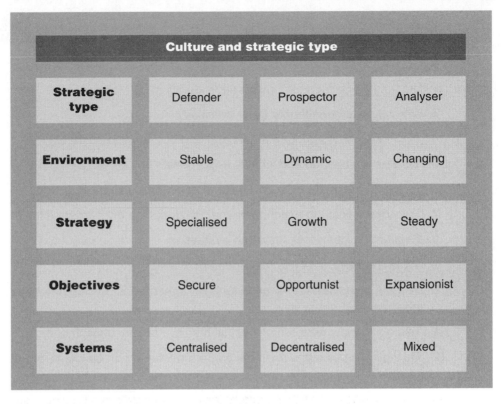

Fig. 4.11 Organisational culture and strategy

tives. Given that this mission statement describes the basic purpose of the organisation, it will have to carefully consider the implications of what it has said. Characteristically, a mission statement will be indistinct and very wide in its scope, without necessarily identifying how it proposes to deal with the objectives. Obviously the organisation does not wish to restrict itself in the future by more clearly defining what it proposes to do. At the very least, it will say what business the organisation is in, who it serves, what benefits it offers and give some reference to its consumers. Naturally enough, the organisation will try to balance all of these, particularly in relation to the possibly conflicting demands of stakeholders and customers.

An organisation would normally seek to avoid changing its mission statement or vision too often. It may choose to simply incorporate an additional statement or sentence in order to encompass any new direction or market development. As we have said a number of times, the organisational culture should seek to reflect the organisational mission statement. Part and parcel of the vision of the organisation will be its culture. There may be a tendency for culture to lag behind the mission statement, but broadly speaking the culture will always be an integral part of the vision, whether this is implicit or explicit in nature.

Review questions

1 Outline the key features of F.W. Taylor's theory on scientific management.

2 List the five classes of human needs identified by Maslow.

3 Why has Maslow's theory been criticised?

4 How can job design form an integral part of motivational theory?

5 What is job rotation and what is its purpose?

6 Explain what is meant by job enlargement and describe its purpose.

7 How do vertical job enrichment and horizontal job enrichment differ?

8 Explain the key principles of job evaluation.

9 What are Fayol's 14 key management qualities and functions?

10 What is Likert's notion of an ideal environment? List his ideas for a good and effective leadership style.

11 Explain the key features of 'best fit' theory and 'pay back' theory.

12 How do organisations reinforce the 'team-based' versus 'them-and-us' points of view?

13 List the advantages that could be enjoyed by developing a single status situation.

14 What are the key stages of group team development?

15 What are the potential advantages of the formation of quality circles?

Further reading

Alderfer, C.P., *Existence, Relatedness and Growth*, 1972, MacMillan.

Argyris, C., *Personality and Organisation*, 1957, Harper & Row.

Argyris, C., *Integrating the Individual and the Organisation*, 1964, Wiley.

Bennis, W.G. and Nanus, B., *Leaders: The Strategies for Taking Charge*, 1985, Harper & Row.

Burns, T. and Stalker, S.M., *The Management of Innovation*, 1966, Tavistock.

Davis, S.M., *Managing Corporate Culture*, 1984, Ballinger.

Deal, T.E. and Kennedy, A.A., *Corporate Cultures: The Rights and Rituals of Corporate Life*, 1982, Addison-Wesley.

Drennan, D., *Transforming Company Culture*, 1992, McGraw-Hill.

Drucker, Peter F., *The Practice of Management*, 1979, Heinemann.

Drucker, Peter F., *The New Society: The Anatomy of the Industrial Order*, 1951, Heinemann.

Fayol, H., *General and Industrial Management*, 1949, Pitman Publishing.

Fielder, F.E., *Theory of Leadership Effectiveness*, 1967, McGraw-Hill.

Hofstede, G., *Cultures and Organisations, Software of the Mind*, 1991, McGraw-HIll.

Hunt, J.W., *Managing People at Work: A Manager's Guide to Behaviour in Organisations*, 1986, McGraw-Hill.

Kanter, R.M., *The Change Masters*, 1983, Simon & Schuster.

Kuhn, J.W. and Shriver, D.W., *Beyond Success: Corporations and their Critics in the 1990s*, 1991, Oxford University Press.

Likert, R. and Likert, J.G., *New Ways of Managing Conflict*, 1976, McGraw-Hill.

Likert, R., *New Patterns of Management*, 1961, McGraw-Hill.

Likert, R., *The Human Organisation*, 1967, McGraw-Hill.

McGregor, D., *The Human Side of Enterprise*, 1960, McGraw-Hill.

Maslow, A., *Motivation and Personality*, 1954, Harper & Row.

Mayo, E., *The Social Problems of an Industrial Civilisation*, 1949, Routledge.

Mintzberg, H., *The Structuring of Organisations*, 1975, Prentice-Hall.

Pavlov, I., *Conditioned Reflexes*, 1927, Oxford University Press.

Quinn, R.E. and McGrath, M.R., *The Transformation of Organisational Cultures: A Competing Values Perspective in Organisational Culture*, edited by Lundberg, C. C. and Martin, J., 1985, Sage.

Schein, E.H., *Organisational Psychology*, 1988, Prentice-Hall.

Further reading

Schein, E.H., *Organisational Culture and Leadership*, 1985, Jossey Bass.

Scholz, C., *Corporate Culture and Strategy: The Problem of Strategic Fit,* 1987.

Stacey, R., *Dynamic Strategic Management for the 1990s*, 1990, Kogan Page.

Stacey, R., *The Chaos Frontier: Creative Strategic Control for Business*, 1991, Butter-worth-Heinemann.

Stacey, R., *Managing Chaos*, 1992, Kogan Page.

Taylor, F.W., *Scientific Management*, 1947, Harper & Row.

Vroom, V.H. and Yetton, P.W., *Leadership and Decision Making*, 1973, University of Pittsburg Press.

Thompson, J.D. and Tuden, A., *Strategy Structures and Processes of Organisational Decision in Comparative Studies in Administration*, 1959, University of Pittsburg Press.

Weber, M., *The Theory of Social and Economic Organisation*, 1964, MacMillan.

Woodward, J., *Industrial Organisation: Theory and Practice*, 1965, Oxford University Press.

 Index